Bloom's Classic Critical Views

STEPHEN CRANE

Bloom's Classic Critical Views

STEPHEN CRANE

Edited and with an Introduction by
Harold Bloom
Sterling Professor of the Humanities
Yale University

BLOOM'S
LITERARY CRITICISM
An imprint of Infobase Publishing

Library of Congress Cataloging-in-Publication Data
Stephen Crane / edited and with an introduction by Harold Bloom.
    p. cm. — (Bloom's classic critical views)
  Includes bibliographical references and index.
  ISBN 978-1-60413-432-2 (hardcover)
  1. Crane, Stephen, 1871–1900—Criticism and interpretation.   I. Bloom, Harold.
II. Title.   III. Series.
  PS1449.C85Z926 2009
  813'.4—dc22   2009001611

Volume editor: Joyce Caldwell Smith
Series design by Erika K. Arroyo
Cover designed by Takeshi Takahashi
Printed in the United States of America
IBT IBT 10 9 8 7 6 5 4 3 2 1

This book is printed on acid-free paper.

All links and Web addresses were checked and verified to be correct at the time of publication. Because of the dynamic nature of the Web, some addresses and links may have changed since publication and may no longer be valid.

Contents

Series Introduction

Bloom's Classic Critical Views is a new series presenting a selection of the most important older literary criticism on the greatest authors commonly read in high school and college classes today. Unlike the Bloom's Modern Critical Views series, which for more than 20 years has provided the best contemporary criticism on great authors, Bloom's Classic Critical Views attempts to present the authors in the context of their time and to provide criticism that has proved over the years to be the most valuable to readers and writers. Selections range from contemporary reviews in popular magazines, which demonstrate how a work was received in its own era, to profound essays by some of the strongest critics in the British and American tradition, including Henry James, G.K. Chesterton, Matthew Arnold, and many more.

Some of the critical essays and extracts presented here have appeared previously in other titles edited by Harold Bloom, such as the New Moulton's Library of Literary Criticism. Other selections appear here for the first time in any book by this publisher. All were selected under Harold Bloom's guidance.

In addition, each volume in this series contains a series of essays by a contemporary expert, who comments on the most important critical selections, putting them in context and suggesting how they might be used by a student writer to influence his or her own writing. This series is intended above all for students, to help them think more deeply and write more powerfully about great writers and their works.

Introduction by Harold Bloom

A prodigy, the Hemingway of America in the 1890s, Crane is the slimmest of classics in the American canon but a classic nevertheless. One novel, *The Red Badge of Courage*, composed in his early twenties, three superb short stories and two or three short poems—that is his permanence. In his brief lifetime (dead at twenty-eight) he filled a vacuum in American literature. Both Henry James and Joseph Conrad, who befriended him during his final, marvelous year of literary and social success in England, perhaps overrated his work. Yet his kind of original impressionism on the verge of exploding into hallucinatory expressionism prophesied Willa Cather, Hemingway, Scott Fitzgerald, Nathanael West, and even aspects of William Faulkner and Cormac McCarthy.

Deeply read, Crane seems to have absorbed crucial lessons from Stendahl, Tolstoy, and Zola. His true mode was phantasmagoria, rendered however with a meticulous nihilism, a deep sense of the meaninglessness of life except for what could be converted into art. The aesthetic of Walter Pater, who accepted only sensations and perceptions as valid, is highly consonant with Crane's work.

It is very difficult to surmise what Crane could have accomplished had he lived past twenty-eight. Conrad and James might have inspired him to create really ambitious fictions, and perhaps these might have been persuasive achievements. I harbor reservations on this. Crane's nihilism probably would have led him even further into the vein of irony that he scarcely could control in the failed novel, *Maggie*. We can be grateful for what he gave us in his brief span.

❖

BIOGRAPHY

❖

Stephen Crane
(1871–1900)

❖

Stephen Crane was born in Newark, New Jersey, on November 1, 1871, the fourteenth and last child of the Reverend Doctor Jonathan Townley Crane. He attended Lafayette College (1890) and Syracuse University (1891), both of which he left without receiving a degree, and then went to New York where he worked, without much success, as a journalist. In 1893, Crane's first novel, *Maggie: A Girl of the Streets,* was printed privately at his own expense. This was followed by *The Red Badge of Courage* (1895), a novel of the Civil War that was widely hailed as a masterpiece of psychological realism. In 1896, Crane left for Jacksonville, Florida, where he met Cora Taylor, who later became his common-law wife. He sailed on the *Commodore* for Cuba, where he planned to report on the war, but the ship sank, and he reached shore only after thirty-three hours in a dinghy with three others. In 1897, he traveled to Greece to report on the Greek-Turkish war, then went to England, where he developed friendships with several writers, including Joseph Conrad, Henry James, and Harold Frederic.

Crane returned to the United States in early 1898 during the Spanish-American War. He signed a contract with Pulitzer's *New York World* to report on the war, sending home some of the war's best dispatches from the front, before returning to New York late in 1898 and sailing to England on the final day of that year. During Christmas week of 1899, Crane suffered a massive tubercular hemorrhage, followed by two more in late March; Cora then took him to Badenweiler, in the Black Forest, in a desperate attempt to restore his health. Crane died on June 5, 1900, almost immediately after his arrival in Germany.

During his lifetime Crane also published two collections of free verse, *The Black Riders and Other Lines* (1895) and *War Is Kind* (1899), three short-story collections *The Little Regiment* (1896), *The Open Boat and Other Tales of Adventures* (1898), and *The Monster and Others Stories* (1899), and two unsuccessful novels, *The Third Violet*

1

(1896) and *Active Service* (1899). *Whilomville Stories* and *Wounds in the Rain*, two other short-story collections, were published posthumously, as was *The O'Ruddy*, an unfinished novel completed by Robert Barr.

❖

PERSONAL

❖

Both during his lifetime and since his death, Stephen Crane has interested readers partly because of his vivid writing and partly because of what some have depicted as a notorious life. From the time he came to the public eye with *The Red Badge of Courage* in 1895, rumors have abounded about the young author. Although an abridged version of *The Red Badge* had appeared in December 1894 in the *Philadelphia Press* and several others newspapers syndicated by Bacheller, Stephen Crane was still largely unknown to the general public until Appleton published the book in late September 1895. American critics reviewed the book widely with mixed results, but when the novel was published in England in early 1896, Crane became internationally recognized.

With that recognition, friends of Crane began publishing reminiscences of the young writer. In this section, Clarence Loomis Peaslee describes Crane when they were both students at Syracuse University. Next Richard Harding Davis, a fellow correspondent covering the Spanish-American War in Cuba, writes of Crane's behavior there. In these two articles, Crane is depicted as fiercely devoted to his writing, so devoted in fact that he put it before a college education and before his personal safety.

The next six pieces were written in 1900, the year of Crane's death, and they lament the loss of the twenty-eight-year-old writer. They reveal the respect and admiration that other prominent literary figures accord Crane, and some give information about specific aspects of his life: what he was like at the end of his life, during his trip to the West and Mexico, during the time he was writing *Black Riders* and *The Red Badge of Courage*, and in the middle of battle in the Spanish-American War. The resulting portrait is of a somewhat shy young man who took death in stride and who helped his friends when they were in need.

The next two articles, written one and three years after his death, are thoughtful reminiscences of Crane in the early part of his writing career. They discuss his habits and routines, his careful attention to his art, and his poverty during that time.

The final piece, written twenty-one years after Crane's death by Ford Madox Ford, is quite unreliable. Although Ford was never a close friend, he was an acquaintance during the time Crane lived in England. Ford romanticizes the young writer, adding fictional flourishes that enhance the legend of Crane's so-called bohemian lifestyle, both at Ravensbrook and later at Brede Place, and inventing conversations or attributing comments to Crane that he did not make, such as his disparagement of Robert Louis Stevenson. In 1923, Thomas Beer published the first book-length biography of Stephen Crane, but it is as unreliable and romanticized as Ford's piece. Beer changed the chronology of Crane's life and invented incidents; he also composed numerous letters supposedly from Crane, a fact suspected but not proved until 1990 by Paul Sorrentino and Stanley Wertheim. Ford's piece, like Beer's book, must be considered more fiction than fact, and the facts for which Ford or Beer are the only sources should be ignored in Crane studies. Unfortunately, material garnered from these two writers for later biographical works is also suspect, so the Stephen Crane biographical stream has been contaminated. The value of the other contemporary writings included here is that they are usually reliable, and they add to the picture of the real Crane.

Clarence Loomis Peaslee
"Stephen Crane's College Days" (1896)

Clarence Loomis Peaslee was one of Crane's friends at Syracuse University, where Stephen Crane resided from September 1890 to June 1891. Peaslee was an aspiring writer as well, publishing poetry and short stories but later earning his living as a lawyer. Still enthusiastic about the possibility of being an author himself, Peaslee wrote this piece at the height of the popularity of *The Red Badge of Courage*.

Peaslee points out that the young Crane was not a dedicated student but was an avid baseball player who went to class sporadically and only studied what he found interesting. He praises Crane's athletic skill and his interest in history.

Peaslee describes the effort that Stephen Crane put into his writing, points out that the young man had a "deep regard for true learning," and credits him for his study of mankind. Even while in college, Crane was writing sketches for various newspapers and reading his short stories and other writings to his fellow students. He depicts an independent young man who refused to go along with tradition when it displeased him. Even after they left school, Peaslee continued to correspond with Crane, quoting from a letter of 1895.

At the beginning of the excerpt, Crane's age at the time is given as eighteen, instead of the correct nineteen, and later his birth date is given as 1872, instead of the correct 1871.

Stephen Crane came to Syracuse University during the college year of '90. He had previously been a student at Lafayette, and while there had been initiated into the Delta Upsilon Fraternity. Upon his arrival in Syracuse he came immediately to the D. U. House, as one of his friends says, "in a cab and a cloud of tobacco smoke."

I well remember my first knowledge of him. Calling one afternoon at the D.U. House to see a friend, I passed up the stairs and was just turning into one of the rooms on the second floor, when the appearance of the room opposite, the door of which stood right open, attracted my attention. College rooms are proverbially disorderly, but this one made the ordinary every day chaos turn to cosmos in comparison. The floor was literally covered with loose sheets of paper, books, football shoes, newspaper clippings, canvas trousers and jackets, baseball masks and bats, running trunks, chest-protectors and other athletic and literary sundries. The table was running over with books and papers and scribblings, together with pipes and tobacco cans, and the walls were hung with pictures, trophies, signs and pen-drawings. Certainly the occupant was nothing unless athletic and literary. The apartment was a large one in the northeast corner of the house, and contained a deep bay-window. It was quite elegantly furnished, some of the pictures being particularly good, for Mr. Crane has always been an ardent admirer of fine paintings. Just then some members of the fraternity were coming along the passage, I asked who lived there, and was told: "A new fellow from Lafayette, 'Steve' Crane." Later in the afternoon, on the athletic field, I met the future novelist, then the new catcher of the 'Varsity nine, a wiry, slender youth, under the average height, with a complexion almost yellow, and very large and expressive eyes. I remember that he did not have one of the old gray 'Varsity suits, but wore a crimson sweater, buff-colored trouser and a pair of broken patent-leather shoes. He was very gritty, and stood up to the plate like a professional. The pitcher at that time was a rather large man, who threw a very swift ball, and Crane was so light that he seemed to bound back with every catch. Little did the motley crowd of students and onlookers that bright April afternoon think that the plucky boy behind the bat would so soon be a character of international interest; for all this happened a little more than six years ago. He was the best player of the nine, and one of the best catchers that the University ever had.

Mr. Crane was then about eighteen years old, small, quiet, and unprepossessing. His face was long and sallow, eyes deep set, and hair very light, almost white. He was very quick and agile in his movements and was a good runner. He had very few intimate friends, cared little for society, and never seemed to be particularly interested in anything that transpired in college except baseball. He was somewhat careless in his dress and negligent of his lectures; was always cool, never worried about anything, smoked infinite tobacco and took life just as it came.

Of Stephen Crane's college life there is little to be said. He was not possessed of a strong individuality. He was simply unimpressive, and his student days gave no promise of the talent he has since displayed. Of the eight or nine hundred students in attendance at Syracuse University during his stay, only a few will remember him at all. From the standpoint of his professors, Mr. Crane's college course was a failure. He was but an indifferent student, not from lack of ability but from want of application. He had no natural taste for study, and never tried to cultivate one. His favorite study was history, and his reading in this branch of instruction has been considerable. He left the University without a degree, and was never enrolled as a student in any regular course, but was classed as a special, taking whatever took his fancy.

Yet the college days of Stephen Crane were not wasted. He preferred to select his own course of instruction rather than follow the cut-and-dried curriculum of a university. Men have always had a greater interest for him than books. When he ought to have been in recitations he was strolling the streets, looking at the faces that passed. One of his favorite haunts was the Central Railroad station, where large numbers of people daily congregated. His course in college was highly "eclectic," and he never pretended to follow it closely. A man of less mental insight and stability would surely have been led amiss by such a general and indifferent method of action, but Stephen Crane had a purpose in view from the very first, and steadily and unswervingly worked to it. He wanted to produce something that would make men think, that would make men feel as he felt, and to do this he early realized that for him it must come through hard work. In the course of a literary correspondence he wrote me a letter, dated at Lincoln, Nebraska, February 12, 1895, in which, after citing various criticism, he says: "As far as myself and my own meager success are concerned, I began the war with no talent, but an ardent admiration and desire. I had to build up. I always want to be unmistakable. That to my mind is good writing. There is a great deal of labor connected with literature. I think that is the hardest thing about it. There is nothing to respect in art, save one's own opinion of it.

It has been charged against Mr. Crane that he scorns scholarship, and is proud of the fact that he has had little or no schooling. Nothing is farther from the truth. He has a deep regard for true learning, but not for the rubbish that often passes under that name, and if he has not burned the midnight oil in search of "school" knowledge, he has worked as but few men have, in the field of observation and the study of mankind.

In college Crane was an omnivorous reader, and sat up late at night, diligently poring over the masterpieces of literature, or trying to pour upon paper his own peculiar views of men and life. It is interesting to note and is an indication of his genius that his stories are all in a new field, and that he is indebted to no "school" of letters or coterie of thinkers for the ideas that he so intensely presents. The outward acts and lives of men are to him but the evidence and outworkings of a strange and unaccountable inner life that is going on in the darkened recesses of the mind. Whether he is stronger as a scene-painter of the great panorama of human action or as a philosopher of life is difficult to determine. He is certainly remarkable for both.

While Stephen Crane was a student in Syracuse University he did a large amount of newspaper hack-work. It was his habit after lunch to repair to the cupola of the Delta Upsilon Chapter house and read, smoke his water-pipe—of which he was very fond—and write sketches which found their way to the *Detroit Free Press* or the various Syracuse dailies. He also did the city correspondence for the *New York Tribune*. It was his delight to block out the plot of a story and then tell his friends about it, putting it in various lights and constructions, and then asking which was more effective. His book, "Maggie: A Girl of the Streets," was thus detailed to some of his acquaintances.

Crane never really enjoyed being treated as a freshman, and always resented any encroachments on his freshman dignity. One day the steward of the club (a senior) was going to sharpen the carving knives. He came into the library, which was crowded, and said: "I want a freshie to turn grindstone; come on, Crane!" "Steve" didn't come, but retorted, with a red face, that he "never had and never would turn grindstone for anybody," which was voted as very bad grace for a freshman. He was always a great admirer of nature, a beautiful landscape or flower appealing strongly to his artistic taste. Coupled with his love of nature was a strong poetical imagination, which was quick to seize on a passing scene. One day, going down the campus, when the fields were fairly yellow with dandelions, he said: "If I could only write poetry I'd tell about the Goddess of Money showering down the gold-pieces."

Mr. Crane was born in Newark, N.J., in 1872, and is therefore only twenty-four years old. His ancestry is English. He is a son of the late Rev. Jonathan T. Crane, D. D., and is a lineal descendant of Stephen Crane, who came from England in 1635 with the company that settled at Elizabethtown, N. J., thus planting the first English colony in that province. His mother was a daughter of Rev. George Peck, D.D., an eloquent Methodist minister and at one time editor of the Christian Advocate, of New York, the official organ of the Methodist Episcopal Church. Stephen Crane's father was a learned divine, a man of broad scholarship and generous enthusiasm, an alumnus of Princeton, president of Pennington Seminary, Pennington, N.J., for nine years, and four times a member of the General Conference, the legislative body of the Methodist Church. He was a manuscript preacher and a writer of rare ability, adorning his discourses with a style of rich beauty. He was also a noted wit, which was particularly evident in debate and private conversation. Stephen Crane inherits much of his intensity of expression from his gifted father. The family tree has produced several clergymen and soldiers. It is an interesting study in heredity to note the influence of these two professions in Mr. Crane's literary work, the one furnishing the basis of style, the other of incident. . . .

—Clarence Loomis Peaslee,
"Stephen Crane's College Days,"
Monthly Illustrator and Home and Country,
August 1896, pp. 27–30

RICHARD HARDING DAVIS
"OUR WAR CORRESPONDENTS IN
CUBA AND PUERTO RICO" (1899)

Richard Harding Davis was both a popular journalist and a writer of romantic fiction. In March 1897, he had met Stephen Crane on the way to the Greek-Turkish War, where they both worked as newspaper correspondents. Later they were both in Cuba reporting the Spanish-American War.

Davis points out that many of Crane's newspaper dispatches later served as the basis of creative pieces; for instance, Crane's story of Nolan appeared first as a newspaper report "Regulars Get No Glory" and later as a short story "The Price of the Harness"; the story of the marine at Guantanamo appeared first in "The Red Badge of Courage Was His Wig-Wag Flag" and later in "Marines Signaling under Fire at Guantanamo."

Davis recounts a story of Crane's utter disregard for his own safety, his extreme interest in studying a situation, and his reluctance to be seen as flaunting his courage.

It is impossible to designate one correspondent as being better than another, because what is important to one does not seem to be of value to his rivals, and their ideas as to their duty differ. One may prefer to stand on the firing-line in order to see what is going forward close at hand, but while he is in greater personal danger, another who watches the battle from an elevation in the rear can obtain a much better view, and a much more correct idea of what is being done in all parts of the field. So the presence of a correspondent on the firing line, or his absence from it, does not prove that he is not doing his full duty to his paper. The best correspondent is probably the man who by his energy and resource sees more of the war, both afloat and ashore, than do his rivals, and who is able to make the public see what he saw. If that is a good definition, Stephen Crane would seem to have distinctly won the first place among correspondents in the late disturbance. . . .

Near the close of the war, a group of correspondents in Puerto Rico made out a list of the events which, in their opinion, were of the greatest news value during the campaign, and a list of the correspondents, with the events each had witnessed credited to his name. Judged from this basis, Mr. Crane easily led all the rest. Of his power to make the public see what he sees it would be impertinent to speak. His story of Nolan, the regular, bleeding to death on the San Juan hills, is, so far as I have read, the most valuable contribution to literature that the war has produced. It is only necessary to imagine how other writers would have handled it, to appreciate that it could not have been better done. His story of the marine at Guantanamo, who stood on the crest of the hill to "wigwag" to the war-ships, and so exposed himself to the fire of the entire Spanish forces, is also particularly interesting, as it illustrates that in his devotion to duty, and also in his readiness at the exciting moments of life, Crane is quite as much of a soldier as the man whose courage he described. He tells of how the marine stood erect, staring through the dusk with half-closed eyes, and with his lips moving as he counted the answers from the war-ships, while innumerable bullets splashed the sand about him. But it never occurs to Crane that to sit at the man's feet, as he did, close enough to watch his lips move and to be able to make mental notes for a later tribute to the marine's scorn of fear, was equally deserving of praise.

Crane was the coolest man, whether army officer or civilian, that I saw under fire at any time during the war. He was most annoyingly cool, with the assurance of a fatalist. When the San Juan hills were taken, he came up them with James Hare, of Collier's. He was walking leisurely, and though the bullets passed continuously, he never once ducked his head. He wore a long rain-coat, and as he stood peering over the edge of the hill, with his hands in his pockets and smoking his pipe, he was as unconcerned as though he were gazing at a cinematograph.

The fire from the enemy was so heavy that only one troop along the entire line of the hills was returning it, and all the rest of our men were lying down. General Wood, who was then colonel of the Rough Riders, and I were lying on our elbows at Crane's feet, and Wood ordered him also to lie down. Crane pretended not to hear, and moved farther away, still peering over the hill with the same interested expression. Wood told him for the second time that if he did not lie down he would be killed, but Crane paid no attention. So, in order to make him take shelter, I told him he was trying to impress us with his courage, and that if he thought he was making me feel badly by walking about, he might as well sit down. As soon as I told him he was trying to impress us with his courage, he dropped on his knees as I had hoped he would, and we breathed again. . . .

—RICHARD HARDING DAVIS, from
"Our War Correspondents in Cuba and
Puerto Rico," Harper's New Monthly Magazine,
May 1899, pp. 938–948

ROBERT BARR "LITERARY NOTES" (1900)

Robert Barr was born in Glasgow, Scotland, grew up in Canada, and moved to London in 1881. He wrote numerous short stories and romantic historical novels, and he edited the monthly *Idler*. Barr met the Cranes when they lived at Ravensbrook, Surrey, in June 1897. Barr, Harold Frederic, Stephen Crane, and their families became close friends during the time Crane lived in England, so close that in this letter Barr refers to the threesome as the Three Musketeers. Often they were joined by Joseph Conrad and his family. Helpful in advising Crane on how to deal with his publishers, Barr credited Crane with being the greatest American writer since Edgar Allan Poe.

When Crane was on his deathbed, Barr reluctantly promised that he would complete his novel, *The O'Ruddy*, which was published in 1903 with Barr writing the last eight chapters.

The letter below shows the close friendship Barr had felt both for Frederic, who had died in 1898, and for Crane.

An exceedingly interesting letter from Robert Barr was published recently in the *New York Herald*, but was given such an inconspicuous position that it has probably escaped the notice of many of the readers of the *Pocket* magazine. There is so much in it that is characteristic of its writer and of the late Stephen Crane that we print it here in full:

"Hillhead, Woldingham, Surrey,
"June 8, 1900

"My Dear * * *—I was delighted to hear from you, and was much interested to see the article on Stephen Crane you sent me. It seems to me the harsh judgment of an unappreciative, commonplace person on a man of genius. Stephen had many qualities which lent themselves to misapprehension, but at the core he was the finest of men, generous to a fault, with something of the oldtime recklessness which used to gather in the ancient literary taverns of London. I always fancied that Edgar Allan Poe revisited the earth as Stephen Crane, trying again, succeeding again, failing again and dying ten years sooner than he did on the other occasion of his stay on earth.

"When your letter came I had just returned from Dover, where I stayed four days to see Crane off for the Black Forest. There was a thin thread of hope that he might recover, but to me he looked like a man already dead. When he spoke, or rather whispered, there was all the accustomed humor in his sayings. I said to him that I would go over to the Schwartzwald in a few weeks, when he was getting better, and that we would take some convalescent rambles together. As his wife was listening he said, faintly, 'I'll look forward to that,' but he smiled at me and winked slowly, as much as to say. 'You d——d humbug, you know I'll take no more rambles in this world.' Then, as if the train of thought suggested what was looked on before as the crisis of his illness, he murmured, 'Robert, when you come to the hedge—that we must all go over—it isn't bad. You feel sleepy—and—you don't care. Just a little dreamy curiosity—which world you're really in—that's all.'

"Tomorrow, Saturday, the 9th, I go again to Dover to meet his body. He will rest for a little while in England, a country that was always good to him, then to America, and his journey will be ended.

"I've got the unfinished manuscript of his last novel here beside me—a rollicking Irish tale, different from anything he ever wrote before. Stephen thought I was the only person who could finish it, and he was too ill for me to refuse. I don't know what to do about the matter, for I never could work up another man's ideas. Even your vivid imagination could hardly conjure anything more ghastly than the dying man, lying by an open window overlooking the English Channel, relating in a sepulchral whisper the comic situations of his humorous hero so that I might take up the thread of his story.

"From the window beside which I write this I can see down in the valley Ravensbrook House, where Crane used to live and where Harold Frederic, he and I spent many a merry night together. When the Romans occupied Britain some of their legions, parched with thirst, were wandering about these dry hills with the choice of finding water or perishing. They watched the ravens and so came to the stream which rises under my place and flows past Stephen's former home, hence the name, Ravensbrook.

"It seems a strange coincidence that the greatest modern writer on war should set himself down where the greatest ancient warrior, Caesar, probably stopped to quench his thirst.

"Stephen died at three in the morning, the same sinister hour which carried away our friend Frederic nineteen months before. At midnight in Crane's fourteenth century house in Sussex we two tried to lure back the ghost of Frederic into that house of ghosts and to our company, thinking that if reappearing were ever possible so strenuous a man as Harold would somehow shoulder his way past the guards, but he made no sign. I wonder if the less insistent Stephen will suggest some ingenious method by which the two can pass the barrier. I can imagine Harold cursing on the other side and welcoming the more subtle assistance of his finely fibered friend.

"I feel rather like the last of the Three Musketeers, the other two gone down in their duel with Death. I am wondering if, within the next two years, I also will get the challenge. If so, I shall go to the competing ground the more cheerfully that two such good fellows await the outcome on the other side. Ever your friend . . .

—ROBERT BARR, "Literary Notes,"
The San Francisco Call, August 12, 1900, p. 12

Willa Cather "When I Knew Stephen Crane" (1900)

Willa Cather, who was to become a great novelist herself—writing *Death Comes for the Archbishop, My Ántonia, The Professor's House,* and other novels, as well as a book of poetry and numerous short stories—met Stephen Crane on his journey through the West and Mexico. Cather interviewed Crane on February 13, 1895, in the office of the *Nebraska State Journal,* where she worked as a drama critic while finishing her degree at Nebraska State University. Cather had earlier copyedited *The Red Badge* for publication in the *Journal,* so she was familiar with his writing when she met him.

Like Crane, a better fiction writer than reporter, Cather partly fictionalizes the event in this obituary written under one of her pseudonyms, Henry Nicklemann, and she includes some inaccuracies. For instance, she reports being a junior in college when she was in fact a senior, and she reports his age at the time as twenty-four, when he was actually twenty-three, and his age at death as twenty-nine rather than the actual twenty-eight. She also dates the article written by Garnett as 1899, instead of the accurate 1898, and she misquotes Garnett slightly.

Despite some minor inaccuracies, this piece is an important first-person account of Crane during his western trip. After graduating from college, Cather, whose first book was published some three years after this article, had supported herself largely through journalism, with some time spent teaching, so she could greatly empathize with the young Crane, who preferred to write creatively but who needed the money from his journalistic pieces. She captures Crane's poverty, and she shows his disregard for everyday concerns such as dress and proper spelling and grammar. She depicts his intense dedication to serious writing and the complexity of his writing process, which resisted following any prescribed rules or logic. Like others who wrote of Crane after his death, she advances the idea that he felt his time to complete his literary mission was short.

———

It was, I think, in the spring of '95, that a slender, narrow-chested fellow in a shabby grey suit, with a soft felt hat pulled low over his eyes, sauntered into the office of the managing editor of the *Nebraska State Journal* and introduced himself as Stephen Crane. He stated that he was going to Mexico to do some work for the Bacheller Syndicate and get rid of his cough, and that he would be stopping in Lincoln for a few days. Later he explained that he was out of money and would be compelled to wait until he got a check from the East before he went further. I was a Junior at the Nebraska State

University at the time, and was doing some work for the *State Journal* in my leisure time, and I happened to be in the managing editor's room when Mr. Crane introduced himself. I was just off the range: I knew a little Greek and something about cattle and a good horse when I saw one, and beyond horses and cattle I considered nothing of vital importance except good stories and the people who wrote them. This was the first man of letters I had ever met in the flesh, and when the young man announced who he was, I dropped into a chair behind the editor's desk where I could stare at him without being too much in evidence.

Only a very youthful enthusiasm and a large propensity for hero worship could have found anything impressive in the young man who stood before the managing editor's desk. He was thin to emaciation, his face was gaunt and unshaven, a thin dark moustache straggled on his upper lip, his black hair grew low on his forehead and was shaggy and unkempt. His grey clothes were much the worse for wear and fitted him so badly it seemed unlikely he had ever been measured for them. He wore a flannel shirt and a slovenly apology for a necktie, and his shoes were dusty and worn gray about the toes and were badly run over at the heel. I had seen many a tramp printer come up the *Journal* stairs to hunt a job, but never one who presented such a disreputable appearance as this story-maker man. He wore gloves which seemed rather a contradiction to the general slovenliness of his attire, but when he took them off to search his pockets for his credentials, I noticed that his hands were singularly fine; long, white, and delicately shaped, with thin, nervous fingers. I have seen pictures of Aubrey Beardsley's hands that recalled Crane's very vividly.

At that time Crane was but twenty-four, and almost an unknown man. Hamlin Garland had seen some of his work and believed in him, and introduced him to Mr. Howells, who recommended him to the Bacheller Syndicate. *The Red Badge of Courage* had been published in the *State Journal* that winter along with a lot of other syndicate matter, and the grammatical construction of the story was so faulty that the managing editor had several times called on me to edit the copy. In this way I had read it very carefully, and through the careless sentence-structure I saw the wonder of that remarkable performance. But the grammar certainly was bad. I remember one of the reporters who had corrected the phrase "it don't" for the tenth time remarked savagely, "If I couldn't write better English than this, I'd quit."

Crane spent several days in the town, living from hand to mouth and waiting for his money. I think he borrowed a small amount from the managing editor. He lounged about the office most of the time, and I frequently encountered him going in and out of the cheap restaurants on

Tenth Street. When he was at the office he talked a good deal in a wandering, absent-minded fashion, and his conversation was uniformly frivolous. If he could not evade a serious question by a joke, he bolted. I cut my classes to lie in wait for him, confident that in some unwary moment I could trap him into serious conversation, that if one burned incense long enough and ardently enough, the oracle would not be dumb. I was Maupassant mad at that time, a malady particularly unattractive in a Junior, and I made a frantic effort to get an expression of opinion from him on *Le Bonheur.* "Oh, you're Moping, are you?" he remarked with a sarcastic grin, and went on reading a little volume of Poe that he carried in his pocket. At another time I cornered him in the Funny Man's room and succeeded in getting a little out of him. We were taught literature by an exceedingly analytical method at the University, and we probably distorted the method, and I was busy trying to find the least common multiple of *Hamlet* and greatest common divisor of *Macbeth,* and I began asking him whether stories were constructed by cabalistic formulae. At length he sighed wearily and shook his drooping shoulders, remarking:

"Where did you get all that rot? Yarns aren't done by mathematics. You can't do it by rule any more than you can dance by rule. You have to have the itch of the thing in your fingers, and if you haven't,—well, you're damned lucky, and you'll live long and prosper, that's all."—And with that he yawned and went down the hall.

Crane was moody most of the time; his health was bad and he seemed profoundly discouraged. Even his jokes were exceedingly drastic. He went about with the tense, preoccupied, self-centered air of a man who is brooding over some impending disaster, and I conjectured vainly as to what it might be. Though he was seemingly entirely idle during the few days I knew him, his manner indicated that he was in the throes of work that told terribly on his nerves. His eyes I remember as the finest I have ever seen, large and dark and full of lustre and changing lights, but with a profound melancholy always lurking deep in them. They were eyes that seemed to be burning themselves out.

As he sat at the desk with his shoulders drooping forward, his head low, and his long, white fingers drumming on the sheets of copy paper, he was as nervous as a race horse fretting to be on the track. Always, as he came and went about the halls, he seemed like a man preparing for a sudden departure. Now that he is dead it occurs to me that all his life was a preparation for sudden departure. I remember once when he was writing a letter he stopped and asked me about the spelling of a word, saying carelessly, "I haven't time to learn to spell." Then, glancing down at his attire, he added with an absent-minded smile, "I haven't time to dress either; it takes an awful slice out of a fellow's life."

He said he was poor, and he certainly looked it, but four years later when he was in Cuba, drawing the largest salary ever paid a newspaper correspondent, he clung to this same untidy manner of dress, and his ragged overalls and buttonless shirt were eyesores to the immaculate Mr. Davis, in his spotless linen and neat khaki uniform, with his Gibson chin always freshly shaven. When I first heard of his serious illness, his old throat trouble aggravated into consumption by his reckless exposure in Cuba, I recalled a passage from Maeterlinck's essay, "The Pre-Destined," on those doomed to early death: "As children, life seems nearer to them than to other children. They appear to know nothing, and yet there is in their eyes so profound a certainty that we feel they must know all.—In all haste, but wisely and with minute care do they prepare themselves to live, and this very haste is a sign upon which mothers can scarce bring themselves to look." I remembered, too, the man's melancholy and his tenseness, his burning eyes, and his way of slurring over the less important things, as one whose time is short.

I have heard other people say how difficult it was to induce Crane to talk seriously about his work, and I suspect that he was particularly averse to discussions with literary men of wider education and better equipment than himself, yet he seemed to feel that this fuller culture was not for him. Perhaps the unreasoning instinct which lies deep in the roots of our lives, and which guides us all, told him that he had not time enough to acquire it.

Men will sometimes reveal themselves to children, or to people whom they think never to see again, more completely than they ever do to their confreres. From the wise we hold back alike our folly and our wisdom, and for the recipients of our deeper confidences we seldom select our equals. The soul has no message for the friends with whom we dine every week. It is silenced by custom and convention, and we play only in the shallows. It selects its listeners willfully, and seemingly delights to waste its best upon the chance wayfarer who meets us in the highway at a fated hour. There are moments too, when the tides run high or very low, when self-revelation is necessary to every man, if it be only to his valet or his gardener. At such a moment, I was with Mr. Crane.

The hoped for revelation came unexpectedly enough. It was on the last night he spent in Lincoln. I had come back from the theatre and was in the *Journal* office writing a notice of the play. It was eleven o'clock when Crane came in. He had expected his money to arrive on the night mail and it had not done so, and he was out of sorts and deeply despondent. He sat down on the ledge of the open window that faced on the street, and when I had finished my notice I went over and took a chair beside him. Quite without invitation on my part, Crane began to talk, began to curse his trade from the first throb of creative desire in a boy to the finished work of the master. The night was oppressively warm; one of those dry winds that are the curse of that country was blowing up from Kansas. The white, western moonlight threw sharp, blue shadows below us. The streets were silent at that hour, and we could hear the gurgle of the fountain in the Post Office square across the street, and the twang of banjos from the lower veranda of the Hotel Lincoln, where the colored waiters were serenading the guests. The drop lights in the office were dull under their green shades, and the telegraph sounder clicked faintly in the next room. In all his long tirade, Crane never raised his voice; he spoke slowly and monotonously and even calmly, but I have never known so bitter a heart in any man as he revealed to me that night. It was an arraignment of the wages of life, an invocation to the ministers of hate.

Incidentally he told me the sum he had received for *The Red Badge of Courage,* which I think was something like ninety dollars, and he repeated some lines from *The Black Riders,* which was then in preparation. He gave me to understand that he led a double literary life; writing in the first place the matter that pleased himself, and doing it very slowly; in the second place, any sort of stuff that would sell. And he remarked that his poor was just as bad as it could possibly be. He realized he said, that his limitations were absolutely impassable. "What I can't do, I can't do at all, and I can't acquire it. I only hold one trump."

He had no settled plans at all. He was going to Mexico wholly uncertain of being able to do any successful work there, and he seemed to feel very insecure about the financial end of his venture. The thing that most interested me was what he said about his slow method of composition. He declared that there was little money in story-writing at best, and practically none in it for him, because of the time it took him to work up his detail. Other men, he said, could sit down and write up an experience while the physical effect of it, so to speak, was still upon them, and yesterday's impressions made today's "copy." But when he came in from the streets to write up what he had seen there, his faculties were benumbed, and he sat twirling his pencil and hunting for words like a schoolboy.

I mentioned *The Red Badge of Courage,* which was written in nine days, and he replied that, though the writing took very little time, he had been unconsciously working the detail of the story out through most of his boyhood. His ancestors had been soldiers, and he had been imagining war stories ever since he was out of knickerbockers, and in writing his first war story he had simply gone over his imaginary campaigns and selected his favorite imaginary experiences. He declared that his imagination was hide-bound; it was there, but it pulled hard. After he got a notion for a story, months passed before he could get any sort of personal contract with it, or feel any potency to handle it. "The detail of a thing has to filter through my blood, and then it comes out like a native product, but it takes forever," he remarked. I distinctly remember the illustration, for it rather took hold of me.

I have often been astonished since to hear Crane spoken of as "the reporter in fiction," for the reportorial faculty of superficial reception and quick transference was what he conspicuously lacked. His first newspaper account of his shipwreck on the filibuster *Commodore* off the Florida coast was as lifeless as the "copy" of a police court reporter. It was many months afterwards that the literary product of his terrible experience appeared in that marvellous sea story "The Open Boat," unsurpassed in its vividness and constructive perfection.

At the close of our long conversation that night, when the copy boy came in to take me home, I suggested to Crane that in ten years he would probably laugh at all his temporary discomfort. Again his body took on that strenuous tension and he clenched his hands, saying, "I can't wait ten years, I haven't time."

The ten years are not up yet, and he has done his work and gathered his reward and gone. Was ever so much experience and achievement crowded into so short a space of time? A great man dead at twenty-nine! That would have puzzled the ancients. Edward Garnett wrote of him in *The Academy* of December 17, 1899: "I cannot remember a parallel in the literary history of fiction. Maupassant, Meredith, Henry James, Mr. Howells and Tolstoy, were all learning their expression at an age where Crane had achieved his and achieved it triumphantly." He had the precocity of those doomed to die in youth. I am convinced that when I met him he had a vague premonition of the shortness of his working day, and in the heart of the man there was that which said, "That thou doest, do quickly."

At twenty-one this son of an obscure New Jersey rector, with but a scant reading knowledge of French and no training had rivaled in technique the foremost craftsmen of the Latin races. In the six years since I met him, a stranded reporter, he stood in the firing line during two wars, knew hairbreadth escapes on land and sea, and established himself as the first writer of his time in the picturing of episodic, fragmentary life. His friends have charged him with fickleness, but he was a man who was in the preoccupation of haste. He went from country to country, from man to man, absorbing all that was in them for him. He had no time to look backward. He had no leisure for *camaraderie*. He drank life to the lees, but at the banquet table where other men took their ease and jested over their wine, he stood a dark and silent figure, sombre as Poe himself, not wishing to be understood; and he took his portion in haste, with his loins girded, and his shoes on his feet, and his staff in his hand, like one who must depart quickly.

—WILLA CATHER, "When I Knew
Stephen Crane," *Library,* June 23, 1900, reprinted
in *Prairie Schooner*, 1949, pp. 2231–2236

HAMLIN GARLAND "STEPHEN CRANE: A SOLDIER OF FORTUNE" (1900)

Hamlin Garland espoused literary realism, or the variety of it that he called veritism. He published his short stories in *Main-Travelled Roads* (1891) and *Prairie Folks* (1893) and his essays in *Crumbling Idols* (1894). He later published several novels, including *Rose of Dutcher's Coolly* (1895), and he published an autobiographical trilogy, with *A Son of the Middle Border* (1917) receiving critical acclaim. Along with the important man of letters William Dean Howells, Garland became an important literary friend of and mentor to Stephen Crane.

Garland met Crane in 1891 when Crane, who was assisting his brother Townley as a shore correspondent for the *New York Tribune*, reported on Garland's lecture on William Dean Howells, one of several talks on American literature that Garland gave at Avon-by-the-Sea, New Jersey, that summer. In August 1892, Garland learned that his new friend had lost his job as a reporter after writing a satiric article on the parade of the Junior Order of United American Mechanics. Garland admired Crane's honesty and literary skill and his early version of *Maggie*, and he used his influence to introduce Crane to various editors, even writing a positive review of the novel in the June 1893 issue of the *Arena*. Their friendship developed as Crane visited Garland at the apartment he shared with his brother in New York in 1894. The brothers frequently fed the young man and loaned him money with which to retrieve half of the manuscript of *The Red Badge* from the typist, who was holding it for payment.

This obituary recounts Garland's friendship with Crane, concentrating on the young man's literary merit and his budding genius. A later piece by Garland published in 1914 in the *Yale Review* recounts much of this same material but adds comments that censure Crane for his bohemian way of life.

The death of Stephen Crane, far away in the mountains of Bavaria, seems to me at this moment a very sorrowful thing. He should have continued to be one of our most distinctive literary workers for many years to come. And yet I cannot say I am surprised. His was not the physical organization that runs to old age. He was old at twenty.

It happened that I knew Crane when he was a boy and have had some years exceptional opportunities for studying him. In the summer of 1888 or 1889 I was lecturing for a seaside assembly at Avon, New Jersey. The report of my first lecture (on "The Local Novelists," by the way) was exceedingly well done in the *Tribune*, and I asked for the name of the reporter. "He is a mere boy," was the reply of Mr. Albert, the manager of the assembly, "and his name is Stephen Crane."

Crane came to see me the following evening, and turned out to be a reticent young fellow, with a big German pipe in his mouth. He was small, sallow and inclined to stoop, but sinewy and athletic for all that—for we fell to talk of sports, and he consented to practice baseball pitching with me. I considered him at this time a very good reporter, and a capital catcher of curved balls—no more, and I said goodbye to him two weeks later with no expectation of ever seeing him again.

In the summer of '91, if I do not mistake, I was visiting Mr. and Mrs. Albert at their school in New York City, when a curious book came to me by mail. It was a small yellow-covered volume, hardly more than a pamphlet, without a publisher's imprint. The author's name was Johnston Smith. The story was called *Maggie, a Girl of the Streets,* and the first paragraph described the battle of some street urchins with so much insight and with such unusual and vivid use of English that I became very much excited about it. Next day I mailed the book to Mr. Howells, in order that he might share the discovery with me. The author had the genius which makes an old world new.

On that very afternoon Crane called upon me and confessed that he had written the book and had not been able to get any one to publish it. Even the firm of printers that put it together refused to place their imprint upon it. He said that the bulk of the edition remained unsold, and that he had sent the book to a number of critics and also to several ministers. On the cover of each copy (as on mine) was written, in diagonal lines, these words or their substance in Crane's beautiful script: "The reader of this story must inevitably be shocked, but let him persist, and in the end he will find this story to be moral." I cannot remember exactly the quaint terms of this admonition, but these words give the idea.

I said to him: "I hardly dare tell you how good that story is. I have sent it to Mr. Howells as a 'find.' Go and see him when he has read it. I am sure he will like it."

He then told me that he had been discharged from the staff of the *Tribune*. He seemed to be greatly encouraged by our conversation, and when he went away I talked with his friends about the book, which appealed to me with great power. I have it still. This desperate attempt of a young author to get a hearing is amusing to an outsider, but it was serious business with Crane then.

I did not see him again until the autumn of 1892, when I went to New York to spend the winter. He wrote occasionally, saying, "Things go pretty slow with me, but I manage to live."

My brother Franklin was in Mr. Herne's Shore Acres Company in those days, and as they were playing an all-season engagement at Daly's theater we decided to take a little flat and camp together for the winter. Our flat was on One Hundred and Fifth Street, and there Crane visited us two or three times a week. He was always hungry and a little gloomy when he came, but my brother made a point of having an extra chop or steak ready for a visitor and Crane often chirped like a bird when he had finished dinner. We often smiled over it then, but it is a pleasure to us now to think we were able to cheer him when he needed it most.

He was living at this time with a group of artists—"Indians," he called them—in the old studio building on East Twenty-third street. I never called to see him there, but he often set forth their doings with grim humor. Most of them slept on the floor and painted on towels, according to his report. Sometimes they ate, but they all smoked most villainous tobacco, for Crane smelled so powerfully of their "smoketalks" that he filled our rooms with the odor. His fingers were yellow with cigarette reek, and he looked like a man badly nourished.

This crowd of artists, according to his story, spent their days in sleep and their nights in "pow-wows" around a big table where they beat and clamored and assaulted each other under a canopy of tobacco smoke. They hated the world. They were infuriated with all hanging committees and art editors, and each man believed religiously in his own genius. Linson was one of those Crane mentioned, and Vosburgh and Green. Together they covenanted to go out some bleak day and slay all the editors and art critics of the city.

Crane at this time wore a light check suit and over it a long gray ulster which had seen much service. His habitual expression was a grim sort of smile. One day he appeared in my study with his outside pockets bulging with two rolls of manuscript. As he entered he turned ostentatiously to put down his hat, and so managed to convey to my mind an impression that he was concealing something. His manner was embarrassed, as if he had come to do a thing and was sorry about it.

"Come now, out with it," I said. "What is the roll I see in your pocket?"

With a sheepish look he took out a fat roll of legal cap paper and handed it to me with a careless, boyish gesture.

"There's another," I insisted, and he still more abruptly delivered himself of another but smaller parcel.

I unrolled the first package, and found it to be a sheaf of poems. I can see the initial poem now, exactly as it was then written, without a blot or erasure—almost without punctuation—in blue ink. It was beautifully legible and clean of outline.

It was the poem which begins thus: "God fashioned the ship of the world carefully."

I read this with delight and amazement. I rushed through the others, some thirty in all, with growing wonder. I could not believe they were the work of the pale, reticent boy moving restlessly about the room.

"Have you any more?" I asked.

"I've got five or six all in a little row up here," he quaintly replied, pointing to his temple. "That's the way they come—in little rows, all made up, ready to be put down on paper."

"When did you write these?"

"Oh! I've been writing five or six every day. I wrote nine yesterday. I wanted to write some more last night, but those 'Indians' wouldn't let me do it. They howled over the other verses so loud they nearly cracked my ears. You see, we all live in a box together, and I've no place to write, except in the general squabble. They think my lines are funny. They make a circus of me." All this with a note of exaggeration, of course.

"Never you mind," I replied; "don't you do a thing till you put all these verses down on paper."

"I've got to eat," he said, and his smile was not pleasant.

"Well, let's consider. Can't we get some work for you to do? Some of these press syndicate men have just been after me to do short stories for them. Can't you do something there?"

"I'll try," he said, without much resolution. "I don't seem to be the kind of writer they want. The newspapers can't see me at all."

"Well, now, let's see what can be done. I'll give you a letter to Mr. Flower, of the *Arena,* and one to Mr. Howells. And I want to take these poems to Mr. Howells tomorrow; I'm sure he'll help you. He's kind to all who struggle."

Later in the meal I said: "Why don't you go down and do a study of this midnight bread distribution which the papers are making so much of? Mr. Howells suggested it to me, but it isn't my field. It is yours. You could do it beyond anybody."

"I might do that," he said; "it interests me."

"Come to-morrow to luncheon," I said, as he went away visibly happier. "Perhaps I'll have something to report."

I must confess I took the lines seriously. If they were direct output of this unaccountable boy, then America had produced another genius, singular as Poe. I went with them at once to Mr. Howells, whose wide reading I knew and relied upon. He read them with great interest, and immediately said:

"They do not seem to relate directly to the work of any other writer. They seem to be the work of a singularly creative mind. Of course they reflect the author's reading and sympathies, but they are not imitations."

When Crane came next day he brought the first part of a war story which was at that time without a name. The first page of this was as original as the verses, and it passed at once to the description of a great battle. Such mastery of details of war was sufficiently startling in a youth of twenty-one who had never smelled any more carnage than a firecracker holds, but the seeing was so keen, the phrases so graphic, so fresh, so newly coined, that I dared not express to the boy's face my admiration. I asked him to leave the story with me. I said:

"Did you do any more 'lines'?"

He looked away bashfully.

"Only six."

"Let me see them."

As he handed them to me he said: "Got three more waiting in line. I could do one now."

"Sit down and try," I said, glad of his offer, for I could not relate the man to his work.

He took a seat and began to write steadily, composedly, without hesitation or blot or interlineation, and so produced in my presence one of his most powerful verses. It flowed from his pen as smooth as oil.

The next day I asked for the other half of the novel. "We must get it published at once," I said. "It is a wonderful study. A mysterious product for you to have in hand. Where is the other part?"

He looked very much embarrassed. "It's in 'hock,'" he said.

"To whom?"

"To the typewriter."

We all laughed, but it was serious business to him. He could see the humor of the situation, but there was a bitter rebellion in his voice.

"How much is it 'hung up' for?"

"Fifteen dollars."

I looked at my brother. "I guess we can spare that, don't you think?"

So Crane went away joyously and brought the last half of *The Red Badge of Courage*, still unnamed at the time. He told us that the coming of that story was just as mysterious as in the case of the verses, and I can believe it. It literally came of its own accord like sap flowing from a tree.

I gave him such words of encouragement as I could. "Your future is secure. A man who can write *The Red Badge of Courage* can not be forever a lodger in a bare studio."

He replied: "That may be, but if I had some money to buy a new suit of clothes I'd feel my grip tighten on the future."

"You'll laugh at all this—we all go through it," said I.

"It's ridiculous, but it doesn't make me laugh," he said, soberly.

My predictions of his immediate success did not come true. *The Red Badge of Courage* and *Maggie* were put through the Syndicate with very slight success. They left Crane almost as poor as before.

In one of his letters, in April, he wrote: "I have not been up to see you because of various strange conditions—notably my toes coming through one shoe, and I have not been going out into society as much as I might. I mail you last Sunday's Press. I've moved now—live in a flat. People can come to see me now. They come in shoals, and say I am a great writer. Counting five that are sold, four that are unsold and six that are mapped out, I have fifteen short stories in my head and out of it. They'll make a book. The *Press* people pied some of *Maggie*, as you will note."

I saw little of him during '93 and '94, but a letter written in May, '94, revealed his condition:

"I have not written you because there has been little to tell of late. I am plodding along on the *Press* in a quiet and effective way. We now eat with charming regularity at least two times a day. I am content and am now writing another novel which is a bird. I am getting lots of free advertising. Everything is coming along nicely now. I have got the poetic spout so that I can turn it on and off. I wrote a Decoration Day thing for the Press which aroused them to enthusiasm. They said in about a minute, though, that I was firing over the heads of the soldiers."

His allusion to free advertising means that the critics were wrangling over *The Black Riders* and *Maggie*. But the public was not interested. I had given him a letter to a Syndicate Press Company, and with them he had left the manuscript of his war novel. In a letter written in November, 1894, he makes sad mention of his lack of success:

"My Dear Friend: So much of my row with the world has to be silence and endurance that sometimes I wear the appearance of having forgotten my best friends, those to whom I am indebted for everything. As a matter of fact, I have just crawled out of the fifty-third ditch into which I have been cast, and now I feel that I can write you a letter which will not make you ill.——put me in one of the ditches. He kept *The Red Badge* six months until I was near mad. Oh, yes—he was going to use it but—Finally I took it to B. They use it in January in a shortened form. I have just completed a New York book that leaves *Maggie* at the post. It is my best thing. Since you are not here I am going to see if Mr. Howells will not read it. I am still working for the *Press*."

At this point his affairs took a sudden turn, and he was made the figure I had hoped to see him two years before. The English critics spoke in highest praise of *The Red Badge,* and the book became the critical bone of contention between military objectors and literary enthusiasts here at home, and Crane became the talk of the day. He was accepted as a very remarkable literary man of genius.

He was too brilliant, too fickle, too erratic to last. Men cannot go on doing stories like *The Red Badge of Courage.* The danger with such highly individual work lies in this—the words which astonish, the phrases which excite wonder and admiration, come eventually to seem like tricks. They lose force with repetition, and come at last to be absolutely distasteful. *The Red Badge of Courage* was marvelous, but manifestly Crane could not go on doing such work. If he wrote in conventional phrase, his power lessened. If he continued to write in his own phrases he came under the charge of repeating himself.

It seems now that he was destined from the first to be a sort of present-day Poe. His was a singular and daring soul, as irresponsible as the wind. He was a man to be called a genius, for we call that power genius which we do not easily understand or measure. I have never known a man whose source of power was so unaccounted for.

The fact of the matter seems to be this. Crane's mind was more largely subconscious in its workings than that of most men. He did not understand his own mental processes or resources. When he put pen to paper he found marvelous words, images, sentences, pictures already to be drawn off and fixed upon paper. His pen was "a spout," as he says. The farther he got from his own field, his own inborn tendency, the weaker he became. Such a man cannot afford to enter the white-hot public thoroughfare, for his genius is of the lonely and the solitary shadow-land.

—HAMLIN GARLAND, "Stephen Crane: A Soldier
of Fortune," *Saturday Evening Post,* July 28, 1900

Edward Marshall "Exciting Life Scenes of Stephen Crane, Journalist" (1900)

Edward Marshall was a journalist and playwright. He first met Stephen Crane in 1894, not the 1890 date given in the following extract. As editor of the *New York Press*, he hired Crane in 1894 to write sketches exposing the squalid living conditions of the city's tenements. One of the first professionals to encourage Crane in his writing, Marshall read *The Black Riders* and *The Red Badge of Courage* in manuscript, suggesting editors who might publish them. He also later wrote favorable reviews of *The Red Badge*, *Maggie*, and *George's Mother*.

This piece reveals Crane as the caring individual his close friends frequently described, one who risked his own livelihood to file a newspaper dispatch for a wounded friend. Marshall was working for a rival newspaper as the two journalists covered the Spanish-American War in Cuba.

⸺⁂⸺ ⸺⁂⸺ ⸺⁂⸺

Crane was not an eccentric character. Many people have said that he was. It was even told in print in this city that he was a drug taker. Such stories were absurd. He was merely the combination of clean, fine youth with genius. When one writes "fine youth" of Stephen Crane the expression is qualified. He was never physically strong. His greatest eccentricity was his habit of all night work. I never saw him wholly at bodily ease. He was not a persistent worker, because his body—a body which suffered from the constant drainings of an intensely active mind—was ever too weak to bear continuous labor. His brain never rested.

Yet when emergencies arose so also did Crane. He was a correspondent on one New York newspaper during the war with Spain. I was a correspondent on another New York newspaper. On June 23 I was told that a battle would occur the next day. I asked Crane if he intended to go to the front. It was insufferably hot, and we had all learned to distrust rumors. He decided not to go. I was amazed by his apparent indolence. I went to the battle and was badly hurt by a bullet. When I regained consciousness, hours after the fight had ended, one of the first faces I saw was that of Stephen Crane. The day was hot. The thermometer—had there been such an instrument in that God forsaken and man invaded wilderness—would have shown a temperature of something like 100 degrees. Yet Stephen Crane—and, mind you, he was there in the interest of a rival newspaper—took the dispatch which I managed to write five or six miles to the coast and cabled it for me. He had to walk, for he could get no horse or mule. Then he rushed about in the heat and arranged with a number of men to bring a stretcher up from the coast and carry me back on it. He was probably as tired then as a man could be and still walk. But he trudged back from the coast in the field hospital where I was lying and saw to it that I was properly conveyed to the coast.

One day in 1890 a young man came to my office with a letter of introduction. He was thin—almost cadaverous. He wanted work and got it. His article—written for a ridiculously low price—on tenement-house fire panics, was one of the best things that he or any other man ever did. It was followed by other strikingly strong stories.

One day he said to me most modestly: "I have written some verse." He handed me a package of manuscript. The next day I left the package on an elevated railroad train. I never told him about it, for within twenty-four hours I had recovered it from the lost property office of the Manhattan L. The manuscript was that of "The Black Riders," which had a tremendous vogue in England.

We were both members of a club made up of writers. The best part of its furnishings was a great open fireplace. Four or five of us sat before it one night and Crane read us parts of a story full of fighting. It was "The Red Badge of Courage." Afterward when we had really seen fighting together I marveled because his stories of actual battle were less realistic than his descriptions of imaginary conflicts in this book. It was that faculty which would have made of Crane a great novelist. He had an accurate and logical imagination.

An episode in his life was unpleasant. He went to a place known as the Broadway Garden to write a descriptive article for a certain newspaper. He was definitely assigned to this work as a soldier might be to guard duty. A woman whom he met there—was a few moments later grossly insulted by a policeman. Crane raised all kinds of trouble for the officer, and in turn was arrested and bothered himself. He took it like a man. He accepted the exceedingly unpleasant notoriety with no comment except that which he made in court.

In losing Crane America lost one of her most promising young writers. But his friends lost more. They lost a chap whom they all knew to be a real man as well as a talented acquaintance.

—EDWARD MARSHALL, "Exciting Life
Scenes of Stephen Crane, Journalist,"
The San Francisco Call, August 12, 1900, p. 12

ELBERT HUBBARD (1900)

Elbert Hubbard, a successful novelist, founded *The Philistine: A Periodical of Protest*, a vehicle for satires of traditional literature. He is best known in

Stephen Crane studies as the one who organized and promoted a dinner in Crane's honor at the Society of the Philistines. The publicity generated was more for his society than for Crane's honor, and Crane actually tried to avoid the event, not having the appropriate dinner clothes for such an occasion and being shy about any sort of public display. Hubbard nevertheless took credit for launching Crane's career, although the banquet came when Crane was already enjoying the popularity of *The Red Badge*.

The dinner was a somewhat rowdy affair with Crane's poetry parodied by several speakers, but Hubbard continued to promote Crane's work, and the two remained friends. Hubbard is somewhat dramatic in his comparison of Stephen Crane with Frederick Chopin, but he illuminates the sensitivity of the young writer to those who were unkind in their reviews of his work.

"Stevie is not quite at home here—he'll not remain so very long," said a woman to me in 1895.

Five years have gone by, and last week the cable flashed the news that Stephen Crane was dead. Dead at twenty-nine, with ten books to his credit, two of them good, which is two more than most of us scribblers will ever write. Yes, Stephen Crane wrote two things that are immortal. *The Red Badge of Courage* is the strongest, most vivid work of the imagination ever fished from ink-pot by an American.

"Men who write from the imagination are helpless when in presence of the fact," said James Russell Lowell. In answer to which I'll point you "The Open Boat," the sternest, creepiest bit of realism ever penned, and Stevie was in the boat.

American critics honored Stephen Crane with more ridicule, abuse and unkind comment than was bestowed on any other writer of his time. Possibly the vagueness, & the loose, unsleeked quality of his work invited the gibes, jeers, and the loud laughter that tokens the vacant mind; yet as half apology for the critics we might say that scathing criticism never killed good work, and this is true, but it sometimes has killed the man.

Stephen Crane never answered back, nor made explanation, but that he was stung by the continual efforts of the press to laugh him down, I am very sure.

The lack of appreciation at home caused him to shake the dust of America from his feet and take up his abode across the sea, where his genius was being recognized, and where strong men stretched out sinewy hands of welcome, and words of appreciation were heard instead of silly, insulting parody. In passing, it is well to note that the five strongest writers of America had their passports to greatness vised in England before they were granted recognition at home. I refer to Walt Whitman, Thoreau, Emerson, Poe and Stephen Crane.

Stevie did not know he cared for approbation, but his constant refusal to read what the newspapers said about him was proof that he did. He boycotted the tribes of Romeike, because he knew that nine clippings out of every ten would be unkind, and his sensitive soul shrank from the pin-pricks.

Contemporary estimates are usually wrong, and Crane is only another of the long list of men of genius to whom Fame brings a wreath and finds her poet dead.

Stephen Crane was a reincarnation of Frederick Chopin. Both were small in stature, slight, fair-haired, and of that sensitive, acute, receptive temperament—capable of highest joy and keyed for exquisite pain. Haunted with the prophetic vision of quick-coming death and with the hectic desire to get their work done, they often toiled the night away and were surprised by the rays of the rising sun.

Shrinking yet proud, shy but bold, with a feminine longing for love and tenderness; mad gaiety, that illy masked a breaking heart, at times took the reins and the spirits of children just out of school seemed to hold the road. At other times—and this was the prevailing mood—the manner was one of placid, patient calm and smooth, unruffled hope; but back and behind all was a dynamo of energy, a brooding melancholy of unrest, & the crouching world-sorrow which this life could never quite unseat. Chopin reached sublimity thru sweet sounds; Crane attained the same heights thru the sense of sight, and words that symboled color, shapes and scenes. In each the distinguishing feature is the intense imagination and active sympathy. Knowledge consists in a sense of values—of distinguishing this from that, for truth lies in the mass. The delicate nuances of Chopin's music have never been equaled by another composer; every note is cryptic, every sound a symbol. And yet it is dance-music, too, but still it tells its story of baffled hope and stifled desire—the tragedy of Poland in sweet sounds. Stephen Crane was an artist in his ability to convey the feeling by just the right word, or a word misplaced, like a lady's dress in disarray, or a hat askew. This daring quality marks everything he wrote. The recognition that language is fluid, and at best only an expedient, flavors all his work. He makes no fetish of a grammar—if the grammar gets in the way so much the worse for the grammar. All is packed with color, and charged with feeling, yet the work is usually quiet in quality and modest in manner.

Art is born of heart, not head; and so it seems to me that the work of these men whose names I have somewhat arbitrarily linked, will live. Each sowed in sorrow and reaped grief. They were tender, kind, gentle, and each possessed a capacity for love that passes the love of women. They were each indifferent to the proprieties, very much as children are. They lived in cloister-like retirement, hidden from the public gaze, or wandered unnoticed & unknown. They founded no schools, delivered no public addresses, and in their day made small impress on the times. Both were sublimely indifferent to what had been said and done—the term precedent not being found within the cover of their bright lexicon of words. In the nature of each was a goodly trace of tincture of iron that often manifested itself in the man's work. They belong to that elect few who have built for the centuries. The influence of Chopin, beyond that of other composers, is alive today, and moves unconsciously, but profoundly, every music-maker; the seemingly careless style of Crane is really lapidaric, and is helping to file the fetters from every writer who has ideas plus, and thoughts that burn.

—ELBERT HUBBARD, obituary,
Philistine, September 1900, pp. 123–128

WILLIAM DEAN HOWELLS
"HINTS FROM THE MAILBAG:
MR. HOWELLS AND STEPHEN CRANE" (1900)

William Dean Howells, the foremost American man of letters during Stephen Crane's life, was a positive influence on the young writer and his reputation. The author of approximately forty novels, Howells also wrote critical essays, plays, poetry, and travel books. Crane looked up to him for his theory of realism, although the writings of the two men differ greatly.

Howells was acquainted with such writers of acclaim as Nathaniel Hawthorne, Ralph Waldo Emerson, Henry David Thoreau, and Walt Whitman, and he became the mentor to many younger writers. He was first assistant editor and then editor of the *Atlantic Monthly*, the most prominent literary magazine of the period. In that role, he wielded great power in literary circles. He was also a columnist for *Harper's Magazine*, where he discussed current literary issues and texts.

Howells did not particularly care for either *The Red Badge of Courage* or *Black Riders*. He praised, however, the original edition of Crane's *Maggie*, after Hamlin Garland had suggested that he send it to the dean of letters, and he supplied a preface of appreciation to the book when it was republished in 1896. Despite its crude dialect, or perhaps because of it, Howells maintained that the novel told the truth about this lower class of society. He urged Crane then to write a novel about a more ordinary family in the slums, and the result was *George's Mother*.

Although Howells was important to Crane for the introductions he arranged with editors and others of influence in publishing, his most important contribution to the young writer was the confidence the older man had in his ability. At the point of meeting Howells, Crane was depressed about the lack of attention he had received from the privately printed first edition of *Maggie*, but Howells boosted Crane's faith in himself to such a degree that he continued diligently working at his writing.

The following letter is one that Howells wrote to Cora Crane after Stephen's death. Admitting that he did not understand some of what Crane had tried to do, Howells reiterates the power that he detected in Crane's early work, especially in *Maggie*. Howells's final sentence raises the value of the young writer to a degree that no other critic had accorded him.

—————   —————   —————

The London Academy has had permission to print the following portion of a letter addressed to Mrs. Stephen Crane by Mr. W. D. Howells:

"Hamlin Garland first told me of 'Maggie,' which your husband then sent me. I was slow in getting at it, and he wrote me a heartbreaking note to the effect that he saw I did not care for his book. On this I read it and found that I did care for it immensely. I asked him to come and see me, and he came to tea and stayed far into the evening, talking about his work and the stress there was on him to put in the profanities which I thought would shock the public from him, and about the semi-savage poor, whose types he had studied in that book. He spoke wisely and kindly about them, and especially about the Tough, who was tough because, as he said, he felt that 'everything was on him.' He came several times afterward, but not at all oftener that I wished, or half so often, and I knew he was holding off from modesty. He never came without leaving behind him some light on the poor, sad life he knew so well in New York, so that I saw it more truly than ever before. He had thought wisely and maturely about it, but he had no plan for it, perhaps not even any hope without a plan.

"He was the great artist which he was because he was in nowise a sentimentalist. Of course I was struck almost as much by his presence as by his mind, and admired his strange, melancholy beauty, in which there was already the forecast of his early death. His voice charmed me, and the sensitive lips from which it came, with their intelligent and ironical smile, and his mystical, clouded eyes. Inevitably there was the barrier between his youth and my age that the years make, and I could not reach him where he lived as a young man might. I cannot boast that I understood him fully; a man of power, before he comes to its full expression, is hard to understand. It is doubtful if he is quite in the secret himself, but I was always aware of his power, and nothing good that he did surprised me. He came to see me last just before he sailed for England the last time, and then he showed the restlessness of the malarial fever that was praying on him; he spoke of having got it in Cuba. But even then, with the sense that we were getting at each other less than ever, I felt his rare quality. I do not think America has produced a more distinctive and vital talent."

—WILLIAM DEAN HOWELLS, "Hints from the
Mailbag: Mr. Howells and Stephen Crane,"
The New York Times, September 8, 1900, p. BR5

R.G. VOSBURGH "THE DARKEST HOUR IN THE LIFE OF STEPHEN CRANE" (1901)

R.G. Vosburgh, one of three artist-illustrators living with Stephen Crane in New York City at the old Art Students League building on East 23rd Street between fall 1893 and spring 1895, describes the money and time Crane put into his efforts to publish his work, spending what was for him a fortune on printing *Maggie*. Vosburgh's description of the writing of *The Red Badge of Courage* reveals the careful attention Crane continued to pay his craft even after the economic failure of his privately printed first book; it also shows how seriously Crane valued his art. Vosburgh confirms the often repeated story that Crane likened battle to the tactics on a football field, a comparison that allowed him to imagine and depict war realistically without ever having seen an actual conflict.

The months following the sinking of the money inherited from his father's estate in the unsuccessful publication of *Maggie: A Girl of the Streets*, marked the lowest ebb in the fortunes of Stephen Crane.

When one firm after another had refused to publish the book, Crane finally invested his own money in the enterprise and lost it all. He then went to live in a boarding house on East Fifty-Seventh street, near Avenue A, and from there moved with the proprietor to West Fifteenth Street. The Fifteenth Street undertaking was not a success, and when the house was given up, Crane went to Lakeview, N.J., for a time. When he returned from Lakeview he was wearing rubber boots because he had no shoes, and he slept and lived at the studios of various artist friends until he was asked to become one of the proprietors of a studio at 145 East Twenty-Third Street.

With Crane the studio had four occupants. He could contribute nothing to its maintenance, but he added very little to the expense, and the others were glad to have him. For seven or eight months, from one autumn until the following summer, the four men lived together. It was during that time that *The Red Badge of Courage* was written. At the time he came to live in the studio, Crane was reading over the descriptive articles on the Civil War published in the *Century*. War and fighting were always deeply interesting to him. The football articles in the newspapers were an especial pleasure. "Ah!" he would say after reading one of them, "that's great. That's bully! That's like war!" And whenever there was a warship coming into the harbor, if he could get the ferry fare, he would go down to Fort Wadsworth and stand on the hill there to watch the vessel come in. He has stood for hours in a drenching rain to see a war vessel enter the harbor.

The articles in the *Century*, then, were full of interest and fascination for Crane, and when he moved to the studio on Twenty-Third street he borrowed the magazines and took them with him to read and study. All of his knowledge of the war and of the country depicted in *The Red Badge of Courage* was gathered from those articles and from the study of maps of that region.

He always worked at night, generally beginning after twelve o'clock, and working until four or five o'clock in the morning, then going to bed and sleeping the greater part of the day. Crane and two of the others slept in a large old-fashioned double bed, taking turns at sleeping in the middle; the fourth man occupied a cot. They pooled their resources, and the first man up was usually the best dressed for the day, unless one of them had a particular reason for wishing to present a good appearance. For men struggling as they were against poverty and privation to force themselves into recognition, there was little incentive to go out except in the search for work. On such occasions, when one of the four men had an idea for getting money, the most presentable combination of clothes that could be made was gotten together for him; and many a time one of them has gone out wearing his friends' clothes bravely over a stomach that had missed more than one meal.

Crane spent his afternoons and evenings studying the war and discussing his stories. Every incident and phase of character in *The Red Badge of Courage* was discussed and argued fully and completely before being incorporated into the story. In this he worked differently from the way in which his short stories were written.

At the time of beginning *The Red Badge of Courage* he was writing sketches of East Side children, some of which have been published since; he could not sell them when they were written. These sketches were quite brief, and most of them were written in one night without previous discussion. After writing a story he would put it away for two or three weeks, and work on something else until his mind was thoroughly clear for a fresh consideration of it. When the story was taken out for revision it would be turned over to his friends for criticism, and Crane would argue with them about the objections they would make. He often accepted suggestions for changes, but it always seemed as though these changes were those he had already decided upon himself before they were mentioned by others. This was also characteristic of the discussions of *The Red Badge of Courage*. He convinced himself; others might help him, but he arrived at his own conclusions.

In his work he always tried for individuality. His daring phrases and short, intense descriptions pleased him greatly. They were studied out with much care, and after they had been trimmed and turned and changed to the final form, he would repeat them aloud and dwell on them lovingly. Impressionism was his faith. Impressionism, he said, was truth, and no man could be great who was not an impressionist, for greatness consisted in knowing truth. He said that he did not expect to be great himself, but he hoped to get near the truth. Although he did not expect to be a great man, he often declared that he would be famous, and sometimes for hours in the intervals when he was not working he would sit writing his name—Stephen Crane—Stephen Crane—Stephen Crane on the books, magazines and loose sheets of paper about the studio. There were plenty of them.

His manuscripts were always scrupulously neat and clean, written in ink on legal cap paper without erasures and without interlineations. In revising his work he would rewrite a whole sheet when a correction was necessary rather than make an erasure, if only to change one word.

The poems published under the title *Black Riders* were also written during this period. Crane himself had a very high opinion of these poems, in which he was confirmed by Hamlin Garland, who, besides William Dean Howells, was his favorite among American authors. The friendship and encouragement of these two men gave him strength and courage in his struggle, and he often spoke of them with pride and gratitude. A critical article by Hamlin Garland comparing Crane and Richard Harding Davis which appeared in the *Arena* during that winter was of immense value to him. The conclusion of the article was that Crane was far superior to Davis, and this opinion Crane often quoted when, under the burden of fresh disappointments, the future seemed to offer no hope. The hard and meagre life—two poor meals a day, a bun or two for breakfast and a dinner of potato salad and sausages warmed over the little stove that heated the room, frequently eaten cold because there was no coal for the stove—could be borne if he were progressing towards his end.

Just after *The Red Badge of Courage* was completed, and two or three months before a publisher was found, Crane received the only commission that he obtained during all of this period. The Wilson Syndicate gave him a commission to write a story about the New York lodging houses. Crane and one of his friends in the studio spent a night and two days as tramps on the Bowery and East Side, about the lodging houses. This was the kind of work that pleased him best, for he said, it was in such places human nature was to be seen and studied. Here it was open and plain, with nothing hidden. It was unvarnished human nature, he said.

—R.G. Vosburgh, "The Darkest Hour
in the Life of Stephen Crane,"
Criterion, February 1901, pp. 26–27

Corwin Knapp Linson
"Little Stories of 'Steve' Crane" (1903)

Stephen Crane was introduced to Corwin Knapp Linson in 1893 by Linson's cousin, Louis C. Senger. The two became close friends during the time Crane was living with some artists in New York City between 1893 and 1895. Linson illustrated Crane's article "In the Depths of a Coal Mine," after both had visited the mines near Scranton, Pennsylvania, and he served as the model for Hawker in Crane's *The Third Violet*. In 1958, the following reminiscence of Crane's time in New York was published posthumously as *My Stephen Crane*. In that version, Linson adds comments on Crane's sense of humor, most often used to poke fun at his own poverty during that time.

Here Linson gives details of Crane's writing of *The Red Badge*, "The Pace of Youth," and the poems for *The Black Riders*. He mentions camping trips that he, Crane, and other friends made to Sullivan County, New York, during the summers, and he shows the sensitivity Crane felt about his writing, in particular his poems, which were often parodied by even his good friends.

———————————

I was closely associated with Stephen Crane during the years just preceding his success, when we both had our feet in the same Slough of Despond. We parted—for a season, I thought—when he went to Athens at the time of the Greek War, after a last evening together in New York.

My first meeting with him was in the winter of 1892–3. One Sunday afternoon, Mr. Louis C. Senger, a cousin who was one of his intimates, brought him to my studio in the old building on West Thirtieth Street and

Broadway. It was a dreary day, and the gray light filtered in through the cobwebby panes of the great sidelight, finding us in a kind of half-gloom. He talked little, sitting on a divan quietly smoking cigarettes. He impressed me as an unusual individuality, at first reserved, but soon expanding in the warmth of our comradeship.

It was a good beginning. His long rain-ulster became a familiar object, for those were slushy, drizzly days, and the winter air was oftener sleety with cold rain than fluffy with feathery snow. One day a pocket contained a yellow-covered book—the Maggie, which was left for me. It was read with enthusiasm and immediately clamored for. His vigorous English and deep human sympathy fairly took me by storm. The book was resigned with a smile. "There are heaps of them left; the public isn't crazy about having them."

And then its history came out; how no publisher would take it, so that he had had it printed at his own expense; how it had been turned down by the newsdealers, icily received by prominent clergymen who did not preach that way, and how two eminent literary men alone had stood by him with encouragement. Afterward I saw the yellow stacks of unsold books in his rooms.

My place was a black den in those days, and my affairs harmonized, so that it was quite a congenial retreat for Crane. It was his daily habit to come and compare notes. When the news-stands declared war, he became savagely caustic; when such men as Howells and Garland, who were to him the last word in American literature, called his books a great performance, he was seriously elated, happy beyond expression. I have often wondered if Mr. Howells knew the deep joy with which his good opinion filled Crane.

His facility used to astonish me. Sitting on my couch, rings of gray smoke circling about him, a pad on his knee, he would turn out a complete story in a half-hour. Sometimes it was a fragment that would be laid by for future use. Several sparkling sketches were invented and written in that atmosphere of melancholy, while I sat at my easel dabbling at a drawing and wondering how a new illustrator could get in his "wedge."

A visit to his rooms one morning discovered him in undress with a wet towel turban-like about his head, feverishly writing. He waved me to a seat, and soon handed me the first pages of a story. "Been at it most of the night, and it's nearly finished." It appeared long after in one of the papers. Its characters were taken from the class that furnishes cheap entertainment at the seaside resorts, and it was slight enough as a tale. But what amazed me was the vivid drawing of these people, his picturing of their life and environment, his insight into their motives and habits, months after he could have been in touch with them at all, revealing keenest observations and understanding.

One might say that like qualities are the common equipment of the artist, but he had them in an uncommon way.

Crane had many loyal friends then, but, unfortunately, they were as poorly situated as himself: young doctors working out their hospital apprenticeship, boyish reporters and artists for obvious reasons unspoiled by prosperity; my cousin, who was none of these but equally at home with all; a half-dozen as ardent souls as ever banded together, widely scattered as to domiciles but easily mobilized for whatever there was afoot, to whom economy was at once a bug-bear and a necessity. There were joyous days, and when fortune once sent us oysters and a beefsteak the notable occasion was duly celebrated.

It was about that time that he had a story of two men who went bathing on the Jersey coast, and, in toying with a derelict raft, were carried out to sea, picked up by a little coast schooner, and taken to New York. He asked me to illustrate it, "on spec," and as I had no other work to do I went through it from title to tailpiece, and never had more fun with anything.

There was no editor hounding me for urgent haste, the author was delighted as things progressed, posed himself for the tall man—he was thin enough!—stuffed a pillow in the clothes of a friend for the fat man (it was funny to see that pillow swelling from beneath a tightly-fitting bathing-suit), and I grimaced in a glass for the bath-ticket seller in his box.

When finished, the whole thing was sent to a magazine, which had already printed a sketch of his. Then I went camping up in Ramapo.

When I returned, the package had also reappeared, having been "considered" for most of the summer. Crane had reported it accepted, and we were correspondingly happy, but somehow it lost its bearings.

The after fate of our effort was unknown, except that it disappeared in the mazy offices of one of the magazines, and never came to the surface.

In the spring of '93 Crane used to spend hours in my place rummaging through old periodicals, poring over the Civil War articles. I did not then grasp his drift, nor did he explain his interest in them. But he was sounding, trying to fathom the inwardness of war through the impressions on record, as I afterward understood. He did express some impatience with the writers, I remember.

"I wonder that some of those fellows don't tell how they felt in those scraps. They spout enough of what they did, but there're as emotionless as rocks."

He was evolving *The Red Badge of Courage.*

He had, also, several short sketches in hand which he casually called the Baby Stories. I had three of them in camp that summer to study for pictures, but nothing came of them. For lucid analysis of the very young human heart I never saw their like. The winter following was a hard one for Crane. It was not honey for me, exactly, but it was growing kindlier, while for him it presented a face of stone. He was now in the old League building on Twenty-third Street, rooming with several young illustrators and newspaper artists.

One morning early, after a blizzardy night, I found him in bed. He looked haggard. He was alone, the others being presumably in pursuit of the art editors.

Pulling a manuscript from mysterious seclusion, he tossed it to me. It was the sketch, "The Men in the Storm," suggested by Mr. Garland. He had been all night at it, out in the storm in line with the hungry men, studying them; then inside, writing it.

This was the period of his tramp studies, written for a press syndicate. He disappeared from view for days, and was suddenly dug up looking as if he had lived in a grave. All this time he had inhabited the tramp lodging-houses nights, and camped on the down-town park benches days. With grim delight he related how an old acquaintance had passed him a foot away, as he sat with a genuine hobo in front of the City Hall, and how the police had eyed his borrowed rags askance, or indicated with official hand that another bench needed dusting.

One evening he came to me, bringing several loose sheets of manuscript.

"What do you think I have been doing?"

"I can imagine anything, Steve."

"I've been writing—poetry!"

"Great Scott! Let me see."

Well as I knew him, I was not prepared for what came. The sheets of legal-cap were handed over, and I read those marvelous short poems. I did not know how good they were. I confessed that they were something new to me, but that they made me see pictures, great pictures.

"Do they, honest?" he asked delightedly.

I added that they moved me profoundly.

"Is that so?" he said seriously.

"Indeed they do, Steve, they're immense! How did you ever think of them?"

"They came."

That seemed to be the way of it, they just "came." And that was my introduction to his new character. I have two of those poems now.

One [friend], happening to be there, seeing some of them and handing them back with, "I don't know much about poetry," called forth an energetic protest after he left.

"I know every one can't like them, but I hate to give a man a chance to hit me in the neck with an ax!"

It was not very long after that an "Authors' Reading" was given, and my cousin Louis went with me, for some things from *The Black Riders* (still unpublished) were to be read. Far from reading his own work, at the idea of which he was aghast, Crane could not be induced even to go and hear—"would not be dragged by the neck"—so in dread was he of a misunderstanding of his work. He could stand up to adverse criticism like a catcher behind the bat, or retort to a gibe, giving better than he received—for his wit had a keen edge, and he was a master of repartee—but cold indifference was the "ax in the neck." The war of the newsdealers upon his *Maggie* was unjust, and he scorned them, but the slight put upon his book by the clergymen to whom he sent it chilled his blood.

So he awaited our report in his room. We made it glowing, for the audience was enthusiastic and the "Lines" had been most effectively read by Mr. Barry.

As to Crane's environment at that time, his statement of it could hardly have been greatly exaggerated. The fellow with whom he lived used to receive his verses as good material for the comic papers, for they jeered at everything. It is the attitude of youth. Once, as we sat by ourselves amid the confusion of tables laden with all the litter of writing and drawing tools, unwashed coffee-cups, newspaper drawing, tobacco, bread, pipes, while about us were crazy chairs, unkept beds, disorderly trunks and shelves, and room-long reach of quaking stoves pipe—everything at war with everything else—he said to me:

"Confound their cheek; they even parody my verse!" Then he laughed and pointed to a pinned-up squib on the wall, with a caricature of himself above it. It was a parody, and clever, so like his style that he might have been its author.

"They make me ill!—but they don't mean it, and I get my innings! They're a husky lot."

There were at least five of them, all on the war-path. More than once I was one of the roomful of "Indians" whose vision of things was distorted in the dim haze of smoke.

Something of this life of his is reflected in *The Third Violet*. We knew all the Cheap-John restaurants together. There was one to which many congenial spirits flittered on Saturday nights; where absolute liberty of emotion was allowed, where a table could break out into song and wild gayety without annoying anyone particularly, where there was much confusion of tongues, where bad wine took the place of "draw one," and where the waiters conjured the knives, forks and spoons from the depths of cavernous breeches" pockets and wiped them on their sleeves! There could be no etiquette in a place like that, except that of good humor. We Americanized its French name into the Buffalo Mode [The Boeuf-a-la-mode, a restaurant on Sixth Avenue], and once each week we carried our troubles to its murkey atmosphere and joyous company. The life of our table—always the middle one of the room—was Crane, and the cheeriest sallies were from his lips.

I had almost forgotten the "towel painting." During that camping summer in the Ramapo backwoods, I had my only two yards of painting canvas slung on a line over my hammock like a roof, to shed the rain, and the next best thing was to make more. The only form of linen up there was in the shape of coarse towels, which I used singly, or sewed together, painting over a coating of glue. They did very well until one of them got rained on, when my hardly secured study flaked off in great spots. But my picture of that year ('94) in the Society was painted on one of those towels!

That summer we were sent to do the mines at Scranton. It was Crane's first assignment from one of the magazines, but he had not enough money to pay his fare from New York. Luckily, I had enough just then to see us through, and we undertook it joyfully. We were expecting after that to do the sea-divers, going down in diving rigs—but it did not happen.

After this, I saw less and less of him, for in '95 he made an extended tour through the West for a press syndicate, going into Mexico, and not returning for some months. A note or two only, from the West and New Orleans, were the only signs I had of his existences.

But he grew rich in material on this trip. He suddenly appeared one evening, and held me breathless and intent with tales of adventure. One of them I saw afterward in print, but his vivid telling was so much more effectives than even his strenuous pen-picture, that the written story seemed to lose color as I contrasted the two in my memory. That his luminous phrasing was not a trick was never more evident than then. It was simply Crane.

His speech was free from the danger that his writing ran, of weakening with repetition. Each scintillation eclipsed the last, but left a complete impression of delight.

He brought back a half-dozen opals, some with the lambent flame of the sunset in their fiery depths. He freely gave me the choice of the lot. I took a little one that flashed at me with the gleam of a rainbow. Crane laughingly added a fine water opal to it. The next morning he said: ·

"It's [a] good thing you came in for a deal yesterday, for the newspaper Indians gave me a dinner last night, and they got my pretty pebbles!"

I frankly regretted that I had made no better use of my opportunity!

And now—'96—our meetings were less frequent. He spent much time away from New York, and I also was absent some months abroad. Finally he sent for a box of manuscript that had been some time in my care, and soon after unexpectedly showed himself at my door, just before his departure for Athens and the Graeco-Turkish war. He was full of his prospective trip. It was a new phase of life, actual war, and the excitement of it was upon him. It was late when we parted, and it was my final "good-by." Almost his last words were references to his almost Sullivan County (New York) which was also my own, provoked by some inane remarks of men at a nearby table at dinner.

"If they only knew it as we do, eh," he said laconically, "they couldn't make such brilliant asses of themselves before old inhabitants."

After that, only occasional reports came, of his living in England, of his presence in Cuba. From a brother with the army at Santiago, I heard of him.

"I met your friend Crane at Santiago. He's going to Manila, he says. He's a hustler, isn't he?"

And then a long blank, until, living in Paris, I heard of his illness in England and before I could realize his condition the news of his death came.

It is inevitable that there must exist a nipping regret at the cutting off of a brilliant individuality in its early development. His was a cometlike career. And undeniably erratic and irresponsible in much as he was, he was lovable to a degree, daring and chivalrous, generous as the air, compelling a genuinely warm affection from those who best knew him; and for his genius I sometimes felt not a little awe, as for a power mysterious and unaccountable.

—Corwin Knapp Linson, "Little Stories of
'Steve' Crane," *Saturday Evening Post*,
April 11, 1903, pp. 19–20

Ford Madox Hueffer [Ford] "Henry James, Stephen Crane and the Main Stream" (1921)

Ford Madox Hueffer, who changed his last name to Ford, was a prolific writer, with thirty-four novels to his credit. He associated with many of the most esteemed writers of his time, including Joseph Conrad, T.S. Eliot, Gertrude Stein, and Ernest Hemingway. Of many of his literary associations he wrote lengthy reminiscences, but in them he became often more of a fiction writer than a biographer, as is evident in the inaccuracies in this piece on Stephen Crane and Henry James. Still, Ford captures something of his feelings about the two writers. For example, he calls Crane "Stevie," a nickname not used in his correspondence with Crane, which always employed a formal mode of address, and he exaggerates the writer's dress and mannerisms. He depicts Crane as having grown up in the Bowery, when he had only visited it. He and Crane were never close, as he intimates, and Crane is not known to have spoken negatively of Stevenson or of Henry James. In fact, James visited the Cranes often, bicycling seven miles from Rye to Brede Place, which sits on a rise and is not in a valley as described by Ford. It was 1897, not 1896, when Edward Garnett introduced Ford to Crane.

Unfortunately, Ford's exaggerations and inaccuracies may have fueled rumors of Crane's eccentricities and excesses. This piece is included to show the contrast between it and the other more reliable reminiscences.

It was perhaps in 1896—I am never very certain of my dates, but it was about then—that Mr. Garnett brought poor, dear, "Stevie" to call upon me. I was then living a very self-consciously Simple Life at Limpsfield in a newly built cottage of huge lumps of rough stone. These Crane, fresh from the other side of the world, muddledly took to be the remains of an ancient fortification. He put in, I remember, a rose tree beside the immensely thick, oaken front door—for all the world like a king planting a memorial oak!—and looking at an outside fire-place remarked:

"That's a bully ol' battlement!"

He told me afterwards that, although he did not, in the ordinary way set much store by corner lots and battle-fields I and my establishment had pretty well seen him for the jack-pot. But the literary point about the interview was this:

At a given moment Mr. Garnett said that Crane—he was then the all-famous author of the *Red Badge of Courage*—must have read a great deal of French imaginative literature. Crane said defiantly that he had never read a word of French in his life. (I dare say the defiance was to my address far more than to Mr. Garnett's.) He had been dragged up in the Bowery, he had, and he hadn't any use for corner lots. When Mr. Garnett persisted and pointed out the great remembrance of his handling of a story to Maupassant's, Crane said:

"Oh well, I've read ol' man James's. . . ." I forget what it was he confessed to having read, but it was one of James's French critical works.

Later, I was requested—this will seem an improbable story—to go one evening to Crane's house at Oxted, near by, to give Mrs. Crane a lesson in dressmaking. The request had been made by a local lady who liked to "bring people together," I not having, out of shyness, I dare say, pursued the acquaintance with Crane. I found Mrs. Crane alone and she did not want a lesson in dressmaking—of the medieval variety. But she begged me to await Crane's return: he had gone up to town on business and she expected he would be nervous and glad of distraction. I think this was the only unsolicited call I ever paid—and that was due to a misapprehension!—and I was nervous enough myself!

He came back—nervous and distracted, truly, and very late—but extraordinarily glad. I have never again seen such gladness as was displayed on that Oxted-night by that great and elf-like writer. For me, Crane came nearer to the otherworldly being than any human soul I have ever encountered: he was indeed what Trelawny has made us believe Shelley was—the Author of emotionalised fiction.

He kept it exaggeratedly beneath the surface. Superficially he was harsh and defiant enough: his small, tense figure and his normal vocabulary were those of the Man of Action of dime drama—very handy in a Far Western fashion, with a revolver. He loved, indeed, to sit about in breeches, leggings, and shirt-sleeves, with a huge Colt strapped to his belt. And he would demonstrate with quite sufficient skill how, on a hot day he could swat a fly on the wall with the bead foresight of his "gun"—all the while uttering Bowery variations on his theme of giving no fancy prices for antiquities. He meant by that that he was not a Poet.

But he was! . . .

What an admirable talent! You had *Maggie*; you had the *Open Boat*, the *Bride Comes to Yellow Sky*, the *Three White Mice*. And I remember with particular emotion the *Third Violet*, a book which Crane's chief admirers did not care for and one which I have not been able to re-read, since it appears to be out of print and I have been able to find no copy.

It is astonishing that any book of Stephen Crane's should be out of print and that one should be able to find no copy. It is lamentable!

He was glad, that night at Oxted; he was astonishingly glad, the joy shining out of him as heat glows sometimes through opaque substances—because his agent, Mr. Pinker, had given him a contract to sign which guaranteed him £20 per thousand words for everything that he chose to write and had advanced him a sum of money sufficient to pay his Oxted debts. So he could get away from Oxted. The motive may seem materialistic to the official-poetic amongst readers. But Crane had hated his suburban villa with a hatred comprehensible enough—and he hated debts with the hatred of a high-strung, nervous but realistic poet.

With the falling from his shoulders of that intolerable load he desired, as Mrs. Crane had foreseen, to talk. And he talked. He kept me there listening, right through the night, until breakfast time. He had the most amazing eyes; large, like a horse's; frowning usually with the gaze of one looking very intently—but shining astonishingly at times. And a deep voice. When he became excited—as that night he was—the studied Americanisms disappeared from his vocabulary, or nearly so, and he talked a rather classical English. He planned then, his glorious future.

They were, his plans, not so much a matter of the world over which he intended to travel, flinging coins from the purse of Fortunatus that had been put by Mr. Pinker into his hands: it was a question, rather, of how he would render that world when he had roved all over it. He talked, in fact, about his technique.

I do not flatter myself that it was to me that he talked; that night he would have talked like that to a broomstick. . . . I had, I suppose, in those days a Pre-Raphaelite or Æsthetic aspect and he seemed to make me responsible for the poems of Rossetti and the prose of Mr. Legallienne. So that, beginning by telling me, like Mr. Conrad, that I could not write and never should be able to write, he went on to tell me how writing should be done—and from time to time denouncing me.

And his formulae were those of the Flaubert-Maupassant-Turgenev school. He had read, naturally, a great deal more French than he had chosen to acknowledge in my unsympathetic presence, to Mr. Garnett. I do not mean to say that his native talent and inspiration did not make him a peculiarly good subject for that contagion. He would no doubt have written simply and forcibly and in the most economical of forms if Maupassant had never written a line. But, under that stimulus he had arrived much more quickly at a "method" and he knew quite well "what he was doing."

And what particularly interested me was his projection before me, then, of a great series of heroic poems that he was planning to write—in Vers Libre. Of these he wrote only one volume—the *Black Riders*, and, if, in this verse he did not attain to the quietness and colloquialism, at which he aimed theoretically—and to which I fancy that even at that date I had attained—he certainly showed some of the way for a whole school. He hated both rhyme and formal metre and at one point he shouted at me—he had never seen a word of mine:

"You ruin . . . ruin . . . ruin . . . all your work by the extra words you drag in to fill up metres and by the digressions you make to get at rhymes!" He possessed, in fact, in a remarkable degree not only the Literary Gift but the Literary Sense—and a devouring passion for words.

The contacts of Henry James and poor Stevie were peculiar. I do not remember to have heard the two of them discuss together anything of material interest. Indeed I only remember to have seen them together at large social functions like the flower shows that Crane and his family interested themselves in, at Brede in Sussex. But I heard the two men discuss each other, often enough.

Crane's attitude toward the Master—except for occasional lapses of irritation in which he would talk of James as Henrietta Maria—was boyishly respectful and enthusiastic. I dare say that, with his marvelous insight, he valued the great man very sufficiently, and when his defiant mood was off him and he was not riding about the country on one of his immense coach-horses, he would readily enough acknowledge himself to be, if not a disciple, at least an attentive scholar of the Old Man's works.

By that time he had taken Brede Place—an immense, haunted and unrestored Elizabethan manor house, lying, unhealthily beshadowed and low in a Sussex valley. I fancy I was responsible for introducing him to the Place; at any rate I had known it for many years before he came there. And with characteristic enthusiasm, though he would still declare that he had no use for battle-fields—he led there the life of an Elizabethan baron. Rushes covered the floors; dogs lay beneath the table to gnaw the bones that fell; a baron of beef and a barrel of ale stood always ready near the back door for every tramp to consume. The house was filled with stray dogs, lost cats, and, as if in tides, indiscriminately chosen bands of irresponsible guests, would fill and recede from, the half-furnished rooms. . . . And in a small room over the great porch of the house Crane would sit writing, to keep it all going.

It used to be terrible to see the words, in a tiny writing, slowly filling the immense sheet of white foolscap; falling from the pen that made that passionate pilgrimage, to keep going that immense house, that not so much riotous as uncalculated hospitality. It was the brave attempt of a gallant soul—and surely there was never a soul more gallant than that of Stephen Crane. . . . But the end was tragic, as it must be in that haunted and foredooming hollow into which the very sunlight seemed to fall with the air of a blight. . . .

Stevie used to rail at English Literature, with its Stevenson and the interjected finger, as being one immense petty, Parlour Game. Our books he used to say were written by men who never wanted to go out of the drawing-rooms for people who wanted to live at perpetual tea-parties. Even our adventure stories, colonial fictions and tales of the boundless prairie were conducted in that spirit. The criticism was just enough. It was possible that James never wanted to live outside tea-parties—but the tea-parties that he wanted were debating circles of a splendid aloofness, of an immense human sympathy, and of a beauty that you do not find in Putney—or in Passy!

It was his tragedy that no such five-o'clock ever sounded for him on the timepieces of this world. And that is no doubt the real tragedy of all of us—of all societies—that we never find in our Spanish Castle our ideal friends living in an assured and permanent republic. Crane's Utopia, but not his literary method, was different. He gave you the pattern in—and the reverse of—the carpet in physical life—in Wars, in slums, in Western saloons, in a world where the "gun" was the final argument. The life that Mr. Conrad gives you is somewhere halfway between the two: it is dominated—but less dominated by the revolver than that of Stephen Crane, and dominated, but less dominated, by the moral scruple than that of James. But the approach to life is the same with all these three: they show you that disillusionment is to be found alike at the tea-table, in the slum and on the tented field. That is of great service to our Republic. . . .

When "poor dear Stevie" at Brede fell sick of his last, protracted illness, the personal concern that James showed was almost fantastic. He turned his days into long debates over this or that benevolence—and he lay all night awake fearing that he might have contemplated something that might wound the feelings or appear patronizing to the sick boy. He would run the gamut of grapes, public subscriptions, cheques. He cabled to New York for sweet-corn and soft-shelled crabs for fear the boy might long for home-food. And when they threw them away—for fear they should make him more homesick!

—Ford Madox Hueffer [Ford],
"Henry James, Stephen Crane and the
Main Stream," *Thus to Revisit: Some Reminiscences*,
New York, E. P. Dutton, 1921, pp. 102–125

❖

GENERAL

❖

The following assessments of Stephen Crane as a writer range from hearty endorsement to disparagement of his work. The first five writers assessed Crane during his lifetime, with the first two selections hailing him as an author who had not been fully appreciated. The third extract, by British critic H.D. Traill, finds neither *The Red Badge of Courage* nor *Maggie: A Girl of the Streets* to be important works, an interesting conclusion in light of the immensely positive reaction to *The Red Badge* on its initial publication there. In particular, he refuses to call these two volumes "realistic," citing the work of a now unknown writer, Arthur Morrison, as being more realistic. The fourth excerpt, by Stephen Gwynn, finds much power in Crane's writing but hopes that his style will improve with time. The final article, written by Edward Garnett, is insightful, providing early specific analysis of Crane's writing and marking the beginning of a long and continuing appreciation of Crane's entire authorial output.

The next five articles, written in the year of his death or shortly thereafter, assess the writer for his overall contribution to literature. Garnett again points out the modern nature of Crane's work and the fact that the young man had managed to produce eleven books during his short lifetime. William L. Alden praises his work of imagination, *The Red Badge*, as superior to his later short stories inspired by actual war. John Northern Hilliard contributes to ideas of Crane's overall methods and literary philosophy by quoting letters that Crane had sent him, and he points out the hurt that Crane had felt from some attacks on his work. He concludes, "It is only justice to add, however, that the very writers who were the severest in their satires and criticisms of Stephen Crane, when he was alive were the first to pay honest and unembittered tributes to his memory."

The best of the contemporary estimates in this group is that of H.G. Wells, who points out the qualities in Crane's works that make them good literature: their originality, their vigor, and their vehement emotion. He marks "The Open Boat" as a masterpiece. In assessing Crane's place in literature, Wells admits that he cannot tell at that point, but he states, "Suffice it that, even before his death, Crane's right to be counted in the hierarchy of those who have made a permanent addition to the great and growing fabric of English letters was not only assured, but conceded."

A disappointment in this group is William Dean Howells's estimation of Crane's contribution to literature, one that still states that *Maggie* is his best work. In trying to arrive at an overall estimation of Crane's place in literature, Howells suggests that Frank Norris may have a higher place, a judgment that has not proved true with time.

The next set of excerpts were written from fourteen to twenty-two years after Crane's death, and they fall into two groups. Hamlin Garland, who had been so supportive of Crane during his early career, continued to believe in the younger writer's genius, but he had been severely affected by the rumors that spread after Crane's death, about his relationship with Cora and his way of life in England, to which there was an element of truth but also much exaggeration. Cora and Stephen were never married because she was not divorced from her husband, and she had operated a hotel in Jacksonville, which was much like a brothel. Joseph Conrad's essay, too, is lukewarm in its praise, pointing out that he thought Crane had written himself out, that he would have made no advancements had he lived.

The final two essays marked the beginning of a sort of resurrection of interest in Stephen Crane's work. Vincent Starrett's article from the *Sewanee Review* is both specific and appreciative of the elements that make the writing continue to live. It came at a time when the imagist movement was gaining force in the United States and when a few critics hailed Crane as the precursor. His iconoclasm was similar to the rebellious nature of imagist poems, and they acknowledge some debt to the earlier poet. Starrett argues correctly that "Crane was an imagist before our modern imagists were known." Starrett was to follow up this essay with his own anthology of Crane's work, *Men, Women and Boats*, published in 1921 by Modern Library. In his introduction to that volume, he tries to establish Crane as a major literary figure but with little success at that time.

The last essay by Edward Garnett does a better job of arguing for Crane's position. It reassesses the elements of the fiction particularly, detailing the strength of his best work and highlighting its modernist characteristics. Both Starrett and Garnett helped to spark a reawakening interest in Stephen Crane's work, and the influential Edmund Wilson carefully joined in; but Wilson was so cautious about bringing attention to what was considered the decadent 1890s that he aroused little interest. It is, however, to the credit of Starrett and Garnett that Crane was brought to the attention of at least some of the modernist writers, several of whom benefitted from reading his works and later admitted his influence on their own writing.

Harry Thurston Peck "Stephen Crane" (1895)

Harry Thurston Peck was an American classical scholar, author, editor, and critic. Associated with Columbia University until 1910 as a tutor and as a professor, he was dismissed from the school after he became involved in a breach-of-promise suit. Four years later, he committed suicide, an event that James Weldon Johnson describes with dismay in his autobiography *Along This Way*.

Peck was the first editor in chief of *The Bookman* magazine, and in that role he created the world's first bestseller list. As a literary critic, he was among the first to recognize in print Stephen Crane's talent. In the following selection, Peck credits Crane for great talent in his writing, detailing the work he has done up to this point.

You will look in vain through the pages of the *Trade Circular* for any record of a story of New York life entitled *Maggie: A Girl of the Streets*, which was published three or four years ago in this city. At the moment of going to press the timorous publishers withdrew their imprint from the book, which was sold, in paper covers, for fifty cents. There seems to be considerable difficulty now in securing copies, but the fact that there is no publisher's name to the book, and that the author appears under the *nom de plume* of "Johnston Smith," may have something to do with its apparent disappearance. The copy which came into the writer's possession was addressed to the Rev. Thomas Dixon a few months ago, before the author went West on a journalistic trip to Nebraska, and has these words written across the cover: "It is inevitable that this book will greatly shock you, but continue, pray, with great courage to the end, for it tries to show that environment is a tremendous thing in this world, and often shapes lives regardlessly. If one could prove that theory, one would make room in Heaven for all sorts of souls (notably an occasional street girl) who are not confidently expected to be there by many excellent people." The author of this story and the writer of these words is Stephen Crane, whose Lines (he does not call them poems) have just been published by Copeland and Day, and are certain to make a sensation.

Stephen Crane is not yet twenty-four years old, but competent critics aver that his command of the English language is such as to raise the highest hopes for his future career. The impression he makes on his literary co-workers is that he is a young man of almost unlimited resource. The realism of his *Maggie*—a story that might have taken a greater hold on the public than even *Chimmie Fadden,* had the publishers been less timid—is of that daring and terrible directness which in its iconoclasm is the very characteristic of rugged undisciplined strength in a youth of genius. We hear the echo of this mood in number XLV of his *Lines:*

Tradition, thou art for suckling children,
Thou art the enlivening milk for babes;
But no meat for men is in thee.
Then —
But, alas, we all are babes.

Mr. Crane started to write for the press when only sixteen, and he has been at newspaper work ever since. He has done very little outside of journalism; some of his stories have been contributed to the *Cosmopolitan,* and a story entitled *The Red Badge of Courage,* which relates the adventures of a recruit under fire for the first time during the Civil War, was one of the most successful serials which the Bachelor Syndicate have handled in a long time. This serial has now been set up in book form, and will be published in the summer by Messrs. Appleton and Company, who think very highly of his work. Among other manuscripts which are now in the publishers' hands is one entitled *A Woman without Weapons.* It is a story of New York Life, like *Maggie,* but its scenes are laid on the borderland of the slums, and not down in the Devil's Row and Rum Alley. When Mr. Hamlin Garland read *Maggie* and reviewed it in the *Arena* on its appearance, he sought out the intrepid young author and introduced him to Mr. W. D. Howells, who in turn extended his kindness to young Crane, and made him acquainted with several of his *confreres* who were likely to encourage his literary aspirations. For over a year Mr. Crane has been on the staff of the Bachelor Syndicate, and he is now in Mexico "writing up" that country for them.

Mr. Crane is a New Yorker, and both his father and mother are dead. All the stanzas in the little volume which has just been published were written in a sudden fit of inspiration, in less than three days, and were polished and finished and sent off within a fortnight. The cover design of *The Black Riders* was drawn by Mr. F. C. Gordon, whose work on the beautiful holiday edition of Tennyson's *Becket,* published last Christmas, met with signal approbation. A review of *The Black Riders* appears in "Some Recent Volumes of Verse" on another page. What Hamlin Garland said of the author a few years ago may be now repeated with a more certain assurance of fulfillment: "With such a technique already in command, with life mainly before him, Stephen Crane is to be henceforth reckoned with."

—HARRY THURSTON PECK, "Stephen Crane,"
The Bookman, May 1895, pp. 229–230

UNSIGNED (1896)

This unsigned excerpt includes the cover design on the dinner menu of the infamous Society of the Philistines's roast to celebrate Stephen Crane's recent publication of *The Red Badge of Courage*. The article also included a portrait of Crane, perhaps the first public visual depiction of him.

The dinner was arranged by Elbert Hubbard, supposedly to bring attention to Crane but largely to draw attention to the society itself; the somewhat shy Crane was hesitant to attend. Hubbard sent out invitations to other writers, publishers, and journalists. A total of thirty men, other than Crane, were in attendance, and they proceeded to read parodies of his poetry in *The Black Riders*, which had also recently been published. Crane took the good-humored ridicule as it had apparently been intended, but the banquet was not particularly instrumental in establishing his reputation, because *The Red Badge* had already made him a public figure.

No one may ask now "Who is Stephen Crane, and what has he done?" Has he not written *The Black Riders* and *The Red Badge of Courage*, and been dined by the Philistines? Mr. Stephen Crane is the first guest to be introduced to the Society of the Philistines, and the dinner given by them in his honor at Buffalo, on December 19th, was no myth, but a very hilarious affair, at which he made a speech, a regular Black Rider poem that scintillated with flashes of wit, to the merriment of all. "Since he had recovered from College," he had thrown off the sophomoric yoke, and was doing what he could to give to the world the best that he had. "I write what is in me," said he, "and it will be enough to follow with obedience the prompting of that inspiration, if it be worthy of so dignified a name." In introducing the guest of honor, Mr. Elbert Hubbard spoke of the "strong voice now heard in America, the voice of Stephen Crane." The Philistines had had a hard time from the beginning, when driven out of their country by a tribe of invaders who had been slaves in Egypt, and had "the pull with the publishers!" Mr. Harry P. Taber, the editor of the "periodical of protest," presided gracefully as toastmaster.

Many regretted that they could not assist at the "Hanging of the Crane." Maurice Thompson would have been given "great pleasure to sit over against Stephen Crane at an eating bout." Miss Louise Imogen Guiney was

"Eyeless in Gaza, at the mill with slaves
Herself in bond (not) under Philistine yoke."

Others doted on Stephen Crane, though they didn't "understand his poetry any more than they understood the inscription on the monolith in Central Park." In a happy spirit of parody, Mr. Hayden Carruth wrote to the Society:

I saw a man reading an invitation,
Anon he chortled like a bull-frog—
Like a billy-be dasted bull-frog.
It was a dinner invitation,
Which accounted for the chortle,
"They will have Grub," quoth the
Man.
"Better yet, Grape Juice: I will go!"
The red chortle died on his white lips.
His shy hand shot into his black
Pocket.
A gray wail burst from his parched,
Brown throat
Like the scarlet yowl of a yellow
Tom Cat.
The Man didn't have the price!
Which accounted for the wail.
I left him cursing the Railroad
Company, with great, jagged,
Crimson curses."

It is gratifying to record the immense success which Mr. Crane's new novel, *The Red Badge of Courage*, is having in England. Since our last issue, in which we stated that Mr. Heinemann had launched Mr. Crane's book with enthusiasm on the English market, we have had successive reports of its warm reception, and the critics seem vying with one another in singing its praises until we understand that Mr. Crane bids fair to be the author of the hour in London. *The New Review*, of which Mr. W. E. Henley is the editor, has a criticism of Mr. Crane's work written by Mr. George Wyndham in its January number, and the same magazine promises to publish a new story of a warlike character by Mr. Crane in February.

Why is it, we might ask again, that in America critics are less sure and readers slower to discover a good book in spite of the genius in it? Except for a review of his *Maggie, a Girl of the Streets*, in *The Arena*, printed a few years ago, in which Mr. Hamlin Garland solitarily hailed the author as one to be reckoned with, THE BOOKMAN was the first, if we are not mistaken, to call attention to Mr. Stephen Crane and his work. This was done in an article which was widely copied throughout the States, printed in the May number of THE BOOKMAN, on the appearance of *The Black Riders, and Other Lines*. Yet he has not received the recognition in his own country which his recent novel at least should evoke—what ever dissentient voices may say about his "Lines"—and which they across the sea have been so quick to award him. The book has its defects—what book by a youth of twenty-four could be without them?—but let us be generous to the genius that has been applied to an experience common to every novice in war so as to make it glow and tingle with a tremendous force of reality. The narrative is stamped with truth. The youth's mind as well as the field of active service in which he is a recruit is a battleground. The dark, fearful, and inglorious moments heading up to his acquittal in the end mark the genuine development of the untried civilian into the capable and daring soldier. Exactly what military courage means for the average man you will learn here. Here also are pictures of war that are masterly. The book is marked throughout by the quiet power that war had proved the hero of it to possess.

—UNSIGNED, *The Bookman*,
February 1896, pp. 468–470

H.D. TRAILL "THE NEW REALISM" (1897)

Henry Duff Traill, a British author and journalist, wrote studies of Coleridge, Sterne, Shaftesbury, Lord Salisbury, and others. Although he was a man of letters respected for his critical acumen, he states that *The Red Badge* is not realistic and that *Maggie: A Girl of the Streets* is amateurish when compared to the English writer Arthur Morrison.

In a day when the spurious is everywhere supposed to be successfully disguised and sufficiently recommended to the public by merely being described as new, it need not surprise us to find our attention solicited by a New Realism, of which the two most obvious things to be said are that it is unreal with the falsity of the half truth, and as old as the habit of exaggeration. One of the latest professors of this doubtful form of art, is the very young American writer, Mr. Stephen Crane, who first attracted notice in this country by a novel entitled *The Red Badge of Courage*. Whether that work was or was not described by its admirers as an achievement in realism, I am not aware. As a matter of fact, and as the antecedents, and indeed the age, of the writer showed, it was not a record of actual observation. Mr. Crane had evidently been an industrious investigator and collator of the emotional experiences of soldiers, and had evolved from them a picture of the mental state of a recruit going into action. It was artistically done and obtained a not undeserved success; but no method, of course, could be less realistic, in the sense on which the professors of the New Realism insist, than the process which resulted in this elaborate study of the emotions of the battlefield from the pen of a young man who has never himself smelt powder.

Since then, however, Mr. Crane has given us two small volumes, which are presumably realistic or nothing. If circumstances have prevented the author from writing about soldiers in action "with his eye on the object," there are no such obstacles to his studying the Bowery and "Bowery boys" from the life; we may take it, therefore, that *Maggie* and *George's Mother* are the products of such study. According to Mr. Howell's effusive "Appreciation," which prefaces it, *Maggie* is a remarkable story having "that quality of fatal necessity which dominates Greek tragedy." Let us see then what this Sophoclean work is like.

The story of *Maggie* opens with a fight between the boys of Rum Alley and those of Devil's Row. Jimmie, the heroine's brother, is a boy of Rum Alley, aged nine, and when the curtain draws up he is the centre of a circle of urchins who are pelting him with stones. "Howls of wrath went up from them. On their small convulsed faces shone the grins of true assassins. As they charged they threw stones and cursed in shrill chorus. . . . Jimmie's coat had been torn to shreds in a scuffle, and his hat was gone. He had bruises on twenty parts of his body, and blood was dripping from a cut in his head. His wan features looked like those of a tiny insane demon. . . . The little boys ran to and fro hurling stones and swearing in barbaric trebles . . . A stone had smashed in Jimmie's mouth. Blood was bubbling over his chin and down upon his ragged shirt. Tears made furrows on his dirt-stained cheeks. His thin legs had begun to tremble and turn weak, causing his small body to reel. His roaring curses of the first part of the fight had changed to a blasphemous chatter. In the yells of the whirling mob of Devil's Row children there were notes of joy like songs of triumphant savagery. The little boys seemed to leer gloatingly at the blood on the other child's face."

A lad of sixteen, afterwards destined to play an important part in the story, then approaches. He smites one of the Devil's Row children on the back of the head, and the little boy falls to the ground and gives a tremendous howl. A reinforcement of the Rum Alley children then arrives, and there is a momentary pause in the fight, during which Jimmie becomes involved in a quarrel with Blue Billie, one of his own side.

They struck at each other, clinched, and rolled over on the cobblestones.

"Smash 'im, Jimmie, kick d' face off 'im," yelled Pete, in tones of delight.

The small combatants pounded and kicked, scratched and tore. They began to weep, and their curses struggled in their throats with sobs. The other little boys clasped their hands and wriggled their legs in excitement. They formed a bobbing circle round the pair.

At this juncture Jimmie's father arrives on the scene and endeavours to separate the combatants with a view of "belting" his son. To this end he begins to kick into the chaotic mass on the ground. "The boy Billie felt a heavy boot strike his head. He made a furious effort and disentangled himself from Jimmie. He tottered away. Jimmie arose painfully from the ground and confronting his father began to curse him." His parent kicked him. "Come home now," he cried, "an' stop yer jawin' or I'll lam the everlasting head off yer." Upon this they go home, the boy swearing "luridly," for he "felt that it was a degradation for one who aimed to be some vague kind of a soldier or a man of blood, with a sort of sublime licence, to be taken home by a father." That is the first chapter much condensed. In the original there are eight pages of it. Is it art? If so, is the making of mud-pies an artistic occupation, and are the neglected brats who are to be found rolling in the gutters of every great city unconscious artists?

In the next chapter Jimmie pummels his little sister, and his mother quarrels with and rates her husband till she drives him to the public-house, remaining at home to get drunk herself. In the third chapter, Jimmie, who has stopped out to avoid an outbreak of her intoxicated fury, steals home again late at night, listens outside the door to a fight going on within between his father and mother, and at last creeps in with his little sister to find both parents prostrate on the floor in a drunken stupor and to huddle in a corner until daybreak, cowering with terror lest they should awaken. For when you are a "realist's" little boy, you have to be very handy and adaptable and do exactly what that realist requires of you: so that, though you may have been defying and cursing your father at one moment, like the daring little imp you have been described as being, you may at the next moment, and for the purpose of another sort of painful picture, have to behave like a cowed and broken-spirited child of a totally different type.

These opening scenes take up about one-fifth of the short book, and those that follow are like unto them. There is a little less fighting, but a good deal more drinking. Jimmie becomes a truck driver, and fights constantly

with other drivers, but the fights are not described at length. His father
dies, probably of drink, and his mother takes to drinking harder than ever.
Maggie is seduced and deserted by Pete, the youth who appeared on the scene
during the opening fight and hits one of the infant fighters on the back of
the head. Jimmie resents the proceedings of the Bowery Lovelace as a breach
of good manners, and, going with a friend to the tavern where Pete acts as
"bar-tender," the two set upon him and there ensues a fight, in the course of
which the lips of the combatants "curl back and stretch tightly over the gums
in ghoul-like grins." It lasts for four pages, and is brought to a close by the
intervention of the police, and the escape of Jimmie "with his face drenched
in blood." How this story continues, how Maggie falls lower and lower and
finally dies, and how after her death her gin-sodden mother is passionately
entreated to forgive her, and at last graciously consents to do so—all this
may be read in Mr. Crane's pages, and shall not here be summarised from
them. Is it necessary to do so? Or to give a *precis* of the companion volume,
George's Mother, the story of a "little old woman" actually of sober and
industrious habits, and of her actually not vicious though weak son, of
whose backslidings she dies? Need I give specimen extracts from it? I hope
not—I think not. The extracts which have been already given are perfectly
fair samples of Mr. Crane's work. Anyone who likes to take it from the writer
of this article, that to read these two little books through would be to wade
through some three hundred and thirty pages of substantially the same stuff
as the above extracts, will do Mr. Crane no injustice. So I will pass from him
to a Realist of considerably larger calibre.

For Mr. Arthur Morrison, author of *Tales of Mean Streets* and A *Child
of the Jago,* undoubtedly carries heavier guns than Mr. Crane. To begin
with, he can tell a story, while Mr. Crane can only string together a series
of loosely cohering incidents. Many of his characters are vividly and
vigorously drawn, while the American writer puts us off for the most part
with sketches and shadowy outlines. Mr. Morrison's ruffians and their
ruffianism are better discriminated, and though there is plenty of fighting
and drinking and general brutality in his last and strongest work—one of
the faction fights in which, indeed, is related at quite inordinate length—he
understands that the description of these things alone will not suffice to
make a satisfactory story even about blackguards, and he has outgrown
that touching *naiveti* displayed in the younger realist's obvious belief in the
perpetual freshness and charm of mere squalor. He perceives that merely
to follow his characters, as Mr. Crane does his, from the drinking-bar to
the low music-hall and thence home again, day after day, with interludes of
brawling and "bashing" and other like recreations, becomes, after a hundred

pages or so, a little monotonous, and that the life of the criminal in his constant struggle with the law, and in perpetual danger from its officers, possesses at least the element of "sport," and presents features of variety and interest which that of the mere sot and tavern-brawler cannot possibly offer. Above all, Mr. Morrison wields a certain command of pathos, a power in which Mr. Crane is not only deficient, but of which he does not even appear to know the meaning; and were it not for a certain strange and, in truth, paradoxical defect, of which more hereafter, in his method of employing it, he would at times be capable of moving his readers very powerfully indeed. In a word, the English writer differs from the American by all the difference which divides the trained craftsman from the crude amateur, and deserves to that extent more serious and detailed criticism.

—H.D. TRAILL, "The New Realism,"
Fortnightly Review, January 1897, pp. 63–66

STEPHEN GWYNN "NOVELS OF AMERICAN LIFE" (1898)

Stephen L. Gwynn was a journalist, poet, and critic who wrote biographies of several writers, including Sir Walter Scott and Robert Louis Stevenson. In this essay, he gives a current estimate of Stephen Crane, finding his *Little Regiment* better than *The Red Badge*. He praises Crane in general but hopes that as he matures "he may slough this crude and violent mannerism."

Mr. Crane merits consideration precisely as a stylist. He made his mark, by universal acclamation, three or four years back, with the *Red Badge of Courage*, written when he was twenty-one. This book is an elaborate study of the psychological experiences undergone by a recruit. It has value not as a record, but as a *tour de force* of the imagination, for Mr. Crane had never seen war; so it is not surprising that many soldiers dissent from his theory of the emotions of combat. According to Mr. Crane, everything passes in a red haze; men advance or retreat as if in a lurid dream; they are something quite different from their everyday selves. A very clever man, who has seen no lack of fighting, Colonel Baden-Powell, comments in a record of South African war upon this theory, read by him somewhere out in the veldt. Man, upon his view, goes into action very much as he goes into a game of football; he is simply more alert, more high-strung, more completely alive, though, in consequence of the tension, subject to fits of blind fury. It must, however, be said that Mr. Crane in his story does not generalise; he takes a single type and individual emotions. Still we have the misfortune not to find credible the processes by which the recruit is coward one day and hero the next; as a psychological document his book appears to us valueless. But there is no doubt that certain impressions of war detach themselves strongly in his work; the blind actions of men, moved by masses, they know not where or why; their total ignorance of whatever lies beyond eyeshot or earshot, the uncertainty as to whether the various movements spell victory or defeat. And certain scenes—the rush across an open against a wood set thick with riflemen, or the sudden coming upon a corpse in a thicket—present themselves to the senses as vividly as in life. That is, of course, Mr. Crane's object, to stimulate sense-perceptions by the use of words. The thing done is very clever, but is it agreeable? He wants, in the first place, to get an impression of confused masses of men weltering through a forest amid a deafening noise; and words are heaped on words to render this, till one feels as if one had been beaten about the head with epithets. Every device is used to quicken the jaded faculty of image-making; words are violently flung together in fanciful collocations and outlandish metaphors; you read of red shouts and green smells, flags 'shaking with laughter,' and cannons talking to each other, 'slightly casual, unexcited in their challenges and warnings.' Men speak, not language, but half-articulate yelps, barely recognisable in their distorted spelling for words. One reads, one thinks how clever it is, and one puts away the book with a sense of relief, feeling as if one had been seeing a curious gymnastic contortion or feat of strength. It is so evident that here is a man straining every nerve to get a certain result, not so much trying to make his readers see as trying to force his own imagination into seeing. Here, for instance, is a picture from *The Little Regiment*, Mr. Crane's volume of short studies of war—a better book than *The Red Badge*, to our thinking:—

> In one mystic changing of the fog as if the fingers of spirits were drawing aside these draperies, a small group of the grey skirmishers, silent, statuesque, were suddenly disclosed to Dan and those about him. So vivid and near were they that there was something uncanny in the revelation. There might have been a second of mutual wonder. Then each rifle in the group was at the shoulder. As Dan's glance flashed along the barrel of his weapon, the figure of a man suddenly loomed as if the musket had been a telescope. The short black beard, the slouch hat, the pose of the man as he sighted to shoot, made a quick picture in Dan's mind. The same moment, it would seem, he pulled his own trigger, and the man, smitten, lurched forward, while his exploding rifle made

a slanting crimson streak in the air, and the slouch hat fell before the body. The billows of the fog, governed by singular impulses, rolled in between.

"You got that feller sure enough," said a comrade to Dan. Dan looked at him absent-mindedly.

If a man were in a fight, would he be thinking of shapes and colours like this? Does a man in a football match have similar impressions? Dan, be it observed, is a veteran; the recruit may have naturally such a confusion of ideas as would be in the mind of a young foreigner put into a side of Rugby football and told to play without knowing the rules. Mr. Crane's description of war does not convince like Mr. Kipling's, in so far as it describes the emotions; it shows entirely false beside what we should take for the touchstone in these matters—Sir Charles Napier's account of his experiences at Corunna. In so far as it aims at rendering external impressions of sight, it seems to us radically bad art, because it tries to do with words what should be done with lines and colours. It may be confidently said that no one unacquainted with the methods of modern impressionist art on canvas will see the pictures that Mr. Crane is trying to convey; and those who are acquainted with them will see that he sees the thing not directly, but, as it were, translated into paint.

Mr. Crane is too young to have written a good novel, and *The Third Violet*, his only attempt at the ordinary story of familiar life, is simply amazing in its futility. But he has written a short study of New York slums which may compare with Mr. Arthur Morrison's Jago sketches and Mr. Maugham's *Liza of Lambeth*. *Maggie* appears with a prefatory commendation from Mr. Howells. We have no objection to stories of slum life; Mr. R. H. Davies's *Gallegher* is a wonderful and attractive picture of the New York street-Arab. But *Maggie* does not seem to us to justify its existence. Given a drunken father, a drunken mother, and their children, a pretty girl and a boy, stunted but as brave as a weasel; this is very likely how the lives will shape themselves. Tragic pathos there certainly is in the girl's devotion to her swaggering lover, a fighting bartender, who deserts her without the shadow of compunction. But it seems as if one needed more than this to repay one for wading through such a mass of revolting details—street fights of little boys, fights of grown men in bars, scenes in dirty beer saloons, and everywhere the dialect of the Bowery, which, as Mr. Crane writes it, is the most hideous representation of human speech that we have ever met with. One may read a book like this as a tract, to keep one alive to the misery existent somewhere in the world; but we can conceive no other motive for reading it. As a work of art we disbelieve in it. Take Mr. Maugham's *Liza*, a work equally unsparing and in some ways more revolting; here you have at least credible human beings, with natural affections. In Mr. Crane's book Maggie's passion for Pete is the one trace of human coherence; there is no other tie between any two of the characters. It is an impression; that is to say, a study made to emphasise certain traits; and an impression of sheer brutality. The admiration for work of this sort savours of the latest modern cant, which preaches that to see things artistically you must see them disagreeably. Mr. Crane has seen a piece of life in a hard superficial way, and rendered it in the spirit of a caricaturist. That is the true formula for producing what, in the cant of the day, is called uncompromising realism.

Mr. Crane, however, stands by himself, and we trust that with advancing maturity he may slough this crude and violent mannerism, alien to all the old traditions of delicacy and reserve whether in style or subject. He has too much talent to be wasted in a wild-goose chase after the ideal of gentlemen in France who write sonnets describing the colours of different vowels. For the present he alone among the writers we have dealt with affords us no human document; his folk in the Bowery have neither country nor class; all he offers is a distorted psychology of combat and an exaggerated theory of style. Yet it is of the essence of talent to go wrong at first and to run into mannerisms.

—STEPHEN GWYNN, from "Novels of
American Life," *Edinburgh Review*,
April 1898, pp. 411–414

EDWARD GARNETT "MR. STEPHEN CRANE: AN APPRECIATION" (1898)

Edward Garnett was a prominent British critic, playwright, and essayist. Stephen and Cora Crane first met Garnett and his wife, Constance, a translator of nineteenth-century Russian novels, when they returned to England from Greece in June 1897. For a short time, the Cranes lived in Limpsfield, Surrey, near the Garnetts' home, and Garnett introduced Crane to Ford Madox Ford, another close neighbor. Because Garnett was the literary adviser to the publishing firms of Fisher Unwin, Heinemann, and Jonathan Cape, he worked with such literary figures as Joseph Conrad, John Galsworthy, Robert Frost, and Liam O'Flaherty, unfortunately turning down James Joyce's *Portrait of the Artist as a Young Man*.

Garnett provides some of the best, most specific contemporary criticism of Stephen Crane's work. He states, "The rare thing about Mr. Crane's art is that he keeps closer to the surface than any living writer, and, like the great portrait-painters, to a great extent makes the surface betray the depths." This insight into Crane's technique is rare in contemporary criticism, revealing techniques later modernists would employ and exploit in their use of everyday "things" to provide information about a character's emotions and motivations. In addition to recognizing Crane's innovative style, Garnett points out the impressionistic aspects of Crane's writing.

⟊ ⟊ ⟊

What Mr. Crane has got to do is very simple: he must not mix reporting with his writing. To other artists the word must often be passed: rest, work at your art, live more; but Mr. Crane has no need of cultivating his technique, no need of resting, no need of searching wide for experiences. In his art he is unique. Its certainty, its justness, its peculiar perfection of power arrived at its birth, or at least at that precise moment in its life when other artists—and great artists too—were preparing themselves for the long and difficult conquest of their art. I cannot remember a parallel case in the literary history of fiction. Maupassant, Meredith, Mr. James, Mr. Howells, Tolstoi, all were learning their expression at the age where Mr. Crane had achieved his, achieved it triumphantly. Mr. Crane has no need to learn anything. His technique is absolutely his own, and by its innate laws of being has arrived at a perfect fullness of power. What he has not got he has no power of acquiring. He has no need to acquire it. To say to Mr. Crane, "You are too much anything, or too little anything; you need concentration, or depth, subtlety, or restraint," would be absurd; his art is always just in itself, rhythmical, self-poising as is the art of a perfect dancer. There are no false steps, no excesses. And, of course, his art is strictly limited. We would define him by saying he is the perfect artist and interpreter of the surfaces of life. And that explains why he so swiftly attained his peculiar power, what is the realm his art commands, and where his limitations come in.

Take *George's Mother,* for example—a tale which I believe he wrote at the ridiculous age of twenty-one. In *method* it is a masterpiece. It is a story dealing simply with the relations between an old woman and her son, who live together in a New York tenement block. An ordinary artist would seek to dive into the mind of the old woman, to follow its workings hidden under the deceitful appearances of things, under the pressure of her surroundings. A great artist would so recreate her life that its griefs and joys became significant of the griefs and joys of all motherhood on earth. But Mr. Crane does neither. He simply reproduces the surfaces of the individual life in so marvellous a way that the manner in which the old woman washes up the crockery, for example, gives us her. To dive into the hidden life is, of course, for the artist a great temptation and a great danger—the values of the picture speedily get wrong, and the artist, seeking to interpret life, departs from the

truth of nature. The rare thing about Mr. Crane's art is that he keeps closer
to the surface than any living writer, and, like the great portrait-painters, to a
great extent makes the surface betray the depths. But, of course, the written
word in the hands of the greatest artist often deals directly with the depths,
plunges us into the rich depths of consciousness that cannot be more than
hinted at by the surface; and it is precisely here that Mr. Crane's natural
limitation must come in. At the supreme height of art the great masters so
plough up the depths of life that the astonished spectator loses sight of the
individual life altogether, and has the entrancing sense that all life is really
one and the same thing, and is there manifesting itself before him. He feels
that, for example, when he watches Duse at her best, or when he stands before
Da Vinci's "La Joconda" in the Louvre and is absorbed by it. I do not think
that Mr. Crane is ever great in the sense of so fusing all the riches of the
consciousness into a whole, that the reader is struck dumb as by an inevitable
revelation; but he is undoubtedly such an interpreter of the significant surface
of things that in a few swift strokes he gives us an amazing insight into what
the individual life is. And he does it all straight from the surface; a few oaths,
a genius for slang, an exquisite and unique faculty of exposing an individual
scene by an odd simile, a power of interpreting a face or an action, a keen
realising of the primitive emotions—that is Mr. Crane's talent. In "The Bride
Comes to Yellow Sky," for example, the art is simply immense. There is a page
and a half of conversation at the end of this short story of seventeen pages
which, as a dialogue revealing the whole inside of the situation, is a lesson
to any artist living. And the last line of this story, by the gift peculiar to the
author of using some odd simile which cunningly condenses the feeling of
the situation, defies analysis altogether. Foolish people may call Mr. Crane a
reporter of genius; but nothing could be more untrue. He is thrown away as
a picturesque reporter: a secondary style of art, of which, let us say, Mr. G. W.
Steevens is, perhaps, the ablest exponent to-day, and which is the heavy clay
of Mr. Kipling's talent. Mr. Crane's technique is far superior to Mr. Kipling's,
but he does not experiment ambitiously in various styles and develop in new
directions, as Mr. Kipling has done. I do not think that Mr. Crane will or can
develop further. Again, I do not think that he has the building faculty, or
that he will ever do better in constructing a perfect whole out of many parts
than he has arrived at in *The Red Badge of Courage.* That book was a series
of episodic scenes, all melting naturally into one another and forming a just
whole; but it was not constructed, in any sense of the word. And, further, Mr.
Crane does not show any faculty of taking his characters and revealing in
them deep mysterious worlds of human nature, of developing fresh riches in
them acting under the pressure of circumstance. His imaginative analysis of

his own nature on a battlefield is, of course, the one exception. And similarly the great artist's arrangement of complex effects, striking contrasts, exquisite grouping of devices, is lacking in him. His art does not include the necessity for complex arrangements; his sure instinct tells him never to quit the passing moment of life, to hold fast by simple situations, to reproduce the episodic, fragmentary nature of life in such artistic sequence that it stands in place of the architectural masses and coordinated structures of the great artists. He is the chief impressionist of this age, as Sterne was the great impressionist, in a different manner, of his age. If he fails in anything he undertakes, it will be through abandoning the style he has invented. He may, perhaps, fail by and by, through using up the picturesque phases of the environment that nurtured him, as Swinburne came to a stop directly he had rung the changes a certain number of times on the fresh rhythms and phrases he created. But that time is not yet, and every artist of a special unique faculty has that prospect before him. Mr. Crane's talent is unique; nobody can question that. America may well be proud of him, for he has just that perfect mastery of form which artists of the Latin races often produce, but the Teutonic and Anglo-Saxon races very rarely. And undoubtedly of the young school of American artists Mr. Crane is the genius—the others have their talents.

—Edward Garnett, "Mr. Stephen Crane:
An Appreciation," *Academy*,
December 17, 1898, pp. 483–484

Edward Garnett "Stephen Crane" (1900)

Edward Garnett wrote the following excerpt after Stephen Crane's death. In it, he again alludes to the modernist nature of Crane's writing, and he points out that Crane's best work is in his short stories, citing a passage from "The Open Boat."

As special correspondent he had seen two wars; he had been wrecked; he had written eleven books, two still in MS., and when he died last Wednesday his years did not number thirty. He was the type of the nervous, nimble-minded American, slight in figure, shy and kind in manner, speaking little, with a great power of work, a fine memory, and an imagination of astonishing psychological insight. Latterly his health had been bad, partly constitutional, and partly through malarial fever contracted in the Cuban campaign. The last two years of his life were spent in the old, huge, fascinating house in Sussex, Brede Place, which he made his home. There he lived, many miles from the nearest railway station, a quiet, domesticated life, welcoming his friends, and writing—always writing. He battled bravely against ill health; but the disease gained ground, and a few weeks ago he was ordered to the Black Forest. It was a forlorn hope, and, although many days were given to the journey, he succumbed at the end to exhaustion.

The Red Badge of Courage was published when he was twenty-five. This study of the psychological side of war, of its effect on a private soldier, justly won for him immediate recognition. Critics of all schools united in praise of that remarkable book, and the more wonderful did the performance appear when it became known that he had never seen a battle, that the whole was evolved from his imagination, fed by a long and minute study of military history. It is said that when he returned from the Greco-Turkish war he remarked to a friend: "The Red Badge is all right." It was all right.

The same swift and unerring characterization, the same keen vision into the springs of motives, the same vivid phrasing, marked *George's Mother*. Here, as in most of his other stories, and in all his episodes, the environment grows round the characters. He takes them at some period of emotional or physical stress, and, working from within outwards, with quick, firm touches, vivifies them into life. Nowhere is this more evident than in the short sketches and studies that were, probably, after *The Red Badge of Courage*, the real expression of his genius. His longer novels, though not wanting in passages that show him at his best, suggest that in time he would have returned to the earlier instinct that prompted him to work upon a small canvas.

As a writer he was very modern. He troubled himself little about style or literary art. But—rare gift—he saw for himself, and, like Mr. Steevens, he knew in a flash just what was essential to bring the picture vividly to the reader. His books are full of images and similes that not only fulfill their purpose of the moment, but live in the memory afterwards. A super-refined literary taste might object to some of his phrases—to such a sentence as this, for example: "By the very last star of truth, it is easier to steal eggs from under a hen than it was to change seats in the dingy," to his colloquialisms, to the slang with which he peppers the talk of his men—but that was the man, who looked at things with his own eyes, and was unafraid of his prepossessions.

His gift of presenting the critical or dramatic moments in the lives of men and women was supreme. We could give a hundred examples. . . .

This youth wandered much over the world in his brief, brilliant life. As we write, his last journey is beginning. He is being taken to his home in America.

—EDWARD GARNETT, "Stephen Crane,"
The Academy, June 9, 1900, p. 491

WILLIAM L. ALDEN
"LONDON LITERARY LETTER" (1900)

William L. Alden was a lawyer, humorist, and editorial writer for *The New York Times*. He also wrote a series of books on the *Adventures of Jimmy Brown*, popular books marketed to boys and totally unlike Stephen Crane's depiction of childhood in the *Whilomville Stories*. Alden was appointed consul general to Rome in 1885 by President Grover Cleveland, moving later to Paris, and then to London, where he contributed editorials to the *Times*.

Alden's editorial on Stephen Crane's death states that Crane's imagination produced better writing than his life experiences, declaring *The Red Badge* superior to his later war sketches.

London, June 22.—In speaking of the death of the late Stephen Crane the opinion has been expressed, almost unanimously, that by far his best work was "The Red Badge of Courage." In that wonderful book Mr. Crane described a battle before he had ever seen one, and the vivid truthfulness of his description is amazing. Afterward he described what passed before his eyes in the Cuban campaign, and clever as his later work unquestionably was, it did not force upon the reader the same conviction of its absolute truthfulness as did the scenes painted in "The Red Badge of Courage." To many people it may seem strange that an author's imagination can be more truthful than his facts; but that this is often the case has been demonstrated times without number. Why should it not be so? Is not the creator superior to the mere reporter? We see the same thing in painting. A portrait is never as true to life in its lines as is a photograph, but it is infinitely truer in its effect. Facts are in the way of a man of real genius when he undertakes descriptive writing. They hamper and restrain him. In a real battle there are many things which the reporter who is present cannot see, but in the imaginary battle the writer plans and fights it through in the way that suits him best. Crane was undeniably a man of genius, although he did his best to mar his work by adherence to his pet theories. He could describe what he saw in Cuba, but he could see only what other men who were with him could also see. When he described his imaginary battle in Virginia he was unhampered, and the result was a truthfulness that his reporting never had. His death is a serious loss. In his way he was unique. Whether he had done his best work in "The Red Badge of Courage," or whether he would in time have surpassed even that brilliant book we shall never know. Probably he would have discarded his theories as he grew older, but with them he might also have discarded the reckless freedom of expression which was to some extent the secret of the fascination of his writing.

He left a novel which was nearly completed, and the task of completing it has been assumed by Mr. Robert Barr. Probably Mr. Barr is better fitted than any other man to carry out this difficult duty for he not only understood Mr. Crane thoroughly, but his familiarity with Americans, gained by his long years of residence in Detroit, enables him to finish Mr. Crane's American portraits without making them absurd, as they would be were they to be completed by almost any Englishman. A volume of short stories, most of which have been published from time to time in the magazines, will also short appear.

—WILLIAM L. ALDEN, "London Literary Letter,"
The New York Times, July 7, 1900, p. BR7

JOHN NORTHERN HILLIARD "STEPHEN CRANE: LETTERS TO A FRIEND ABOUT HIS AMBITION, HIS ART, AND HIS VIEWS OF LIFE" (1900)

John Northern Hilliard, a reporter in Chicago and New York City and later a literary editor and critic for the *Rochester Union and Advertiser* and the *Rochester Post Express*, contributed critical articles to numerous newspapers. He became a close friend of Stephen Crane during Crane's early years in New York, and he later wrote about their relationship.

Hilliard points out that the "abuse" Crane's work received in the United States, especially those criticisms targeting *The Red Badge* and *Black Riders*, had deeply bothered Crane. Hilliard also notes the many positive attributes of Crane's personality and the emphasis that some had placed on what they labeled a bohemian lifestyle. Hilliard quotes three letters Crane had sent him to illustrate the young writer's disappointment with such inaccurate judgments.

The comments of the American press on the death of Stephen Crane and the estimates of his position in native literature are in striking contrast to the comments of the same press five years ago. When "The Red Badge of Courage" and "The Black Riders" were put upon the market their author was the most thoroughly abused writing man between the Atlantic and Pacific. The slim little volume of verse was the particular target of nearly every critic, joker, and parodist in the country. Nor were these lampooners content with making merely fun of the book. They hurled epithets at it that would have put to shame the editor of a partisan Western weekly. Idiocy, garbage, rot bombast, drivel, indecent, besotted, opium-laden, fustian, bluster, balderdash, stupid, swell-head stuff, were but a few of the mildest adjectives maximed at the book.

It is only justice to add, however, that the very writers who were the severest in their satires and criticisms of Stephen Crane when he was alive were the first to pay honest and unembittered tributes to his memory. Mr. Crane never replied to his critics, even when they descended to personalities; he welcomed honest criticism; he was always ready to accept advice given in good faith, but many of the unkind things hurt him to the quick, for he was very sensitive, and it was this state of affairs that led to his living in England, though he was always a stanch advocate and defender of his native land. Mr. Crane's attitude toward his critics may be gathered from the following letter, which he wrote shortly after the publication of "The Red Badge of Courage" and "The Black Riders," when ridicule and personalities were volley across the net of criticism:

"The one thing that deeply pleases me in my literary life—brief and inglorious as it is—is the fact that men of sense believe me to be sincere. 'Maggie,' published in paper covers, made me the friendship of Hamlin Garland and W. D. Howells, and the one thing that makes my life worth living in the midst of all this abuse and ridicule is the consciousness that never for an instant have these friendships at all diminished. Personally I am aware that my work does not amount to a string of dried beans—I always calmly admit it. But I also know that I do the best that is in me, without regard to cheers or damnation. When I was the mark for every humorist in the country I went ahead, and now, when I am the mark for only 50 per cent, of the humorists of the country, I go ahead, for I understand that a man is born into the world with his own pair of eyes and he is not at all responsible for his quality of personal honesty. To keep close to my honesty is my supreme ambition. There is a sublime egotism in talking of honesty. I, however, do not say that I am honest. I merely say that I am as nearly honest as a weak mental machinery will allow. This aim in life struck me as being the only thing worth while. A man is sure to fail at it, but there is something in the failure."

This personal document reveals the real Stephen Crane—simple, unostentatious, sincere, and very far removed from the eccentric personality that was evolved in the careless arrangement of irresponsible types. Crane's rather free and bohemian life, his scorn of the conventionalities of life and literature, the vividness and often crude vigor of his style, the lack of proportion and perspective in his mental equipment were some of the factors that made this misunderstanding possible. It were not difficult for the fancy to conjure up a Stephen Crane from his published writing, but the real Stephen Crane was as far removed from the creation of the mind as the equator is from the poles. He was no more eccentric than nine and ninety men you meet on the street every day; and if a penchant for working all night and smoking innumerable pipes during the day are among the oddities of genius, then Crane was undeniably odd. Otherwise he was a quiet, undemonstrative fellow, quick and agile in his movements, and with an abnormally active brain. Except in his relations with a limited number of intimate friends, he was shy and reserved. When he was at college he was prominent only for his skill as a shortstop and the amount of tobacco he consumed. At that time he was not possessed of any strong individuality—in fact was unimpressive—and of the thousand students who attended Syracuse University during his stay, probably not more than a dozen will remember him at all. He was not a favorite with the Faculty, and his scholarship was a negative quality. He was never enrolled as a student in any regular course, but took what studies struck his fancy, principally history and psychology. In a letter written two years after leaving college, when his name was first becoming known, he dwelt on this point as follows:

"As far as myself and my own meager success are concerned, I began the battle of life with no talent, no equipment, but an ardent admiration and desire. I did little work at school, but confined my abilities, such as they were, to the diamond. Not that I disliked books, but the cut-and-dried curriculum of the college did not appeal to me. Humanity was a much more interesting study. When I ought to have been at recitations I was studying faces on the streets, and when I ought to have been studying my next day's lessons I was watching the trains roll in and out of the Central Station. So, you see, I had, first of all, to recover from college. I had to build up, so to speak. And my chiefest desire was to write plainly and unmistakably, so that all men (and some women) might read and understand. That to my mind is good writing. There is a great deal of labor connected with literature. I think that is the hardest thing about it. There is nothing to respect in art save one's own opinion of it."

That was his opinion when he was struggling for a precarious living in New York City writing local reports and sketches for the newspapers that did not meet with the approbation of city editors, and working at odd times on his story of the civil war. He had his ideals then, and he was true to them; but when widespread success followed the publication of "The Red Badge of Courage," and all England and America were talking about the book, he did not let good fortune interfere with the life work he had planned in the Delta Upsilon chapter house in Syracuse. In a letter to me, written in England, when Crane was in the first flush of his fame, he wrote modestly as follows:

"I have only one pride—and may it be forgiven me. This single pride is that the English edition of 'The Red Badge' has been received with praise by the English reviewers. Mr. George Wyndham, Under Secretary for

War in the British Government, says, in an essay, that the book challenges comparison with the most vivid scenes of Tolstoi's 'War and Peace' or of Zola's 'Downfall'; and the big reviews here praise it for just what I intended it to be, a psychological portrayal of fear. They all insist that I am a veteran of the civil war, whereas the fact is as you know, I never smelled even the powder of a sham battle. I know what the psychologists say, that a fellow can't comprehend a condition that he has never experienced, and I argued that many times with the Professor. Of course, I have never been in a battle, but I believe that I got my sense of the rage of conflict on the football field, or else fighting is a hereditary instinct, and I wrote intuitively; for the Cranes were a family of fighters in the old days, and in the Revolution every member did his duty. But be that as it may, I endeavored to express myself in the simplest and most concise way. If I failed, the fault is not mine. I have been very careful not to let any theories or pet ideas of my own creep into my work. Preaching is fatal to art in literature. I try to give to readers a slice out of life; and if there is any moral or lesson it, I do not try to point it out. I let the reader find it himself. The result is more satisfactory to both the reader and myself. As Emerson said, 'There should be a long logic beneath the story, but it should be kept carefully out of sight.' Before 'The Red Badge of Courage' was published, I found it difficult to make both ends meet. The book was written during this period. It was an effort born of pain, and I believe that it was beneficial to it as a piece literature. It seems a pity that this should be so—that art should be a child of suffering; and yet such seems to be the case. Of course there are fine writers who have good incomes and live comfortably and contentedly; but if the conditions of their lives were harder, I believe that their work would be better. Bret Harte is an example. He has not done any work in recent years to compare with those early California sketches. Personally, I like my little book of poems, 'The Black Riders,' better than I do 'The Red Badge of Courage.' The reason is, I suppose, that the former is the more ambitious effort. In it I aim to give my ideas of life as a whole, so far as I know it, and the latter is a mere episode, or rather an amplification. Now that I have reached the goal, I suppose that I ought to be contented; but I am not. I was happier in the old days when I was always dreaming of the thing I have now attained. I am disappointed with success, and I am tired of abuse. Over here, happily, they don't treat you as if you were a dog, but give every one an honest measure of praise or blame. There are no disgusting personalities."

There was one more side to his character. Personally he was a courageous gentleman at all times, and as generous and kind-hearted as he was brave. I think that he was the coolest and bravest man I have ever known. He was, in a way, a fatalist, and his favorite saying was that "what is to be is not to be dodged, and let worry go hang." But his was not altogether the courage of a fatalist. It was in the blood. His people were pioneers and fighters. One was a member of the Continental Congress until within a week of the signing of the Declaration of Independence. Another was shot to death upon the ramparts of Quebec, and still another was bayoneted by Hessians because he refused to give information as to the whereabouts of an American camp. Family pride was one of Crane's finest traits. As to his personal courage, others have eloquently testified to what Richard Harding Davis has written that Crane was the coolest man under fire that he had every seen, and he cites Crane's description of the marines signaling under fire at Guantanamo as the best piece of descriptive writing during the war with Spain. Crane had often told the writer of this article that his fondest desire was to die in battle, as was meet in one whose ancestors had given up their lives for their country. Certainly it was one of the little ironies of life that, after facing all sorts of dangers by sea and land, he should pass away quietly and conventionally in a German health resort.

—John N. Hilliard, "Stephen Crane:
Letters to a Friend about His Ambition,
His Art, and His Views of Life,"
The New York Times, July 14, 1900, p. BR2

H.G. Wells "Stephen Crane: From an English Standpoint" (1900)

H.G. Wells, a successful English novelist, was a close friend of Crane's during the last year of his life, when he was residing at Brede Place in Sussex. Because Wells had had tuberculosis in his youth, he was greatly concerned about Crane, even bicycling through freezing rain to a local doctor in the neighboring town of Rye when the young writer had a serious attack. Wells was one of several friends who visited Crane in Dover, prior to his crossing the English Channel en route to the Black Forest, where he died at the age of twenty-eight, not at thirty as Wells claims in this selection. Confusing the time of Crane's shipwreck during an earlier aborted trip to Cuba in January 1897, Wells mistakenly thought the wreck occurred during the Spanish-American War in 1898 and that it had contributed to his health problems. Crane contracted tuberculosis in Cuba during his reporting of the Spanish-American War but not from the shipwreck.

Wells was not only a good friend to Crane, he was also one of the best contemporary critics of his work. He writes that Crane has "made a

permanent addition to the great and growing fabric of English letters,"
and he cites "The Open Boat" as the best of his work, castigating those
critics who did not give his short stories the credit they deserve. Like
many others, he highly values *The Red Badge*, but he laments that very
little credit had been given to either *Maggie* or *George's Mother*, which he
finds equally effective. Wells points out Crane's "freshness of method,"
his "vigor of imagination," and his "force of color" and "essential freedom
from many traditions," but he fears that popular criticism may have
coerced Crane into writing the inferior *Third Violet* and *Active Service*.

The untimely death at thirty of Stephen Crane robs English literature of an
interesting and significant figure, and the little world of those who write, of a
stout friend and a pleasant comrade. For a year and more he had been ailing.
The bitter hardships of his Cuban expedition had set its mark upon mind and
body alike, and the slow darkling of the shadow upon him must have been
evident to all who were not blinded by their confidence in what he was yet to
do. Altogether, I knew Crane for less than a year, and I saw him for the last
time hardly more than seven weeks ago. He was then in a hotel at Dover, lying
still and comfortably wrapped about, before an open window and the calm and
spacious sea. If you would figure him as I saw him, you must think of him as a
face of a type very typically American, long and spare, with very straight hair
and straight features and long, quiet hands and hollow eyes, moving slowly,
smiling and speaking slowly, with that deliberate New Jersey manner he had,
and lapsing from speech again into a quiet contemplation of his ancient enemy.
For it was the sea that had taken his strength, the same sea that now shone, level
waters beyond level waters, with here and there a minute, shining ship, warm
and tranquil beneath the tranquil evening sky. Yet I felt scarcely a suspicion
then that this was a last meeting. One might have seen it all, perhaps. He was
thin and gaunt and wasted, too weak for more than a remembered jest and a
greeting and good wishes. It did not seem to me in any way credible that he
would reach his refuge in the Black Forest only to die at the journey's end. It will
be a long time yet before I can fully realize that he is no longer a contemporary
of mine; that the last I saw of him was, indeed, final and complete.

Though my personal acquaintance with Crane was so soon truncated, I
have followed his work for all the four years it has been known in England.
I have always been proud, and now I am glad, that, however obscurely, I
also was in the first chorus of welcome that met his coming. It is, perhaps,
no great distinction for me; he was abundantly praised; but, at least, I was
early and willing to praise him when I was wont to be youthfully jealous of
my praises. His success in England began with *The Red Badge of Courage*,

which did, indeed, more completely than any other book has done for many years, take the reading public by storm. Its freshness of method, its vigor of imagination, its force of color and its essential freedom from many traditions that dominate this side of the Atlantic, came—in spite of the previous shock of Mr. Kipling—with a positive effect of impact. It was a new thing, in a new school. When one looked for sources, one thought at once of Tolstoi; but, though it was clear that Tolstoi had exerted a powerful influence upon the conception, if not the actual writing, of the book, there still remained something entirely original and novel. To a certain extent, of course, that was the new man as an individual; but, to at least an equal extent, it was the new man as a typical young American, free at last, as no generation of Americans have been free before, of any regard for English criticism, comment or tradition, and applying to literary work the conception and theories of the cosmopolitan studio with a quite American directness and vigor. For the great influence of the studio on Crane cannot be ignored; in the persistent selection of the essential elements of an impression, in the ruthless exclusion of mere information, in the direct vigor with which the selected points are made, there is Whistler even more than there is Tolstoi in *The Red Badge of Courage*. And witness this, taken almost haphazard:

At nightfall the column broke into regimental pieces, and the fragments went into the fields to camp. Tents sprang up like strange plants. Camp fires, like red, peculiar blossoms, dotted the night . . . From this little distance the many fires, with the black forms of men passing to and fro before the crimson rays, made weird and satanic effects.

And here again; consider the daring departure from all academic requirements, in this void countenance:

A warm and strong hand clasped the youth's languid fingers for an instant, and then he heard a cheerful and audacious whistling as the man strode away. As he who had so befriended him was thus passing out of his life, it suddenly occurred to the youth that he had not once seen his face.

I do not propose to add anything here to the mass of criticism upon this remarkable book. Like everything else which has been abundantly praised, it has occasionally been praised "all wrong;" and I suppose that it must have been said hundreds of times that this book is a subjective study of the typical soldier in war. But Mr. George Wyndham, himself a soldier of experience, has pointed out in an admirable preface to a re-issue of this and other of Crane's war studies, that the hero of the *Red Badge* is, and is intended to be, altogether a more sensitive and imaginative person than the ordinary man. He is the idealist, the dreamer of boastful things brought suddenly to the test of danger and swift occasions and the presence of death. To this theme Crane returned several times, and particularly in a story called "Death and the Child" that was written after the Greek war. That story is considered by very many of Crane's admirers as absolutely his best. I have carefully reread it in deference to opinions I am bound to respect, but I still find it inferior to the earlier work. The generalized application is, to my taste, a little too evidently underlined; there is just that touch of insistence that prevails so painfully at times in Victor Hugo's work, as of a writer not sure of his reader, not happy in his reader and seeking to drive his implication (of which also he is not quite sure) home. The child is not a natural child; there is no happy touch to make it personally alive; it is THE CHILD, something unfalteringly big; a large, pink, generalized thing, I cannot help but see it, after the fashion of a Vatican cherub. The fugitive runs panting to where, all innocent of the battle about it, it plays; and he falls down breathless to be asked, "Are you a man?" One sees the intention clearly enough; but in the later story it seems to me there is a new ingredient that is absent from the earlier stories, an ingredient imposed on Crane's natural genius from without—a concession to the demands of a criticism it had been wiser, if less modest, in him to disregard—criticism that missed this quality of generalization and demanded it, even though it had to be artificially and deliberately introduced.

Following hard upon the appearance of *The Red Badge of Courage* in England came reprints of two books, *Maggie* and *George's Mother,* that had already appeared in America six years earlier. Their reception gave Crane his first taste of the peculiarities of the new public he had come upon. These stories seem to me in no way inferior to the *Red Badge;* and at times there are passages, the lament of Maggie's mother at the end of *Maggie,* for example, that it would be hard to beat by any passage from the later book. But on all hands came discouragement or tepid praise. The fact of it is, there had been almost an orgy of praise—for England, that is; and ideas and adjectives and phrases were exhausted. To write further long reviews on works displaying the same qualities as had been already amply discussed in the notices of the *Red Badge* would be difficult and laborious; while to admit an equal excellence and deny an equal prominence would be absurd. But to treat these stories as early work, to find them immature, dismiss them and proceed to fresher topics, was obvious and convenient. So it was, I uncharitably imagine, that these two tales have been overshadowed and are still comparatively unknown. Yet, they are absolutely essential to a just understanding of Crane. In these stories, and in these alone, he achieved tenderness and a compulsion of sympathy for other than vehement emotions, qualities that the readers of *The Third Violet* and On *Active Service,* his later love stories, might well imagine beyond his reach.

And upon the appearance of these books in England came what, in my present mood, I cannot but consider as the great blunder and misfortune of Crane's life. It is a trait of the public we writers serve, that to please it is to run the gravest risk of never writing again. Through a hundred channels and with a hundred varieties of seduction and compulsion, the public seeks to induce its favorite to do something else—to act, to lecture, to travel, to jump down volcanoes or perform in music halls, to do anything, rather than to possess his soul in peace and to pursue the work he was meant to do. Indeed, this modern public is as violently experimental with its writers as a little child with a kitten. It is animated, above all things, by an insatiable desire to plunge its victim into novel surroundings, and watch how he feels. And since Crane had demonstrated, beyond all cavil, that he could sit at home and, with nothing but his wonderful brain and his wonderful induction from recorded things, build up the truest and most convincing picture of war; since he was a fastidious and careful worker, intensely subjective in his mental habit; since he was a man of fragile physique and of that unreasonable courage that will wreck the strongest physique; and since, moreover, he was habitually a bad traveller, losing trains and luggage and missing connections even in the orderly circumstances of peace, it was clearly the most reasonable thing in the world to propose, it was received with the applause of two hemispheres as a most right and proper thing, that he should go as a war correspondent, first to Greece and then to Cuba. Thereby, and for nothing but disappointment and bitterness, he utterly wrecked his health. He came into comparison with men as entirely his masters in this work as he was the master of all men in his own; and I read even in the most punctual of his obituary notices the admission of his journalistic failure. I have read, too, that he brought back nothing from these expeditions. But, indeed, even not counting his death, he brought back much. On his way home from Cuba he was wrecked, and he wrote the story of the nights and days that followed the sinking of the ship with a simplicity and vigor that even he cannot rival elsewhere.

"The Open Boat" is to my mind, beyond all question, the crown of all his work. It has all the stark power of the earlier stories, with a new element of restraint; the color is as full and strong as ever, fuller and stronger, indeed; but those chromatic splashes that at times deafen and confuse in *The Red Badge,* those images that astonish rather than enlighten, are disciplined and controlled. "That and 'Flanagan,'" he told me, with a philosophical laugh, "was all I got out of Cuba." I cannot say whether they were worth the price, but I am convinced that these two things are as immortal as any work of any living man. . . .

"The Open Boat" gives its title to a volume containing, in addition to that and "Flanagan," certain short pieces. One of these others, at least, is also to my mind a perfect thing, "The Wise Men." It tells of the race between two bar-tenders in the city of Mexico, and I cannot imagine how it could possibly have been better told. And in this volume, too, is that other masterpiece—the one I deny—"Death and the Child."

Now I do not know how Crane took the reception of this book, for he was not the man to babble of his wrongs; but I cannot conceive how it could have been anything but a grave disappointment to him. To use the silly phrase of the literary shopman, "the vogue of the short story" was already over; rubbish, pure rubbish, provided only it was lengthy, had resumed its former precedence again in the reviews, in the publishers' advertisements and on the library and book-sellers' counters. The book was taken as a trivial by-product, its author was exhorted to abandon this production of "brilliant fragments"—anything less than fifty thousand words is a fragment to the writer of literary columns—and to make that "sustained effort," that architectural undertaking, that alone impresses the commercial mind. Of course, the man who can call "The Open Boat" a brilliant fragment would reproach Rodin for not completing the edifice his brilliant fragments of statuary are presumably intended to adorn, and would sigh, with the late Mr. Ruskin for the day when Mr. Whistler would "finish" his pictures. Moreover, he was strongly advised—just as they have advised Mr. Kipling—to embark upon a novel. And from other quarters, where a finer wisdom might have been displayed, he learned that the things he had written were not "short stories" at all; they were "sketches" perhaps, "anecdotes"—just as they call Mr. Kipling's short stories "anecdotes;" and it was insinuated that for him also the true, the ineffable "short story" was beyond his reach. I think it is indisputable that the quality of this reception, which a more self-satisfied or less sensitive man than Crane might have ignored, did react very unfavorably upon his work. They put him out of conceit with these brief intense efforts in which his peculiar strength was displayed.

It was probably such influence that led him to write *The Third Violet*. I do not know certainly, but I imagine, that the book was to be a demonstration, and it is not a successful demonstration, that Crane could write a charming love story. It is the very simple affair of an art student and a summer boarder, with the more superficial incidents of their petty encounters set forth in a forcible, objective manner that is curiously hard and unsympathetic. The characters act, and on reflection one admits they act, *true,* but the play of their emotions goes on behind the curtain of the style, and all the enrichments of imaginative appeal that make love beautiful are omitted. Yet, though the story as a whole fails to satisfy, there are many isolated portions of altogether happy effectiveness, a certain ride behind an ox cart, for example. Much more surely is *On Active Service* an effort, and in places a painful effort, to fit his peculiar gift to the uncongenial conditions of popular acceptance. It is the least capable and least satisfactory of all Crane's work.

While these later books were appearing, and right up to his last fatal illness, Crane continued to produce fresh war pictures that show little or no falling off in vigor of imagination and handling; and, in addition, he was experimenting with verse. In that little stone-blue volume, *War Is Kind,* and in the earlier *Black Riders,* the reader will find a series of acute and vivid impressions and many of the finer qualities of Crane's descriptive prose, but he will not find any novel delights of melody or cadence or any fresh aspects of Crane's personality. There remain some children's stories to be published and an unfinished romance. With that the tale of his published work ends, and the career of one of the most brilliant, most significant and most distinctively American of all English writers comes to its unanticipated *finis.*

It would be absurd, here and now, to attempt to apportion any relativity of importance to Crane, to say that he was greater than A, or less important than B. That class-list business is, indeed, best left forever to the newspaper plebiscite and the library statistician; among artists, whose sole, just claim to recognition and whose sole title to immortality must necessarily be the possession of unique qualities, that is to say, of unclassifiable factors, these gradations are absurd. Suffice it that, even before his death, Crane's right to be counted in the hierarchy of those who have made a permanent addition to the great and growing fabric of English letters was not only assured, but conceded. To define his position in time, however, and in relation to periods and modes of writing will be a more reasonable undertaking; and it seems to me that, when at last the true proportions can be seen, Crane will be found to occupy a position singularly cardinal. He was a New Englander of Puritan lineage, and the son of a long tradition of literature. There had been many Cranes who wrote before him. He has shown me a shelf of books, for the most part the pious and theological works of various antecedent Stephen Cranes. He had been at some pains to gather together these alien products of his kin. For the most part they seemed little, insignificant books, and one opened them to read the beaten *cliches,* the battered outworn phrases, of a movement that has ebbed. Their very size and binding suggested a dying impulse, that very same impulse that in its prime had carried the magnificence of Milton's imagery and the pomp and splendors of Milton's prose. In Crane that impulse was altogether dead.

He began stark—I find all through this brief notice I have been repeating that in a dozen disguises, "freedom from tradition," "absolute directness" and the like—as though he came into the world of letters without ever a predecessor. In style, in method and in all that is distinctively *not* found in his books, he is sharply defined, the expression in literary art of certain enormous repudiations. Was ever a man before who wrote of battles so abundantly as he has done, and never had a word, never a word from first to last, of the purpose and justification of the war? And of the God of Battles, no more than the battered name; "Hully Gee!"—the lingering trace of the Deity! And of the sensuousness and tenderness of love, so much as one can find in *The Third Violet!* Any richness of allusion, any melody or balance of phrase, the half quotation that refracts and softens and enriches the statement, the momentary digression that opens like a window upon beautiful or distant things, are not merely absent, but obviously and sedulously avoided. It is as if the racial thought and tradition had been razed from his mind and its site ploughed and salted. He is more than himself in this; he is the first expression of the opening mind of a new period, or, at least, the early emphatic phase of a new initiative—beginning, as a growing mind must needs begin, with the record of impressions, a record of a vigor and intensity beyond all precedent.

—H.G. WELLS, "Stephen Crane: From an
English Standpoint," *North American Review,*
August 1900, pp. 233–242

WILLIAM DEAN HOWELLS
"FRANK NORRIS" (1902)

William Dean Howells, unlike most critics, values *The Red Badge of Courage* less than *Maggie* and *George's Mother*. In this essay looking back at Stephen Crane's literary output, Howells contends that *"Maggie* remains the best thing he did."

The physical slightness, if I may so suggest one characteristic of Crane's vibrant achievement, reflected the delicacy of energies that could be put forth only in nervous spurts, in impulses vivid and keen, but wanting in breadth and bulk of effect. Curiously enough, on the other hand, this very lyrical spirit, whose freedom was its life, was the absolute slave of reality. It was interesting to hear him defend what he had written, in obedience to his experience of things, against any change in the interest of convention. "No," he would contend, in behalf of the profanities of his people, "that is the way they *talk*. I have thought of that, and whether I ought to leave such things out, but if I do I am not giving the thing as I *know* it." He felt the constraint of those semi-savage natures, such as he depicted in *Maggie,* and *George's Mother,* and was forced through the fealty of his own nature to report them as they spoke no less than as they looked. When it came to *The Red Badge of Courage,* where he took leave of these simple aesthetics, and lost himself in a whirl of wild guesses at the fact from the ground of insufficient witness, he made the failure which formed the break between his first and his second manner, though it was what the public counted a success, with every reason to do so from the report of the sales.

The true Stephen Crane was the Stephen Crane of the earlier books, the earliest book; for *Maggie* remains the best thing he did. All he did was lyrical, but this was the aspect and accent as well as the spirit of the tragically squalid life he sang, while *The Red Badge of Courage,* and the other things that followed it, were the throes of an art failing with material to which it could not render an absolute devotion from an absolute knowledge. He sang, but his voice erred up and down the scale, with occasional flashes of brilliant melody, which could not redeem the errors. New York was essentially his inspiration, the New York of suffering and baffled and beaten life, of inarticulate or blasphemous life; and away from it he was not at home, with any theme, or any sort of character. It was the pity of his fate that he must quit New York, first as a theme, and then as a habitat; for he rested nowhere else, and wrought with nothing else as with the lurid depths which he gave proof of knowing better than any one else. Every one is limited, and perhaps no one is more limited than another; only, the direction of the limitation is different in each. Perhaps George Douglas, if he had lived, would still have done nothing greater than *The House with the Green Shutters,* and might have failed in the proportion of a larger range as Stephen Crane did. I am not going to say that either of these extraordinary talents was of narrower bound than Frank Norris; such measures are not of the map. But I am still less going to say that they were of finer quality because their achievement seems more poignant, through the sort of physical concentration which it has. Just as a whole unhappy world agonizes in the little space their stories circumscribe, so what is sharpest and subtlest in that anguish finds its like in the epical breadths of Norris's fiction.

—WILLIAM DEAN HOWELLS,
"Frank Norris," *North American Review,*
December 1902, pp. 770–771

HAMLIN GARLAND "STEPHEN CRANE AS I KNEW HIM" (1914)

Hamlin Garland, who had been so important to Stephen Crane and his career—feeding him, loaning him money, introducing him to Howells and other important literary contacts—grew more socially judgmental with time. In particular, he came to disapprove of the lifestyle he thought Crane had adopted. Apparently the news that Stephen and Cora Crane were never married and the details of her previous marriages and her proprietorship of the Hotel de Dream finally reached the ears of the increasingly conservative Garland. In this later version recounting his meeting with Crane, he repeats much of the previously cited article, but he ends it with references to Crane's "irresponsibility" and his "living in sin."

Despite the obvious condemnation of Crane's lifestyle, Garland still calls him a genius and predicts that his work will "live long in the libraries of those who esteem the man who is able to create original characters and to make old words seem new."

. . . when "The Black Riders" came out, I was touched to find it dedicated to me. It was a thin volume of less than a hundred small pages, but it seemed to me then and seems to me yet one of the most imaginative little books ever published in this country. Its originality, its high thought, its large images in small compass, made it difficult to estimate or catalogue. No one reads it now and few read "The Red Badge of Courage," and yet I maintain they were both daring and vivid pieces of literary craftsmanship. Perhaps they were too unconventional.

There was something essentially unwholesome about his philosophy, something bitter, ironic, despairing; and it may be that his work, so powerfully individual, and his diction, so striking and so vivid, worked against his advancement in the end. It is a strange reflection and a melancholy fact that his books, so delightful in the freshness of their appeal, should have passed (in the space of fifteen years) almost entirely out of the consideration of even the highest class of readers.

He was not born for long life and he was not born for development. His work did not change except for the worse. It remained fragmentary and severe. "The Red Badge" in its printed form did not in my judgment have the quality that was in the manuscript which came to me in the boy's pocket. The prodigious opening sentence which so impressed me on that memorable day disappeared entirely from his copy and the printed book lacked many other of the most notable pages of the original manuscript. Nevertheless, it remains one of the most vivid pictures of battle in our literature.

It had a most unfortunate effect, however; for it led McClure and other editors to insist on his doing other battle scenes. The war with Spain came on, he became field correspondent, and the power which had filled his first manuscripts gradually failed. His development was forced along journalistic lines, and the books which he produced afterward were in a sense only reflections of "The Red Badge of Courage." Vivid, concise, and powerful as they often were, his books remained episodic. They failed of high, sustained design. He could not construct.

In a later volume of verse, "War is Kind," he struck the love-note and struck it vibrantly, for his love-life was stormy; but his book was only for the few, for those who worship the right placing of words, and admire the expression of a bitter and essentially tragic personality. Forced to earn a living with his prose, he more and more conformed, but in his verse he remained himself. He could not sing, he was not lyric, but he produced a kind of subconscious, distinctive music.

I saw but little of him after the close of the Spanish War. He went abroad, somewhat shadowed by an experience which he hints at in these lines:

I

There was a man and a woman
Who sinned.
Then did the man heap the punishment
All upon the head of her,
And went away gaily.

II

There was a man and a woman
Who sinned.
And the man stood with her.
As upon her head, so upon his,
Fell blow and blow,
And all people screaming, "Fool!"
He was a iron heart.

III

He was a braver heart.
Would you speak with him, friend?
Well, he is dead,
And there went your opportunity.
Let it be your grief
That he is dead

And your opportunity gone;
For, in that, you were a coward.

A strange, short-lived, marvelous boy! He never seemed to be other than a boy to me. He never arrived at full responsibility and citizenship. He was a genius, as erratic as he was unaccountable, a rocket whose very speed assisted in the wasting of his substance, and yet the work he did will live long in the libraries of those who esteem the man who is able to create original characters and to make old words seem new.

—HAMLIN GARLAND,
"Stephen Crane as I Knew Him,"
The Yale Review, April 1914, pp. 494–506

JOSEPH CONRAD "STEPHEN CRANE: A NOTE WITHOUT DATES" (1919)

Joseph Conrad, the author of *Heart of Darkness*, *Nostromo*, *Lord Jim*, and several other novels, became to Stephen Crane a close friend and literary intimate, the two often talking about their respective projects and work in progress. They read and admired each other's writing, and they and their families exchanged frequent visits while the Cranes lived in England.

When the two first met, Crane had achieved greater recognition than Conrad, but Crane had read Conrad's *Nigger of the "Narcissus,"* thought it great literature, and asked to meet the author. Once the two became acquainted, they spent many hours in each other's company, discussing their work. After Joseph and Jessie Conrad welcomed the birth of their first son, Borys, the Conrads spent ten days at the Cranes's home. Crane, with his long-held love of dogs and horses, had insisted that every boy must have a dog, and when Borys was older Crane presented him with one.

The sincere admiration and friendship of the two cannot be doubted, so it is surprising when Conrad remarks, "It was a great loss to his friends, but perhaps not so much to literature." Conrad had genuinely valued the work that Crane had done, but in this piece he seems to feel that Crane would not have realized any further advances in his art had he lived.

My acquaintance with Stephen Crane was brought about by Mr. Pawling, partner in the publishing firm of Mr. William Heinemann.

One day Mr. Pawling said to me: "Stephen Crane has arrived in England. I asked him if there was anybody he wanted to meet and he mentioned two names. One of them was yours." I had then just been reading, like the rest of the world, Crane's "Red Badge of Courage." The subject of that story was war, from the point of view of an individual soldier's emotions. That individual (he remains nameless throughout) was interesting enough in himself, but on turning over the pages of that little book which had for the moment secured such a noisy recognition I had been even more interested in the personality of the writer. The picture of a simple and untried youth becoming through the needs of his country part of a great fighting machine was presented with an earnestness of purpose, a sense of tragic issues, and an imaginative force of expression which struck me as quite uncommon and altogether worthy of admiration.

Apparently Stephen had received a favourable impression from the reading of the "Nigger of the *Narcissus*," a book of mine which had also been published lately. I was truly pleased to hear this.

On my next visit to town we met at a lunch. I saw a young man of medium stature and slender build, with very steady, penetrating, blue eyes, the eyes of a being who not only sees visions but can brood over them to some purpose.

He had indeed a wonderful power of vision, which he applied to the things of this earth and of our mortal humanity with a penetrating force that seemed to reach, within life's appearances and forms, the very spirit of life's truth. His ignorance of the world at large—he had seen very little of it—did not stand in the way of his imaginative grasp of facts, events, and picturesque men.

His manner was very quiet, his personality at first sight interesting, and he talked slowly with an intonation which on some people, mainly Americans, had, I believe, a jarring effect. But not on me. Whatever he said had a personal note, and he expressed himself with a graphic simplicity which was extremely engaging. He knew little of literature, either of his own country or of any other, but he was himself a wonderful artist in words whenever he took a pen into his hand. Then his gift came out—and it was seen then to be much more than mere felicity of language. His impressionism of phrase went really deeper than the surface. In his writing he was very sure of his effects. I don't think he was ever in doubt about what he could do. Yet it often seemed to me that he was but half aware of the exceptional quality of his achievement.

This achievement was curtailed by his early death. It was a great loss to his friends, but perhaps not so much to literature. I think that he had given his measure fully in the few books he had the time to write. Let me not be misunderstood: the loss was great, but it was the loss of the delight his art could give, not the loss of any further possible revelation. As to himself, who can say how much he gained or lost by quitting so early this world of the living, which he knew how to set before us in the terms of his own artistic vision? Perhaps he did not lose a great deal. The recognition he was accorded was rather languid and given him grudgingly. The worthies welcome he secured for his tales in the country was from Mr. W. Henley in the *New Review* and later, towards the end of his life, from the late Mr. William Blackwood in his magazine. For the rest I must say that during his sojourn in England he had the misfortune to be, as the French say, *mal entouré*. He was beset by people who understood not the quality of his genius and were antagonistic to the deeper fineness of his nature. Some of them have died since, but dead or alive they are not worth speaking about now. I don't think he had any illusions about them himself; yet there was a strain of good-nature and perhaps of weakness in his character which prevented him from shaking himself free from their worthless and patronizing attentions, which in those days caused me secret irritation whenever I stayed with him in either of his English homes. My wife and I like best to remember him riding to meet us at the gate of the Park at Brede. Born master of his sincere impressions, he was also a born horseman. He never appeared so happy or so much to advantage as on the back of a horse. He had formed the project of teaching my eldest boy to ride and meantime, when the child was about two years old, presented him with his first dog.

I saw Stephen Crane a few days after his arrival in London. I saw him for the last time on his last day in England. It was in Dover, in a big hotel, in a bedroom with a large window looking on to the sea. He had been very ill and Mrs. Crane was taking him to some place in Germany, but one glance at that wasted face was enough to tell me that it was the most forlorn of all hopes. The last words he breathed out to me were: "I am tired. Give my love to your wife and child." When I stopped at the door for another look I saw that he had turned his head on the pillow and was staring wistfully out of the window at the sails of a cutter yacht that glided slowly across the frame, like a dim shadow against the grey sky.

Those who have read his little tale, "Horses," and the story "The Open Boat," in the volume of that name, know with what fine understanding he loved horses and the sea. And his passage on this earth was like that of a horseman riding swiftly in the dawn of a day fated to be short and without sunshine.

—Joseph Conrad, "Stephen Crane:
A Note without Dates," *London Mercury*,
December 1919, pp. 192–193

Vincent Starrett "Stephen Crane: An Estimate" (1920)

Vincent Starrett was born on October 26, 1886, in Toronto, moving with his family to Chicago in the late 1890s. He worked for the *Chicago Daily News* as a crime reporter, a feature writer, and from 1914 to 1915 as a war correspondent in Mexico. Starrett also wrote mystery and supernatural fiction for pulp magazines in the 1920s and 1930s. His most famous work, *The Private Life of Sherlock Holmes*, was published in 1933. In 1965, he retired from *The Chicago Tribune* where he had written a book column for twenty years.

Starrett is virtually alone in keeping up Stephen Crane's reputation after a number of obituary or remembrance articles appeared in the early 1900s. Starrett probably felt some kinship with Crane due to his own newspaper reporting, both of city affairs and of war. His estimate of Crane's value seems to have been inspired by the fairly recent World War I.

Starrett points out that Crane's "prose was finer poetry than his deliberate essays in poesy," an observation sometimes made by several later critics, and he refers to *The Red Badge of Courage* as a psychological study. He prefers Crane's short stories in *The Open Boat*, *Wounds in the Rain*, and *The Monster and Other Stories*. Unlike most early critics, Starrett observes Crane's use of beauty in war and humor in otherwise serious events. This estimate by someone who had no direct connection with Crane is an excellent appraisal of his work overall, valuing the elements that others had seen as affectations or faults.

It hardly profits us to conjecture what Stephen Crane might have written about the World War had he lived. Certainly, he would have been in it, in one capacity or another. No man had a greater talent for war and personal adventure, nor a finer art in describing it. Few writers of recent times could so well describes the poetry of motion as manifested in the surge and flow of battle, or so well depict the isolated deed of heroism in its stark simplicity and terror.

To such an undertaking as Henri Barbusse's *Under Fire*, that powerful, brutal book, Crane would have brought an analytical genius almost clairvoyant. He possessed an uncanny vision; a descriptive ability photographic in its clarity and in its care for minutiae—yet unphotographic in that the big central thing is often omitted, to be felt rather than seen in the occult suggestion of detail. Crane would have seen and depicted the grisly horror of it all, as Barbusse did, but he would have seen also the glory and the ecstasy and the wonder of it, and over that his poetry would have been spread.

While Stephen Crane was an excellent psychologist, he was also a true poet. Frequently his prose was finer poetry than his deliberate essays in poesy. His most famous book, *The Red Badge of Courage,* is essentially a psychological study, a delicate clinical dissection of the soul of a recruit, but it is also a *tour de force* of the imagination. When he wrote the book he had never seen a battle: he had to place himself in the situation of another. Years later, when he came out of the Greco-Turkish *fracas,* he remarked to a friend: "*The Red Badge* is all right."

Written by a youth who had scarcely passed his majority, this book has been compared with Tolstoy's *Sebastopol* and Zola's *La Débacle,* and with some of the short stories of Ambrose Bierce. The comparison with Bierce's work is legitimate; with the other books, I think, less so. Tolstoy and Zola see none of the traditional beauty of battle; they apply themselves to a devoted— almost obscene—study of corpses and carnage generally; they lack the American's instinct for the commonplace, the natural, which so materially aids his realism. In *The Red Badge of Courage* invariably the tone is kept down where one expects a height: the most heroic deeds are accomplished with studied awkwardness.

Crane was an obscure free-lance when he wrote this book. The effort, he says, somewhere, "was born of pain—despair, almost." It was a better piece of work, however, for that very reason, as Crane knew. It is far from flawless. It has been remarked that it bristles with as many grammatical errors as with bayonets; but it is a big canvas, and I am certain that many of Crane's deviations from the rules of polite rhetoric were deliberate experiments, looking to effect—effect which, frequently, he gained.

Stephen Crane "arrived" with this book. There are, of course, many who never have heard of him, to this day, but there was a time when he was very much talked of. That was in the middle nineties, following the publication of *The Red Badge of Courage,* although even before that he had occasioned a brief flurry with his weird collection of poems called *The Black Riders and Other Lines.* He was highly praised, and highly abused, and laughed at, but he seemed to be "made." We have largely forgotten since. But Crane still lives and will live.

Personally, I prefer his short stories to his novels and his poems; those, for instance, contained in *The Open Boat,* in *Wounds in the Rain,* and in *The Monster.* The title-story in that first collection is perhaps his finest piece of work. Yet what is it? A truthful record of an adventure of his own in the filibustering days that preceded our war with Spain; the faithful narrative of the voyage of an open boat, manned by a handful of shipwrecked men. But Captain Bligh's account of *his* small boat journey, after he had been sent adrift by the mutineers of the *Bounty*, seems tame in comparison, although of the two the English sailor's voyage was the more perilous.

In *The Open Boat* Crane again gains his effects by keeping down the tone where another writer might have attempted "fine writing" and have been lost. In it perhaps is most strikingly evident the poetic cadences of his prose: its rhythmic, monotonous flow is the flow of the gray water that laps at the sides of the boat, that rises and recedes in cruel waves, "like little pointed rocks." It is a desolate picture, and the tale is one of our greatest short stories. In the other tales that go to make up the volume are wild, exotic glimpses of Latin-America. I doubt whether the color and spirit of that region have been better rendered than in Stephen Crane's curious, distorted, staccato sentences.

War Stories is the laconic sub-title of *Wounds in the Rain*. It was not war on a grand scale that Crane saw in the Spanish-American complication, in which he participated as a war correspondent; no such war as the recent horror. But the occasions for personal heroism were no fewer than always, and the opportunities for the exercise of such powers of trained and appreciative understanding and sympathy as Crane possessed, were abundant. For the most part, these tales are episodic reports of isolated instances—the profanely humorous experiences of correspondents, the magnificent courage of signalmen under fire, the forgotten adventure of a converted yacht—but all are instinct with the red fever of war, and are backgrounded with the choking smoke of battle. Never again did Crane attempt the large canvas of *The Red Badge of Courage*. Before he had seen war, he imagined its immensity and painted it with the fury and fidelity of a Verestschagin; when he was its familiar, he singled out its minor, crimson passages for briefer but no less careful delineation.

In this book, again, his sense of the poetry of motion is vividly evident. We see men going into action, wave on wave, or in scattering charges; we hear the clink of their accoutrements and their breath whistling through their teeth. They are not men going into action at all, but men going about their business, which at the moment happens to be the capture of a trench. They are neither heroes nor cowards. Their faces reflect no particular emotion save, perhaps, a desire to get somewhere. They are a line of men running for a train, or following a fire engine, or charging a trench. It is a relentless picture, ever changing, ever the same. But it contains poetry, too, in rich, memorable passages.

In *The Monster, and Other Stories*, there is a tale called *The Blue Hotel*. A Swede, its central figure, toward the end manages to get himself murdered. Crane's description of it all is just as casual as that. The story fills half a dozen pages of the book; but the social injustice of the whole world are hinted in that space: the upside downness of creation, right prostrate, wrong triumphant,—a mad, crazy world. The incident of the murdered Swede is just part of the backwash of it all, but it is an illuminating fragment. The Swede was slain, not by the gambler whose knife pierced his thick hide; he was the victim of a condition for which he was no more to blame than the man who stabbed him. Stephen Crane thus speaks through the lips of one of the characters.—

"We are all in it! This poor gambler isn't even a noun. He is a kind of an adverb. Every sin is the result of a collaboration. We, five of us, have collaborated in the murder of this Swede. Usually there are from a dozen to forty women really involved in every murder, but in this case it seems to be only five men—you, I, Johnnie, old Scully, and that fool of an unfortunate gambler came merely as a culmination, the apex of a human movement, and gets all the punishment."

And then this typical land arresting piece of irony: —

"This corpse of the Swede, alone in the saloon, had its eyes fixed upon a dreadful legend that dwelt atop of the cash-machine: This registers the amount of your purchase."

In *The Monster*, the ignorance, prejudice and cruelty of an entire community are sharply focused. The realism is painful; one blushes for mankind. But while this story really belongs in the volume called *Whilomville Stories*, it is properly left out of that series. The Whilomville stories are pure comedy, and The Monster is a hideous tragedy.

Whilomville is any little village one may happen to think of. To write of it with such sympathy and understanding, Crane must have done some remarkable listening in Boyville. The truth is, of course, he was a boy himself—"a wonderful boy," somebody called him—and was possessed of the boy mind. These tales are chiefly funny because they are so true—boy stories written for adults; a child, I suppose, would find them dull. In none of his tales is his curious understanding of human minds and emotions better shown.

A blind critic once pointed out that Crane, in his search for striking effects, had been led into "frequent neglect of the time-hallowed rights of certain words," and that in his pursuit of color he "falls occasionally into almost ludicrous mishap." The smug pedantry of the quoted lines is sufficient answer to the charges, but in support of these assertions the critic quoted certain passages and phrases. He objected to cheeks "scarred" by tears, to "dauntless" statues, and to "terror-stricken" wagons. The very touches of poetic impressionism that make largely for Crane's greatness, are cited to prove him an ignoramus. There is the finest of poetic imagery in the suggestions subtly conveyed by Crane's tricky adjectives, the use of which was as deliberate with him as his choice of a subject. But Crane was an imagist before our modern imagists were known.

This unconventional use of adjectives is marked in the Whilomville tales. In one of them Crane refers to the "solemn odor of burning turnips." It is the most nearly perfect characterization of turnips conceivable; can anyone improve upon that "solemn odor"?

Stephen Crane's first venture was *Maggie: A Girl of the Streets*. It was, I believe, the first hint of naturalism in American letters. It was not a best-seller; it offers no solution of life; it is an episodic bit of slum fiction, ending with the tragic finality of a Greek drama. It is a skeleton of a novel rather than a novel, but it is a powerful outline, written about a life Crane had learned to know as a newspaper reporter in New York. It is a singularly fine piece of analysis, or a bit of extraordinarily faithful reporting, as one may prefer; but not a few French and Russian writers have failed to accomplish in two volumes what Crane achieved in two hundred pages. In the same category is *George's Mother*, a triumph of inconsequential detail piling up with a cumulative effect quite overwhelming.

Crane published two volumes of poetry—*The Black Riders* and *War Is Kind*. Their appearance in print was jeeringly hailed; yet Crane was only pioneering in the free verse that is today, if not definitely accepted, at least tolerated. . . .

—Vincent Starrett, "Stephen Crane:
An Estimate," *Sewanee Review*,
July 1920, pp. 405–413

Edward Garnett "Stephen Crane" (1922)

Edward Garnett, a friend and early supporter of Stephen Crane, looks back over a quarter century to the time when Crane was lauded for *The Red Badge of Courage*. Garnett reassesses Crane's work after not having read it for many years, and he points out Crane's "wonderful insight into, and mastery of the primary passions, and his irony deriding the swelling emotions of the self." Unlike Conrad's faltering interest in Crane's writing, Garnett's reappraisal comes to the conclusion that "if America has forgotten or neglects Crane's achievements, above all in 'Maggie' and 'The Open Boat,' she does not yet deserve to produce artists of rank. Crane holds a peculiar niche in American literature."

Garnett has proved to be prophetic, as Crane scholarship, which had virtually disappeared at the time this article was written, began to burgeon in the 1970s and has continued to grow and become more sophisticated over the years.

A short time ago I picked up on a London book-stall, the first edition of "The Red Badge of Courage." Its price was sixpence. Obviously the bookseller lay no store by it, for the book had been thrown on the top of a parcel of paper-covered novels among the waifs and strays of literature. Chancing to meet a young American poet I asked him, curiously, how his countrymen esteemed today that intensely original genius, Crane, the creator of "The Open Boat," "George's Mother," "Maggie," "The Black Riders." He answered, "One rarely hears Crane's name mentioned in America. His work is almost forgotten, but I believe it has a small, select circle of admirers." I confess I was amused, especially when a little later a first edition of "Almayer's Folly," the first Conrad, was sold at auction for five hundred times the amount of the early Crane. And Conrad was also amused when I told him, and we suggest a title for an allegorical picture yet to be painted—the Apotheosis of an Author crowned by Fashion, Merit and Midas. For we both had in mind the years when the critics hailed "The Nigger of the Narcissus" as a worthy pendent to the battle-pictures presented in "The Red Badge of Courage," and when Sir, then Mr. Authur Quiller-Couch spoke of "The Nigger," as "having something of Crane's insistence."

We talked together over Crane and his work and cast our memories back over twenty years when we were both in couch with "poor Steve," he more than I. And we agreed that within its peculiar limited compass Crane's genius was unique. Crane, when living at Oxted, was a neighbour of mine, and one day, on my happening to describe to him an ancient Sussex house, noble and grey with the passage of five hundred years, nothing would satisfy him but that he must become the tenant of Brede Place. It was the lure of romance that always thrilled Crane's blood, and Brede Place had had indeed, an unlucky, chequered history. I saw Crane last, when he lay dying there, the day before his wife was transporting him, on a stretcher bed, to a health resort in the Black Forest, in a vain effort to arrest the fatal disease, and I see again his bloodless face and the burning intensity of his eyes. He had lived at too high pressure and his consumptive physique was ravaged by the exhausting strain of his passionate life, and sapped by the hardships of the Cuban campaign, which he suffered as a war-correspondent. Crane's strange eyes, with their intensely concentrated gaze, were those of a genius and I recall how on his first visit to our house I was so struck by the exquisite symmetry of his brow and temples, that I failed to note, what a lady pointed out when he had left, the looseness of his mouth. Yes, the intensity of genius burned in his eyes, and his weak lips betrayed his unrestrained temperament. Crane' genius, his feeling for style were wholly intuitive and no study had fostered them. On first reading "The Red Badge of Courage," I concluded had been influenced by the Russian masters, but I learned when I met him, that he had never read a line of them. Would that he had! For Crane, as Conrad reminded me, never knew how good his best work was. He simply never knew. He never recognized that in the Volume "The Open Boat," he had achieved the perfection of his method. If he had comprehend that in "The Bride Comes to Yellow Sky" and in "Death and the Child" he had attained then, his high water mark, he might perhaps have worked forward along the lines of patient, ascending effort; but after "The Open Boat," 1898, his work dropped to lower levels. He wrote too much, he wrote against time, and he wrote while dunned for money. At first sight it appears astonishing that the creator of such a miracle of style as "The Bride Comes to Yellow Sky" should publish in the same year so mediocre a novel as "On Active Service." But Crane ought never to have essayed the form of the novel. He had not handled it satisfactorily in "The Third Violet," 1897, a love story charming in its impressionistic lightness of touch, but lacking in forces, in concentration, in characterization. My view of Crane as a born impressionist and master of the short story, I emphasized in an Appreciation in 1898, and since it is germane to my purpose here, I reprint the criticism:

[Reprints the earlier article]

On the above criticism Conrad wrote me at the time, "The Crane thing is just—precisely just a ray of light flashed in and showing all there is."

II

But when I wrote that criticism, that journalistic novel "On Active Service" was yet to be published, and I did not fully comprehend Crane's training and his circumstances. I sounded a warning note against "reporting," but though he had emerged from journalism, he was still haunted by journalism and was encircled by a—well! by a crew of journalists. I remarked, "I do not think Mr. Crane can or will develop further," but pressing him were duns and debts and beckoning him was the glamour of the war-correspondent's life, and before him were editors ready for ephemeral stuff, while they shook their heads sadly over such perfect gems as "The Pace of Youth." Crane had seen much for a man of his years, but he was still thirsting for adventure and the life of action, and he had not time to digest his experiences, to reflect, to incubate and fashion his work at leisure in the two or three hurried years that remained to him after the publication of "The Open Boat," he created some notable things, but the dice of fate were loaded by all his circumstances against his development as craftsman.

We must therefore be thankful that his instinct for style emerged when his psychological genius broke out and so often possessed him in the teeth of the great stucco gods and the chinking of brass in the market place. He had written his best things without advice or encouragement, urged by the demon within him, and his genius burned clear, with its passionate individuality, defying all the inhibitions and conventions of New England. Was that genius ever appreciated by America? I doubt it, though Americans were forced to accept him, first because of the fame which "The Red Badge of Courage" brought Crane in England, and secondary because his subject was the American Civil War, a subject that could not be disregarded. On re-reading "The Red Badge of Courage" I am more than ever struck by the genius with which Crane, in imagination, pierced to the essentials of War. Without any experiences of war at the time, Crane was essentially true to the psychological core of war—if not to actualities. He naturally underestimated the checks placed by physical strain and fatigue on the faculties, as well as war's malignant, cold ironies, its prosaic dreadfulness, its dreary, deadening tedium. But as Goethe has pointed out, the artist has a license to ignore actualities, if he is obeying inner, aesthetic laws. And Crane' subject was the passions, the passions of destruction, fear, pride, rage, shame and exaltation in the heat of action. The deep artistic unity of "The Red Badge of Courage," is fused in its flaming, spiritual intensity, in the fiery ardour with which the shock of the Federal and Confederate armies is imaged. The torrential force and impetus, the check, sullen recoil and reforming of shattered regiments, and the renewed onslaught and obstinate resistances of brigades and divisions are visualized with extraordinary forces and colour. If the sordid grimness of carnage, is partially screened, the feeling of War's cumulative rapacity, of its breaking pressure and fluctuating tension is caught with wonderful fervour and freshness of style. It is of course, the work of ardent youth, but when Crane returned from the Graeco-Turkish war he said to Conrad, "My picture of war was all right! I have found it as I imagined it." And his imaginative picture he supplemented, four years later, in that penetrating, somber, realistic piece "Memories of War" in "Wounds in the Rain," his reminiscences of the Cuban campaign that in fact had death's secret mark already on him. I may note, too, how Crane, sitting in our garden, described that on questioning Veterans of the Civil War about their feelings when fighting, he could get nothing out of them but one this, viz, "We just went there and did so and so."

III

And here I must enlarge and attend my criticism of 1898 by saying that two qualities in especial, combined to form Crane's unique quality, viz his

wonderful insight into, and mastery of the primary passions, and his irony
deriding the swelling emotions of the self. It is his irony that checks the
emotional intensity of his delineation, and suddenly reveals passion at high
tension in the clutch of the implacable tides of life. It is the perfect fusion of
these two forces of passion and irony that creates Crane's spiritual background,
and raises his work, at its finest, into the high zone of man's tragic conflict
with the universe. His irony is seen in its purest form in "Black Riders,"
1896, a tiny collection of *vers libres*, as sharp in their naked questioning as
a sword blades. These verses pierce with dreadful simplicity certain illusions
of unregarding sages, whose earnest commentaries pour, and will continue
to pour from the groaning press. In "Maggie," 1896, that little masterpiece
which drew the highest tribute from the veteran, W. D. Howells, again it is the
irony that keeps in right perspective Crane's remorseless study of New York
slum and Bowery morals. The code of herd law by which the inexperienced
girl, Maggie, is pressed to death by her family, her lover and the neighbours,
is seen working with strange finality. The Bowery inhabitants, as we, can be
nothing other than what they are; their human nature responds inexorably to
their brutal environment; the curious habits and code of the most primitives
savage tribes could not be presented with a more impartial exactness, or with
more sympathetic understanding.

"Maggie" is not a story *about* people; it is primitive human nature itself
set down with perfect spontaneity and grace of handling. For pure aesthetic
beauty and truth no Russian, not Tchehov himself, could have bettered
this study, which, as Howells remarks, has the quality of Greek tragedy.
The perfection of Crane's style, his unique quality, can, however, be studied
best in "The Open Boat," 1898. Here he is again the pure artist, brilliant,
remorselessly keen, delighting in life's passions and ironies, amusing, tragic
or grimacing. Consider the nervous audacity, in phrasing, of the piece "An
Experiment in Misery," which reveals the quality of chiaroscuro of a master's
etching. No wonder the New York editors looked askance at such a break
with tradition. How would they welcome the mocking verve and sinister
undertone of such pieces as "A Man and Some Others," or the airy freshness
and flying spontaneity of "The Pace of Youth?" In the volume "The Open
Boat" Crane's style has a brilliancy of tone, a charming timbre peculiar
to itself. As with Whistler, his personal note eschews everything obvious,
everything inessential, as witness "Death and the Child," that haunting
masterpiece where a child is playing with pebbles and sticks on the great
mountain-side, while the smoke and din of the battlefield, in the plain below,
hide the rival armies of pigmy men busy reaping with death. It is in the calm
detachment of the little child playing, by which the artist secures his poetic

background; man, pigmy man, watched impassively by the vast horizons of life, is the plaything of the Fates. The irony of life is here implicit. Perfect also is that marvel of felicitous observation "An Ominous Babe," where each touch is exquisitely final; sketch in which the instincts of the babes betray the roots of all wars, past and to come. This gem ought to be in every anthology of American prose.

The descent of Crane in "On Active Service" 1898, to a clever, journalistic level, was strange. It was a lapse into superficiality; much stronger artistically was "The Monster," 1901, a book of stories of high psychological interest, which might indeed have made another man's reputation, but a book which is ordinary in atmosphere. The story "The Blue Hotel" is, indeed, a brilliant exploration of fear and its reactions, and "His New Mittens" is a delightful graphic study of boy morals, but we note that when Crane breathes an everyday, common atmosphere his aesthetic power always weaken. One would give the whole contents of "Whilomville Stories," 18902, for the five pages of "An Ominous Baby"; and the heterogeneous contents of "Last Words," 1902, a volume of sweepings from Crane's desk, kick the balance when weighed against the sketch "A Tale of Mere Chance," the babblings of a madman, which Dostoevsky might be proud to claim. The companion sketch "Manacled" (in "The Monster") bears also the authentic stamp of Crane's rare vision.

To conclude, if America has forgotten or neglects Crane's achievements, above all in "Maggie" and "The Open Boat," she does not yet deserve to produce artists of rank. Crane holds a peculiar niche in American literature. Where it is weak, viz in the aesthetic and psychologically truthful delineation of passion, Stephen Crane is a master. And masters are rare, yes how rare are masters, let the men of Crane's generation, looking back on the twenty years since his death, decide.

—Edward Garnett, "Stephen Crane,"
*Friday Nights: Literary Criticism and
Appreciations*, New York: Alfred A
Knopf, 1922, pp. 201–217

❖

WORKS

❖

In March 1893, after rejection by several publishers, *Maggie: A Girl of the Streets* was privately printed under the pseudonym Johnston Smith. Stephen Crane had been left some coal stock upon his mother's death, and he used the money from the sale of the stock to have his first full-length manuscript printed. After mailing copies to various friends and critics, Crane was rewarded with virtually no publicity, the sole exception that year being Hamlin Garland's positive review in the *Arena*. Two years later Rupert Hughes's review, which was also complimentary, was published in *Godey's Magazine*, and Nancy Huston Banks's negative review, which compares *Maggie* unfavorably with the recently published *Red Badge of Courage*, appeared in the *Bookman*.

When an expurgated version of *Maggie* was brought out by D. Appleton & Company in June 1896, Crane had already published *The Black Riders and Other Lines* in early May 1895 and *The Red Badge* in late September 1895. The reviews of *Maggie* were mixed. William Dean Howells and H.G. Wells enthusiastically praised the book, but others such as Edward Bright found little to admire and much to rebuke.

When *Black Riders* appeared, it generated some attention, with positive reviews from Thomas Wentworth Higginson and Mark Antony de Wolfe Howe and an extravagantly affirmative review by Elbert Hubbard, who later organized the infamous Philistine dinner for Crane. The other review here by Josephine Dodge Daskam praises some poems and denounces others. Unlike many friends and critics who parodied the poems, she reviews them seriously, even comparing Crane unfavorably with Emerson and favorably with Whitman.

In contrast to the reception of these two works, *The Red Badge of Courage* reached almost instant popularity, both in the United States in late 1895 and in England where it was published a few months later.

The reviews were largely flattering, but some were so negative as to begin an all-out sparring contest with the *Dial*, whose owner Alexander C. McClurg attacked the book, declaring it popular in England because it is "a vicious satire upon American soldiers and American armies." His extremely disapproving letter was followed up by a *Dial* review by J.L. Onderdonk, supporting McClurg's opinion. In that same issue, D. Appleton & Company, Crane's publisher, corrects McClurg's mistaken ideas on *The Red Badge's* publication history. As a result of these heated responses, a number of controversial reviews, both negative and positive, followed. All this publicity, painful as some of it must have been, served to keep Crane's masterpiece in the literary spotlight with both English and American critics vying for their part in having recognized Crane's genius.

The most perceptive criticism on *The Red Badge* is found in the reviews by Sydney Brooks, Harold Frederic, and George Wyndham, all of whom recognized the art of the book and pointed out its specific contributions to literature. The final article on the novel, written shortly after Crane's death, takes credit for *The New York Times* as the first to have had a long notice of the work in print.

Although Crane had finished *George's Mother* in November 1894, he did not submit it for publication until after the success of *The Red Badge*. *George's Mother*, published in May 1896, received mixed reviews. Henry Thurston Peck, who just a year earlier had written a glowing review of *Maggie* in its first edition, begins his review with "This is sorry stuff." Frank Rinder notes that *George's Mother* has defects, but he finds it overall "a strong study." John D. Barry, in an article published six months after the book appeared, defends it from those who had already declared it dead, calling it "a great book."

As George Parsons Lathrop states emphatically in his review of *The Little Regiment*, "It goes without saying that these war stories cannot compare with *The Red Badge* in merit." *The Red Badge* is the standard that Stephen Crane never again achieved in his lifetime. Crane perhaps deservedly attracted little positive attention with *The Third Violet* and *Active Service*, but as H.G. Wells has pointed out, his collections of short stories seemed to have been largely unappreciated because the genre itself is accorded less respect than the novel. A few of Crane's shorter works, such as "The Open Boat" and *The Monster*, received limited attention, but his collection *Wounds in the Rain* received almost none. His last volume of poetry, *War Is Kind,* was reviewed with "grave doubts of his ultimate success" in poetry.

MAGGIE: A GIRL OF THE STREETS

HAMLIN GARLAND "AN AMBITIOUS FRENCH NOVEL AND A MODEST AMERICAN STUDY" (1893)

Hamlin Garland was one of the first to recognize the value of Stephen Crane's writing, having been given a copy of the original privately printed *Maggie: A Girl of the Streets*. In this early review, he praises the book enthusiastically, a contrast to his later disillusionment following rumors of Crane's bohemian life in England.

———

This [*Maggie*] is of more interest to me, both because it is the work of a young man, and also because it is a work of astonishingly good style. It deals with poverty and vice and crime also, but it does so, not out of curiosity, not out of salaciousness, but because of a distinct art impulse, the desire to utter in truthful phrase a certain rebellious cry. It is the voice of the slums. It is not written by a dilettante; it is written by one who has lived the life. The young author, Stephen Crane, is a native of the city, and has grown up in the very scenes he describes. His book is the most truthful and unhackneyed study of the slums I have yet read, fragment though it is. It is pictorial, graphic, terrible in its directness. It has no conventional phrases. It gives the dialect of the slums as I have never before seen it written—crisp, direct, terse. It is another locality finding voice.

It is important because it voices the blind rebellion of Rum Alley and Devil's Row. It creates the atmosphere of the jungles, where vice festers and crime passes gloomily by, where outlawed human nature rebels against God and man.

The story fails of rounded completeness. It is only a fragment. It is typical only of the worst elements of the alley. The author should delineate the families living on the next street, who live lives of heroic purity and hopeless hardship.

The dictum is amazingly simple and fine for so young a writer. Some of the works illuminate like flashes of light. Mr. Crane is only twenty-one years of age, and yet he has met and grappled with the actualities of the street in almost unequalled grace and strength. With such a technique already at command, with life mainly before him, Stephen Crane is to be henceforth reckoned with. "Maggie" should be put beside "Van Bibber" to see the extremes of New York as stated by two young men. Mr. Crane need not fear comparisons so far as technique goes, and Mr. Davis will need to step forward right briskly or he may be overtaken by a man who impresses the reader with a sense of almost unlimited resource.

—HAMLIN GARLAND,
"An Ambitious French Novel
and a Modest American Study,"
Arena, June 1893, pp. 11–12

RUPERT HUGHES (1895)

Rupert Hughes was a historian, novelist, film director, and composer. Born in Lancaster, Missouri, in 1872, he was the uncle of Howard Hughes, the famous aviation magnate and filmmaker. Although his other writing is virtually unknown now, Hughes's three-volume scholarly biography of George Washington, which was lauded by historians, broke new ground in demythologizing the first president of the United States. He was assistant editor of *Godey's Magazine* in the 1890s. In this review, published under the pseudonym of "Chelifer," Hughes enthusiastically discusses Stephen Crane's privately printed *Maggie: A Girl of the Streets*.

. . . probably the strongest piece of slum writing we have is *Maggie*, by Stephen Crane, which was published some years ago with a pen-name for the writer and no name at all for the publishers. But merit will out, and the unclaimed foundling attracted no little attention, though by no means as much as it deserves. The keenness of the wit, the minuteness of the observation, and the bitterness of the cynicism resemble Morrison's work. The foredoomed fall of a well-meaning girl reared in an environment of drunkenness and grime is told with great humanity and fearless art, and there is a fine use of contrast in the conclusion of the work, where the brutal mother in drunken sentimentality is persuaded with difficulty to "forgive" the dead girl whom she compelled to a harsh fate by the barren cruelty of home-life. The subjects chosen . . . compel an occasional plainness of speech which may give a shock to spasmic prudishness, but there is nothing to harm a healthy mind, and they all should have the effect of creating a better understanding and a wiser, more active sympathy for the unfortunates who must fill the cellar of the tenement we call life. To do this is far better even than to be artistic.

—RUPERT HUGHES,
Godey's Magazine, October 1895,
pp. 431–432

N.H.B. [NANCY HUSTON BANKS]
"THE NOVELS OF TWO JOURNALISTS" (1895)

Nancy Huston Banks was a staff reviewer for *The Bookman*; she also published several popular novels. In this review, she compares Edward W. Townsend and Stephen Crane, both journalists and novelists whose subject was the slums of New York. Although she sees merit in *Maggie*, she states that Townsend's novel is "all story" and Crane's is "no story at all." Indeed, she finds Crane's work unnatural, needing "sunlight" and "normal growth."

The question whether journalism helps or hinders a writer to create literature has recently been discussed by the local press with fresh interest, and the discussion is likely to continue for a long time, inasmuch as the controversialists seek to reach general conclusions where no general conclusion can be reached. Meantime, two novels from newspaper men of New York furnish a contribution to the revival of the subject, whether or not they be accepted as proof on the one side or the other. The authors, Mr. Stephen Crane and Mr. Edward W. Townsend, are both engaged in active journalism, and in the work which first distinguished them from the army of anonymous writers there is a degree of resemblance. Each in his first work of fictions deals with the slums, finding the light of his art in the shadows of the under-world which his profession forced him to penetrate. *Maggie, a Girl of the Streets,* Mr. Crane's first expression of the deep feeling of life thus imbibed is among the saddest books in our language. Mr. Townsend, writing from the same standpoint, touches these terrible problems with alleviating humour, thus increasing rather than lessening the conviction of his sympathy and earnestness. Smiles at "Chimmie Fadden's" extravagances serve to make more acute the pathos of his early life, as the readiest laughter lies always closest to the quickest tears. So far the literary careers of the two journalists may be said to have run on somewhat parallel lines; but in their new books they part company widely, one taking a different theme and the other a different manner. It is a far cry from the field in which Mr. Crane first appeared to *The Red Badge of Courage*, his last book—so very far indeed that he seems to have lost himself as well as his reader. . . .

Whereas Mr. Townsend's is all story, Mr. Crane's is no story at all. The latter may perhaps be best described as a study in morbid emotions and distorted external impressions. The short, sharp sentences hurled without sequence give one the feeling of being pelted from different angles by hail—hail that is hot. The reader longs to plead like Tony Lumpkin, that the author "not keep dinging it, dinging it into one so." The few scattered bits of description are like stereopticon views insecurely put on the canvas. And yet there is on the reader's part a distinct recognition of power—misspent perhaps—but still power of an unusual kind. . . .

. . . whatever the influence journalism may or may not have had upon Mr. Crane's literary training, he does not write like a journalist when he undertakes literature. It is in truth rather awful to image what an old newspaper editor would do with these pages if he wished to give the author a memorable lesson in what not to do, or, as Dickens says: "how not to do it." A literary editor, on the contrary, would perhaps smile on the same pages as he never would on those of Mr. Townsend's; so that the wisdom of life in this case, as in all others, consists in addressing one's message to the mind that needs it. As for these two volumes, the root of literature seems to lie in Mr. Crane's; but the root seems to be terribly buried, and much in need of being assisted into sunlight and a natural, normal growth.

—N.H.B. [Nancy Huston Banks],
"The Novels of Two Journalists,"
The Bookman, November 1895, pp. 217–220

William Dean Howells
"An Appreciation" (1896)

William Dean Howells greatly admired *Maggie: A Girl of the Streets* after reading the original privately printed version, and he wrote enthusiastically of the novel after an expurgated version was published by D. Appleton in June 1896. Howells continued to value this short novel above the rest of Stephen Crane's work, including *The Red Badge of Courage*. Howells points out what he sees as the slim volume's resemblance to Greek tragedy, and he assures the reader that his own "rhetoric scarcely suggests the simple terms the author uses to produce the effect."

Howells's endorsement of Crane's writing meant much to the emerging writer, both in terms of reputation and more importantly of his own confidence in his writing ability.

I think that what strikes me most in the story of *Maggie* is that quality of fatal necessity which dominates Greek tragedy. From the conditions it all had to be, and there were the conditions. I felt this in Mr. Hardy's *Jude*, where the principle seems to become conscious in the writer; but there is apparently no consciousness of any such motive in the author of *Maggie*. Another effect is that of an ideal of artistic beauty which is as present in the working out of this poor girl's squalid romance as in any classic fable. This will be foolishness, I know, to the many foolish people who cannot discriminate between the material and the treatment in art, and think that beauty is inseparable from daintiness and prettiness, but I do not speak to them. I appeal rather to such as feel themselves akin with every kind of human creature, and find neither high nor low when it is a question of inevitable suffering, or of a soul struggling vainly with an inexorable fate. My rhetoric scarcely suggests the simple terms the author uses to produce the effect which I am trying to repeat again. They are simple, but always most graphic, especially when it comes to the personalities of the story; the girl herself, with her bewildered wish to be right and good, with her distorted perspective, her clinging and generous affections, her hopeless environments; the horrible old drunken mother, a cyclone of violence and volcano of vulgarity; the mean and selfish lover, dandy, rowdy, with his gross ideals and ambitions; her brother, an Ishmaelite from the cradle, who with his warlike instincts beaten back into cunning, is what the b'hoy of former times has become in our more strenuously policed days. He is, indeed, a wonderful figure in a group which betrays no faltering in the artist's hand. He, with his dull hates, his warped good-will, his cowed ferocity, is almost as fine artistically as Maggie, but he could not have been so hard to do, for all the pathos of her fate is rendered without one maudlin touch. So is that of the simple-minded and devoted and tedious old woman who is George's mother in the book of that name. This is scarcely a study at all, while Maggie is really and fully so. It is the study of a situation merely; a poor inadequate woman, of a commonplace religiosity, whose son goes to the bad. The wonder of it is the courage which deals with persons so absolutely average, and the art which graces them with the beauty of the author's compassion for everything that errs and suffers. Without this feeling the effects of his mastery would be impossible, and if it went further, or put itself into the pitying phrases, it would annul the effects. But it never does this; it is notable how in all respects the author keeps himself well in hand. He is quite honest with his reader. He never shows his characters or his situations in any sort of sentimental glamour; if you will be moved by the sadness of common fates you will feel his intention; but he does not flatter his portraits of people on conditions to take your fancy.

—WILLIAM DEAN HOWELLS, "An Appreciation,"
Maggie: A Girl of the Streets, 1896, preface,
previously published in the New York *World,*
July 26, 1896, p. 18

EDWARD BRIGHT (1896)

Edward Bright is unknown today, but his review of *Maggie* is typical of the negative criticism the novel engendered. He calls the book "lurid melodrama," and he maintains that in this book Stephen Crane "is a caricaturist, not an artist; and, to make matters worse, he is a caricaturist without humor." Bright admires *The Red Badge*, but he feels *Maggie* maligns the children of the slums.

A novel by Stephen Crane, entitled *Maggie: A Girl of the Streets*, has just been published by D. Appleton & Co. It is the last of the talented young author's works to see the light, but it is the first in point of composition. I base this inference on the fact that it was put in type and copyrighted three years ago. Now, allowing six months for the writing, this ought to take us back to the dawn of a career still in its infancy.

I have thought it best to emphasize this circumstance, because I wish to be absolutely just to the author. I have done so, furthermore, because I have found it extremely difficult to reconcile my undisguised admiration for Mr. Crane's *The Red Badge of Courage* with any dissatisfaction with *Maggie*. The difference between these two books is so great that, were I to neglect chronology, I should have to confess that Mr. Crane's talents are in a process of degeneration.

My objection might be phrased differently—and perhaps more accurately—were I to say that as between *The Red Badge of Courage* and *Maggie*, the dissimilarity is mainly noticeable in the greater conventionality of the latter. This is extraordinary, considering the well-known character of the author's work, and, according to my view, can be explained only on the ground that *Maggie* is an immature effort in a most ambitious field of literary art.

In further explanation of my meaning, let the reader reflect that the slums presents itself to the imagination of most prosperous and well-bred people under one of two aspects: Either it is a locale replete with the raw material of sentiment, or it is a battle-ground of unspeakable sordidness, a loathsome pit infested by monsters in human form, who pass their lives preying on one another—a menace to respectable society, a source of dread even to the well-armed policeman.

Now, it is because, knowing somewhat of the slums of New York and having arrived at certain definite conclusions from my experience, I have for several years contended that Richard Harding Davis's sentimental slum sketches are as false to the actual conditions as I am now reluctantly forced to own is Mr. Crane's presentation of the life of the same locality. There is little to choose between hollow sentimentality and lurid melodrama.

In the bare facts of Maggie's career I am able to believe. Credulity is not taxed by learning that her home—or the miserable tenement which passed for a home—was sordid; neither am I surprised to be told that she drifted easily into a still more hapless life. There is something shocking but quite natural in the fact that Pete was the instrument of her ruin.

Yes! Mr. Crane has used his note-book to good effects; his story bears unmistakable evidences of being observed, and observed on the spot. I will go so far as even to admit that there are a few scenes and passages of dialogue in Mr. Crane's story of masterly vigor and convincing reality. I make no objection to the details—or to most of them. My quarrel with the author begins and ends with his general conception of the life of the slums.

To change the form of expression, he might be likened to an artist who knows how to draw but cannot paint. He has "laid in" an admirable sketch, which raises one's hopes high for the success of the finished picture. But the moment he begins to lay on his colors it is evident that he is a caricaturist, not an artist; and, to make matters worse, he is a caricaturist without humor.

Space does not permit me to prove my indictment by quotations, but I would call the reader's attention to the fight with which the book opens, and would ask that special attention be given to the adjectives employed in describing the affray. There are gentler modes of exercise than an East-Side fight, but I protest that even the sturdy children of the tenements are maligned by Mr. Crane's adjectives.

—EDWARD BRIGHT, *Illustrated American*,
July 11, 1896, p. 94

H.G. WELLS (1896)

Although H.G. Wells had not met Stephen Crane when he wrote this review, he already recognizes Crane's talent and calls *Maggie* a "work of art." He points out what he considers "pretty effects" marring the book, and he considers it not up to the stature of *The Red Badge*.

The literature of the slum multiplies apace; and just as the mud of the Port of London has proved amenable to Mr. Whistler, so the mud of the New York estuary has furnished material for artistic treatment to Mr. Crane. Mr. Crane, in *Maggie*, shows himself the New York equivalent of Mr. Morrison, with perhaps a finer sense of form and beauty and a slenderer physique. He is the light weight of the two. He is far more alert for what the industrious playwright calls the effective "line," and every chapter cocks its tail with a point to it. He sketches, for instance, the career of Maggie's brother James, and tells of his lusts and brutality. "Nevertheless," ends the chapter, "he had on a certain starlit evening said wonderingly and quite reverently, 'Dah moon looks like h—l, don't it?'" And with that the chapter, rather self-consciously, pauses for your admiration. Of Mr. Morrison's "Dick Perrott" it is not recorded that he ever saw the beauty of moonlight or the stars. But one may doubt, even after the chromatic tumult of the *Red Badge of Courage*, whether Mr. Crane is anywhere equal to Mr. Morrison's fight between Perrott and Leary. To read that and to turn to Mr. Crane's fight between Maggie's brother and her seducer is to turn from power to hysterics. The former is too strong and quiet to quote—it must be read; but of the latter. . . .

Which is very fine, no doubt, but much more suggestive of a palette dipped in vodki than of two men fighting. Yet, on the other hand, the emotional power of that concluding chapter of *Maggie* seems a little out of Mr. Morrison's reach—an old woman, drink sodden and obese, stricken with the news of her daughter's death and recalling her one vivid moment of maternal pride.

"Jimmy, boy, go get yer sister! Go get yer sister an' we'll put dah boots on her feet!"

The relative merits of the Red *Badge of Courage* and *Maggie* are open to question. To the present reviewer it seems that in *Maggie* we come nearer to Mr. Crane's individuality. Perhaps where we might expect strength we get merely stress, but one may doubt whether we have been hasty in assuming Mr. Crane to be a strong man in fiction. Strength and gaudy colour rarely go together; tragic and sombre are well nigh inseparable. One gets an impression from the *Red Badge* that at the end Mr. Crane could scarcely have had a gasp left in him—that he must have been mentally hoarse for weeks after it. But here he works chiefly for pretty effects, for gleams of sunlight on the stagnant puddles he paints. He gets them, a little consciously perhaps, but, to the present reviewer's sense, far more effectively than he gets anger and fear. And he has done his work, one feels, to please himself. His book is a work of art, even if it is not a very great or successful work of art—it ranks above the novel of commerce, if only on that account.

—H.G. WELLS, *Saturday Review,*
December 19, 1896, p. 655

THE BLACK RIDERS AND OTHER LINES

THOMAS WENTWORTH HIGGINSON (1895)

Thomas Wentworth Higginson was known as a man of letters, a prolific essayist, a radical theologian, a suffragist and outspoken defender of equal rights for women, and a prominent abolitionist. After leading a group of black volunteer soldiers during the Civil War, Higginson eventually became involved in the literary field; he is now best known as a mentor to Emily Dickinson, whose poetry he helped edit after her death.

In this review, Higginson recognizes the power of Stephen Crane's poetry in *The Black Riders*, but he predicts that it will not be successful, much as Dickinson's had not been at that period of time.

It is worthwhile considering wherein lies the charm that attaches, it appears to The Black Riders, and Other Lines, by Stephen Crane. It is an attraction which makes young people learn it by heart, carry it into the woods with them, sleep with it under their pillows, and perhaps suggest that it should be buried with them in their early graves. Undoubtedly it offers new sensations: the brevity of its stanzas, its rhymelessness and covert rhythm, as of a condensed Whitman on an amplified Emily Dickinson; a certain modest aggressiveness, stopping short of actual conceit. The power lies largely in the fact that this apparent affectation is not really such, and that there is behind it a vigorous earnestness and a fresh pair of eyes. Even the capitalization of every word seems to imply that the author sought thus to emphasize his "lines"—just as Wordsworth printed "The White Doe of Rylstone," in quarto—to express his sense of their value. A mere experiment will show how much each page loses by being reduced to what printers call "lower-case" type; and yet this result itself seems unsatisfactory because anything which is really good, one might say, could bear to be printed in letters as small as in those microscopic newspapers sent out of Paris under pigeons' wings during the siege. The total effect of the book is that of poetry torn up by the roots—a process always interesting to the botanist, yet bad for the blossoms. As formless, in the ordinary sense, as the productions of Walt Whitman, these "lines" are in other respects the antipodes of his; while Whitman dilutes mercilessly, Crane condenses almost as formidably. He fulfils Joubert's wish, to condense a page into a sentence and a sentence into a word. He grasps his thought as nakedly and simply as Emily Dickinson; gives you a glance at it, or, perhaps, two glances from different points of view, and leaves it there. If it be a paradox, as it commonly is, so much the better for him. Thus:

In a Lonely place,
I encountered a sage
Who sat, all still,
Regarding a newspaper.
He accosted me:

"Sir, what is this?"
Then I saw that I was greater,
Aye, greater than this sage.
I answered him at once,
"old, old man, it is the wisdom of the age."
The sage looked upon me with admiration.

That is all, but it tells its own story, and is the equivalent of many columns. At other times he not merely intimates his own problem, but states it, still tersely:

Behold the grave of a wicked man,
And near it a stern spirit.
There came a drooping maid with violets,
But the spirit grasped her arm.
"No flowers for him," he said.
The maid wept.
"Ah, I loved him,"
But the spirit, grim and frowning,
"No Flowers for him."

Now this is it
If the spirit was just,
Why did the maid weep?

Again, he gives his protest against superstition:

A man went before a strange God—
The God of many men, sadly wise.
And the Deity thundered loudly,
"Kneel, mortal, and cringe
And grovel and do homage
To my particularly sublime Majesty."
The man fled.
Then the man went to another God—
And this one looked at him
With soft eyes
Lit with infinite condescension,
And said, "My poor child!"

Better, perhaps, than any of these polemics are those "lines" which paint, with a terseness like Emily Dickinson's, some aspect of nature. Since Browning's fine description, in "England in Italy," of the "infinite movement" of a chain of mountains before the traveler, the same thing has not been more vividly put than here:

On the horizon the peaks assembled,
And, as I looked,
The march of the mountains began.
As they marched, they sang,
"Aye, we come! We come!"

That is all; but it is fine, it tells its own story. If it be asked whether it is also poetry, one can only remember Thoreau's dictum, that no matter how we define poetry, the true poet will presently set the whole definition aside. If it be further asked whether such a book gives promise, the reply must be that experience points the other way. So marked a new departure rarely leads to further growth. Neither Whitman nor Miss Dickinson ever stepped beyond the circle they first drew.

—Thomas Wentworth Higginson,
Nation, October 24,
1895, p. 296

Mark Antony de Wolfe Howe (1896)

Mark Antony de Wolfe Howe was an American author and editor who served as assistant editor of the *Atlantic Monthly* from 1893 to 1895. This generally positive review points out the similarity of Stephen Crane's poetry to Emily Dickinson's poetry, and it lauds the "freshness of conception" while questioning whether the poems are too modern or blasphemous.

The strange little lines of which The Black Riders is made up are not even rhymed and have but a faint rhythmic quality. Surpassing the college exercise in verse, to which the shrewd instructor made objection that every line began with a capital letter, these small skeletons of poetry are printed entirely in capitals, and in the modern fashion which hangs a few lines by the shoulders to the top of the page, as if more had meant to come below, but had changed its mind. The virtue of these lines, however, is that they often have enough freshness of conception to set the reader thinking, and so perhaps the blank spaces are filled. The spirit of the lines is generally rebellious and modern in the extreme, occasionally blasphemous to a degree which even cleverness will not reconcile to a liberal taste. One feels that a long journey has been taken since the Last Poems of Mr. Lowell were read. But it is too much to think that the writer always takes himself seriously. Many of the lines are intentionally amusing, and the satiric note sometimes serves to mollify the profanity. The parable form into which many of the fragments are cast gives them half their effectiveness. The audacity of their conception, suggesting a mind not without kinship to Emily Dickinson's, supplies the rest. Instead of talking more about them or discussing the possibility of their production before Tourgenieff's Prose Poems, let us quote, without all its capital letters, this characteristic bit, which might serve either as a *credo* for the modern pessimist or as a felicitous epigram at his expense:—

> In the desert
> I saw a creature, naked, bestial,
> Who, squatting upon the ground
> Held his heart in his hands,
> And ate of it.
> I said, "Is it good, friend?"
> "It is bitter—bitter," he answered;
> "But I like it
> Because it is bitter,
> And because it is my heart."

Throughout the little book, nevertheless, there is some eating other viands, for the sweet is mixed with the bitter. Just another parable we must transcribe, since it is thoroughly typical of Mr. Crane's performances, and will serves as an excellent "sixthly and lastly" for any critic who has spoken his mind: —

> Once there was a man, —
> Oh, so wise!
> In all drink
> He detected the bitter,
> And in all touch
> He found the sting.
> At last he cried thus:
> "There is nothing, —
> No life,
> No joy,
> No pain, —
> There is nothing save opinion,
> And opinion be damned."

—MARK ANTONY DE WOLFE HOWE,
Atlantic Monthly, February 1896, pp. 271–272

ELBERT HUBBARD (1896)

Elbert Hubbard, whose dinner for Stephen Crane at the Society of the
Philistines in December 1895 had garnered much publicity, praises Crane's
poetry in this review of *The Black Riders*, tending to exaggerate the romantic and sentimental aspects of the work. He states that "there is a great
moral truth taught in each of Crane's poems."

Stephen Crane possesses genius. Just what genius is the world has not
determined, for, like the ulster, the word covers a multitude of sins. But if
pushed for a definition, I would say that genius is only a woman's intuition
carried one step further. It is essentially feminine in its tributes, and the men
of genius (as opposed to men of talent) have always been men with marked
feminine qualities. The genius knows because he knows, and if you should
ask the genius whence comes this answer, he would answer you (if he knew)
in the words of Cassius: "My mother gave it me."

Every genius has had a splendid mother. Had I space, I could name you
a dozen great men—dead and gone—who were ushered into this earth-life
under about the following conditions: A finely-organized, receptive, aspiring
woman is thrown by fate into an unkind environment. She thirsts for
knowledge, for sweet music, for beauty, for sympathy, for attainment. She has
a heart-hunger that none about her comprehend; she strives for better things
but those nearest her do not understand. She prays to God, but the heavens
are but brass. When in this peculiar mental condition a child is born to her.
This child is heir to all of his mother's spiritual desires, but he develops a man's
strength and breaks the fetters that held her fast. He surmounts obstacles that
she could never overcome. The woman's prayer was answered. God listened
to her after all. But, like Columbus, who gave the world a continent, she dies
in ignorance of what she has achieved.

Earth's buffets are usually too severe for her; she cannot endure its
contumely; she goes to her long rest, soothed only by the thought that she did
her work as best she could. In summer, wild flowers nod in the breeze above
her forgotten grave, and in winter, the untracked snow covers with bridal
white the spot where she sleeps. But far away in the gay courts of great cities
the walls echo the praises of her son, and men say, Behold, a Genius!

She died that others might live. Her prayer was answered, as every sincere
prayer is: for every desire of the heart has somewhere its gratification. But
Nature cares not for the individual—her thought is only for the race. Do you
know the history of Nancy Hanks? She is the universal type of women who
give the world its men of genius.

When in 1891 Stephen Crane wrote *Maggie, A Girl of the Streets*, Mr. Howells read the story, and after seeing its author said, "This man has sprung into life full-armed." And that expression of Mr. Howells fully covers the case. I can imagine no condition of life that might entangle a man or woman within its meshes that Stephen Crane could not fully comprehend and appreciate. Men are only great as they possess sympathy. Crane knows the human heart through and through, and he sympathizes with its every pulsation. From the beggar's child searching in ash barrels for treasure, to the statesman playing at diplomacy with his chief thought on next fall's election, Stephen Crane knows the inmost soul of each and all. Whether he is able to translate it to you or not is quite another question; but in the forty or more short stories and sketches he has written I fail to find a single false note. He neither exaggerates nor comes tardy off.

The psychologists tell us that a man cannot fully comprehend a condition that he has never experienced. But theosophy explains the transcendent wisdom of genius by saying that in former incarnations the man passed through these experiences. Emerson says: "We are bathed in an ocean of intelligence, and under right conditions the soul knows all things." These things may be true, but the secret of Crane's masterly delineation is that he is able to project himself into the condition of others. He does not describe men and women—he is that man. He loses his identity, forgets self, abandons his own consciousness, and is for the moment the individual who speaks. And whether this individual is man, woman or child, makes no difference. Sex, age, condition, weigh not in the scale.

During the latter half of the year 1895 no writing man in America was so thoroughly hooted and so well abused as Stephen Crane. I have a scrap-book of newspaper clippings that is a symposium of Billingsgate mud-balls, with Crane for the target. Turning the leaves of this scrap-book I find used in reference to a plain little book called *The Black Riders*, these words: Idiocy, drivel, bombast, rot, nonsense, puerility, untruth, garbage, hamfat, funny, absurd, childish, drunken, besotted, obscure, opium-laden, blasphemous, indecent, fustian, rant, bassoon-poetry, swell-head stuff, bluster, balderdash, windy, turgid, stupid, pompous, gasconade, gas-house ballads, etc., etc.

There are also in this scrapbook upward of a hundred parodies on the poems. Some of these are rather clever, but they differ from Crane's work in this, that there is not a molecule of thought in one of them, while there is a great moral truth taught in each of Crane's poems. It's so easy to write a parody; a parody is a calico cat stuffed with cotton; it pleases the little boys who wear dresses. Usually, people—even sensible people—will not take time to find it. But one might as well accuse Aesop of idiocy when he has a fox talk to a goose. Of course. We could truthfully swear that no fox ever carried on a conversation with a goose since the world began. But to assume that Aesop was therefore a fool would be proof that the man who made the assumption was a fool and not Aesop.

The 'Lines' in *The Black Riders* seem to me very wonderful: charged with meaning like a storage battery. But there is a fine defy in the flavour that warns the reader not to take too much or it may strike in. Who wants a meal of horseradish? When I hear intelligent people jeer at *The Black Riders* (and intelligent people do jeer at *The Black Riders*) I think of those Chicago hand-me-out restaurants where men woo dyspepsia, (and win the termagant) fighting like crimson devils for pie, and gulp things red hot because Time and the Stock Exchange wait for no man; or perhaps of Paul Bourget who swallowed three fingers of Worcestershire Sauce on a Pullman Dining Car and then made a memorandum in his note book that American wines are very bad.

Any man who has a tuppence worth of philosophy in his clay, and a little of God's leisure at his disposal that will allow him to take his mental aliment with pulse at normal, will find a good honest nugget of wisdom in every sentence of Copeland & Day's unique little work. Yet I admit that in a certain mood the brevity of expression is rather exasperating, and the independence of spirit which shows that the author can do without you is the quip modest, if not the reproof valiant, that is not always pleasant. But granting that there are some things in *The Black Riders* that I do not especially like, I yet have no quarrel with the book. I accept it and give thanks.

But granting for argument's sake that *The Black Riders* is "rot," it then must be admitted that it was a great stroke of worldly wisdom. For Stephen Crane now has the ear of the world. Publishers besiege him with checks in advance, and the manuscript of a story he has just completed has been bid on by four different firms, with special offer for the English copyright. Tradition has it that the sixty-eight short poems in *The Black Riders* were all written in the space of two days and a night—in a time of terrible depression. The work was then handed to a dear friend. This friend thought he saw the deep burning thought of a prophet in the lines, and he conceived the plan of publishing them. A thousand copies were printed and sold inside of six months. If you want a first edition of *The Black Riders* now, it will cost you five dollars, and if you can pick up a *Maggie* on the streets for twice that, you'd better do it—and do it quick.

Stephen Crane attended Lafayette College for a time in his nineteenth year. The teachers there write me that they remember him only as "a yellow, tow-haired youth, who would rather fight than study." They advised him to "take a change," so he went to Syracuse University—his guardian being anxious he should be "educated." His fame at Syracuse rests on the fact that he was the best shortstop ever on pile University baseball team. He soon became captain, this on account of his ability to hold his own when it came to an issue with certain scrapping antagonists.

Once when he was called upon to recite in the psychology class, he argued a point with the teacher. The Professor sought to silence him by an appeal to the Bible: "Tut, tut—what does St. Paul say, Mr. Crane, what does St. Paul say?" testily asked the old Professor.

"I know what St. Paul says," was the answer, "but I disagree with St. Paul."

Of course no Methodist college wants a student like that; and young Crane wandered down to New York and got a job reporting on the *Herald*.

Since then he has worked on the editorial staff of various papers. He is now, however, devoting his whole time to letters, living at Hartwood, Sullivan County, N.Y. Hartwood has a store, a blacksmith shop and a tavern. When the train comes in all of the citizens go down to the station to see 'er go through. Should you ask one of these citizens who Stephen Crane is, he would probably answer you as he did me:

"Mr. Crane, Mr. Crane! You mean Steve Crane?"

"Yes. Why, he's—he's Steve Crane an' a dern good feller!"

Mr. Crane is now in his twenty-fifth year. He is a little under the average height, and is slender and slight in build, weighing scarcely one hundred and thirty pounds. He is a decided blonde: his eyes blue. His intellect is as wide awake as the matin chimes, and his generosity is as ample as the double chin of Col. Ingersoll. His handsome, boyish face and quiet, half-shy, modest manner make him a general favorite everywhere with women. And to me, it is rather curious that women should flock around and pet this sort of a man, who can read their inmost thoughts just as that Roentgen invention can photograph things inside of a box, when a big, stupid man with a red face and a black mustache they are very much afraid of.

At a recent banquet given by the Society of the Philistines, in honor of Mr. Crane, thirty-one men sat at the feast. These men had come from Chicago, New York, Boston, and elsewhere to attend the dinner. Several lawyers, one eminent physician, and various writers were there. Crane was the youngest individual at the board, but he showed himself the peer of any man present. His speech was earnest, dignified, yet modestly expressed. His manner is singularly well poised, and his few words carry conviction.

Still he can laugh and joke, and no man has a better appreciation of humor. He loves the out-doors, and in riding horseback by his side across country I have admired his happy abandon, as he sits secure, riding with loose rein and long stirrup in a reckless rush.

In the New York *Times* for January 26 is a two-column letter from London, by that distinguished critic, Mr. Harold Frederic. The subject of the entire article is Stephen Crane. . . .

There is a class of reviewers who always wind up their preachments by saying: "This book gives much promise, and we shall look anxiously for Mr. Scribbler's next." Let us deal in no such cant. A man's work is good or it is not. As for his "next," nobody can tell whether it will be good or not. There is a whole army of men about to do something great, but the years go by and they never do it. They are like those precocious children who stand on chairs and recite "pieces." They never make orators. As to Crane's "future work," let us keep silent. But if he never produces another thing, he has done enough to save the fag-end of the century from literary disgrace; and look you, friends, that is no small matter!

—ELBERT HUBBARD, *Lotos,*
March 1896, pp. 674–678

JOSEPHINE DODGE DASKAM
"THE DISTINCTION OF OUR POETRY" (1901)

Josephine Dodge Daskam, a novelist and writer of short stories, produced one volume of poetry in 1903. This review lauds Stephen Crane for what she considers his best poems and chastises him for his worst.

If, in the one, philosophy slipped into mysticism, inspired brevity into curtness, intensity of conviction into dogmatism; if his exquisite facility has sometimes led the other into work more remarkable for that quality than for inspiration, they yet remain the most perfect types, the most valuable examples, and the safest criterions of the American genius; and it is their influence on our most notable recent verse, direct or implied, that subsequent illustration, unaided by much analysis or comment, may be trusted to bring out.

But if it is a question of native force and original spirit, why not present that more strikingly vigorous personality, Walt Whitman?

Simply because that titanic force, that sweeping annihilation of all accepted canons, that unregulated if colossal genius, is manifestly unrelated, and voluntarily so, to any school or characteristic system. It is a law unto itself, and to stretch it further, to allow it to cover the crudities and vulgarities, the vagueness and incoherence, the cheap sentimentality and meaningless cosmopolitanism, into which an unrestrained imitation of it would surely degenerate, would bring a condition of things for which the most unqualified admirer of his work would surely hesitate to be made responsible.

At his best, the poet of "When lilacs last in the dooryard bloomed" is inimitable; if not to be claimed as typically American, at least to be cherished as one of the great universal brotherhood who have risen most adequately to the expression of a deep and lofty feeling; at his worst, however, he falls to a level which is precisely the level reserved for the American of genius in his most unfortunate lapses. Walt Whitman is more akin to us in our failures than in our legitimate and characteristic successes. To illustrate this : —

> "On the horizon the peaks assembled;
> And as I looked,
> The march of the mountains began.
> As they marched they sang,
> Aye! we come! we come!"

Now, in its repression, its strength, its atmosphere so perfectly adequate to the conception, the telling quality of every word, this is equal to almost the best of Emerson. In its large, sympathetic, bold treatment of an unusual theme Whitman should not have scorned it. And yet the young man who can catch so perfectly the temper and instant impression of a row of shouldering peaks, and in such a brief flash of poetic insight set them before us, in the next breath is capable of this : —

> "'Think as I think,' said a man,
> 'Or you are abominably wicked.
> You are a toad.'
> And after I had thought of it,
> I said, 'I will, then, be a toad.'"

Whatever heights of philosophical achievement this may have represented to Stephen Crane, it certainly is not poetry. Thus far Emerson could never drop; the most sententious of his aphorisms has a certain grave dignity, a pleasing and aristocratic quality of phrase, that, if it does not intoxicate or illumine, at least does not insult the muse. Yet compared with some of the amazing combinations of Walt Whitman, it is classic.

> Consider this : —
> "The ocean said to me once,
> 'Look!
> Yonder on the shore

Is a woman weeping.
I have watched her:
Go yon and tell her this, —
Her love I have laid
In cool green hall.
There is wealth of golden sand
And pillars, coral-red;
Two white fish stand guard at his bier.
'Tell her this
And more, —
That the king of the seas
Weeps, too, old, helpless man.
The bustling fates
Heap his hands with corpses
Until he stands like a child
With surplus of toys.'

This might almost be a literal translation from Heine; and yet there is a subtle note, a clean, abstract, universal pathos in it, that the self-centred German could not have given us.

—JOSEPHINE DODGE DASKAM,
"The Distinction of Our Poetry,"
Atlantic Monthly, May 1901, pp. 696–705

THE RED BADGE OF COURAGE

UNSIGNED (1895)

This early review of *The Red Badge of Courage* expresses many of the concerns of later critics: Stephen Crane's concentration on the unheroic aspects of war, his stylistic affectations, and his pictorial realism. Comparing Crane's novel to Bret Harte's *Clarence*, the reviewer credits Kipling and Tolstoy as influences in addition to kindly saving the reader from the novel's "oaths and other horrors."

. . . the other, *The Red Badge of Courage* is, if we mistake not, the first sustained effort in fiction of a young author, Stephen Crane, throughout whose previous occasional work in prose and in verse there has peeped the bud of promise. . . . Mr. Crane's book may be called a military romance only through courtesy, there being nothing whatever of a romantic quality in his graphic narrative of a single episode of the Civil War. Let us consider the volumes separately. . . .

For, it should be premised, Mr. Crane's book is nothing more or less than a series of battle pictures. *The Red Badge of Courage* describes the sensations of a young soldier receiving his baptism of fire. There is so little of personal or romantic interest in it that one learns only in the middle of the book and then quite as though by accident, his name. Other than himself only several figures show vaguely through the smoke. Now, this performance of Mr. Crane is remarkable for one or two reasons. First, that so young a writer, born after the war, should have evolved from his imagination purely what strikes the reader as a most impressive and accurate record of actual personal experiences. To be sure, one's wonder at this is tempered presently by noting the unmistakable influences upon the writer of Tolstoi and Rudyard Kipling. It is not so much that he obviously, if unconsciously, mimics the manner of Kipling; but one hears throughout the thrilling strife the echo of Sebastopol, and, above all, of 'The Drums of the Fore and Aft.' The other noticeable fact in Mr. Crane's brilliant fanciful study is his ample recognition of the demands of art in the reproduction of the most tragic scenes. He keeps himself in admirable control; he does more than that he quite effaces himself. Whereas Tolstoi, in denying the genius of generalship, would exalt the courage and the power of the common soldier, young Mr. Crane reduces the general to the ranks (inasmuch as he makes him swear like a trooper), at the same time that he impeaches the courage of the raw recruit. In a word, his book is intended to show us how a simple country youth first withstood and then fled from the fire of the enemy, and then faced it again, and from wavering acquired the Bersekir rage and so was graduated from the shame of cowardice to the high honor of *The Red Badge of Courage*. . . .

We have selected this passage from Mr. Crane's book, not because it is a particularly fine one, but because it is fairly representative of the author's style and is singularly free from oaths and other horrors. So, our readers may make their choice. Here are two stories of the great war. In one it is clothed with romance; in the other it is stripped of it. And thus stand the elder and the younger writers of fiction.

—Unsigned, Philadelphia *Press,*
October 13, 1895, p. 30

Unsigned "The Latest Fiction" (1895)

This review comments on the imaginative quality of *The Red Badge of Courage,* provides details of the plot, and concludes that the book is strong but has affectations of style: "When he begins a sentence with 'too,' for instance, he makes a sensitive reader squirm." The review shows more insight into grammar than style.

Stephen Crane is very young—not yet twenty-five, it is said—and this picture he presents of war *(The Red Badge of Courage)* is therefore a purely imaginative work. The very best thing that can be said about it, though, is that it strikes the reader as a statement of facts by a veteran. The purpose of the book is to set forth the experiences of a volunteer soldier in his first battle. The poetical idea of the hero and the coward in war was long since abandoned by well-informed writers. A recent autobiographical account of actual experiences in our civil war bears testimony that every soldier is frightened at the moment of entering battle, and his fright increases rather than diminishes as he grows old in service and more familiar with the dangers he has to encounter. It is true, also, that once in battle all men are much alike. They fight like beasts. Cowards and skulkers are the exception, and cowardice is often the result of some sudden physical disability.

The young private soldier who is the central personage in this remarkable work was a farm boy in one of the Middle States, probably Ohio, though certain peculiarities of the dialect in which Mr. Crane chooses to clothe the speech of all his persons, belong also to Western Pennsylvania and the Hoosier country. Except for those few expressions, such as "Watch out" for "Look out," the talk is a very fair phonetic equivalent for the common speech in parts of this State and Connecticut. The boy does not enlist at the beginning of the war, but his duty to go to the front weighs upon him day and night. He is the only son of his mother, and she is a widow and a typical American woman of the old New-England stock, who ever conceals her emotions, and seems to possess no imaginative faculty whatever. She is peeling potatoes when her boy, in his new blue clothes, says "Goodbye," and the exhortation she then delivers is perfectly practical and devoid of all sentiment. There is a black-eyed girl, nameless in the story, who looks after the youth as he trudges down the road, but when he looks back pretends to be gazing at the sky.

In other words, the early environment of Mr. Crane's hero is absolutely typical, differing in no particular from that of tens of thousands of young men who went to the front in the interval between the Sumter episode and the fall of Richmond. But as to his temperament and the quality of his mind, we cannot speak so positively. He is certainly of a more emotional type than any one of his comrades. His aspirations, perhaps, are no higher than theirs, his mental capacity no larger, his will, certainly, no stronger. But there is a touch of poetry in his nature which most men lack.

Probably Mr. Crane has put some of his own mental traits into the composition of his otherwise commonplace hero. Therefore, it is not possible to accept this graphic study of his mind under the stress of new and frightful experiences as an exact picture of the mental states of every green soldier under his first fire. All its complexities are surely not typical.

Yet it is as a picture which seems to be extraordinarily true, free from any suspicion of ideality, defying every accepted tradition of martial glory, that the book commends itself to the reader. The majesty, the pomp and circumstance of glorious war, Mr. Crane rejects altogether. War, as he depicts it, is a mean, nasty, horrible thing; its seeming glories are the results of accident or that blind courage when driven to bay and fighting for life that the meanest animal would show as strongly as man. For it must be remembered that the point of view is consistently that of the humblest soldier in the ranks, who never knows where he is going or what is expected of him until the order comes, who never comprehends the whole scheme, but only his small share of it, who is frequently put forward as an intentional sacrifice, but yet it is a sentient human being, who is bound to have his own opinions founded on the scanty knowledge he possesses, his own hopes and fears and doubts and prejudices.

Private Henry Fleming goes to war a hot-headed young patriot with his mind brimful of crude ideas of glory and a settled conviction that his capacity for heroism is quite out of the common. Weary months of drill in camp reduce him seemingly to the proper machinelike condition. He learns many things, among them that the glories of war have been greatly exaggerated in books, that the enemy is not composed chiefly of bragging cowards, that victory is rare and dear, and that the lot of a private soldier is very hard. On the eve of his first battle he has about abandoned all hope of ever getting a chance to distinguish himself. Yet when the hour comes it brings depression instead of exhilaration. He communes with himself, and fears that he is a coward.

The battle Mr. Crane describes is one of those long and bloody conflicts of our civil war that we now freely admit were badly mismanaged through lack of good generalship, which had no particular result except the destruction of human life, and were claimed as prodigious victories by both sides. The green regiment is part of a brigade which is in the centre at first, and for a long while it has nothing to do. Then it has to stand on the edge of a piece of woods and receive the enemy's fire, and return it. This is a short and sharp proceeding, and while it lasts Private Henry Fleming acquits himself creditably. When the enemy's fire stops, he feels himself a hero and feels also that he has done the greatest day's work of his life. The nervous tension has been awful, the revulsion of feeling is correspondingly great. When the enemy's fire is resumed, a few minutes later, he is entirely unprepared. Panic seizes him, he drops his musket and runs for his life.

All that day he is a skulker in the rear of a great battle. His emotions, his mental vagaries, his experiences with the dead and dying, and the terrible nervous ordeal he undergoes are depicted by Mr. Crane with a degree of vividness and original power almost unique in our fiction. The night of the first day finds him back in the camp of his own regiment, lauded by his surviving comrades as a wounded hero. His scalp was cut by a blow of a musket by a retreating soldier, whose flight he tried to stop, for no reason, and he has tied his handkerchief over the wound. He is physically exhausted and his conscience troubles him sorely.

In the next day's conflict he remains with his regiment. His nervous excitement has increased, but he is no longer so greatly shocked by the spectacle of the dead and dying. He has lost all control of his tongue, and he jabbers oaths incessantly. When his regiment is called upon to repel an advance of the enemy, he excels all his comrades in the ferocious rapidity of his fire. He is again extolled as a hero, but scarcely comprehends the praise. His regiment, esteemed by the division officers, apparently with good reason, as nearly worthless is selected to make a charge which is intended merely to check a contemplated attack of the enemy on the left until reinforcements can be forwarded to that point. It is not expected that any member of the regiment will return alive, and some rude remarks of a staff officer to this effect reach the ears of the men and transform them into demons, but very impotent and purposeless demons. The order is only half carried out. A file of soldiers in gray, behind a rail fence, keeps the blue fellows at bay. They stand like lost sheep, and scarcely return the fire which is destroying them. Yet, on their retreat, they combat bravely enough with a small Confederate body which tries to cut them off. Returning to their own lines, they are received with derision, while their Colonel is roundly abused by his superior. The charge has been a failure, yet it has transformed Private Henry Fleming. He has saved the colors, and he has sounded his own depths. He feels that he will never run away again.

At last his eyes seem to open to some new ways. He found that he could look back upon the brass and bombast of his earlier gospels and see them truly. He was gleeful when he discovered that he now despised them. With this conviction came a store of assurance. He felt a quiet manhood, non-assertive, but of sturdy and strong blood. He knew that he would no more quail before his guides wherever they should point. He had been in touch with the great death, and found that after all, it was but the great death. He was a man.

The book is written in terse and vigorous sentences, but not without some unpleasant affectations of style which the author would do well to correct. His natural talent is so strong that it is a pity its expression should be marred by petty tricks. When he begins a sentence with "too," for instance, he makes a sensitive reader squirm. But he is certainly a young man of remarkable promise.

—UNSIGNED, "The Latest Fiction,"
The New York Times, October 19, 1895, p. 3

WILLIAM DEAN HOWELLS (1895)

Still expressing his preference for *Maggie*, William Dean Howells points out the psychological realism of *The Red Badge*, although he does not use that term. He also predicts greater works will be produced by the author in the future.

Of our own smaller fiction I have been reading several books without finding a very fresh note except in *The Red Badge of Courage*, by Mr. Stephen Crane. He is the author of that story of New York tough life, *Maggie*, which I mentioned some time ago as so good but so impossible of general acceptance because of our conventional limitations in respect of swearing, and some other traits of the common parlance. He has now attempted to give a dose-at-hand impression of battle as seen by a young volunteer in the civil war, and I cannot say that to my inexperience of battle he has given such a vivid sense of it as one gets from some other authors. The sense of deaf and blind turmoil he does indeed give, but we might get that from fewer pages than Mr. Crane employs to impart it. The more valuable effect of the book is subjective: the conception of character in the tawdry-minded youth whom the slight story gathers itself about, and in his comrades and superiors of all sorts. The human commonness (which we cannot shrink from without vulgarity) is potently illustrated throughout in their speech and action and motive; and the cloud of bewilderment in which they all have their being after the fighting begins, the frenzy, the insensate resentment, are graphically and probably suggested. The dialect employed does not so much convince me; I have not heard people speak with those contractions, though perhaps they do it; and in commending the book I should dwell rather upon the skill shown in evolving from the youth's crude expectations and ambitions a quiet honesty and self-possession manlier and nobler than any heroism he had imagined. There are divinations of motive and experience which cannot fail to strike the critical reader, from time to time; and decidedly on the psychological side the book is worth while as an earnest of the greater things that we may hope from a new talent working upon a high level, not quite clearly as yet, but strenuously.

—WILLIAM DEAN HOWELLS, *Harper's Weekly*,
October 26, 1895, p. 1013

ATTRIBUTED TO SYDNEY BROOKS (1896)

Sydney Brooks, the probable author of this review, lauds *The Red Badge* and Stephen Crane, "whose picture of the effect of actual fighting on a raw regiment is simply unapproached in intimate knowledge and sustained imaginative strength." Brooks later remarked, in a letter he wrote in defense of Crane's artistry, that he was one of the American's first English reviewers.

In a brief preview notice, published a week before this review was published, Brooks lauds the book as "the most realistic description ever published of modern war from the purely subjective standpoint of a private soldier. The author does not appear to be an artist; he seems to be concerned merely with giving an exact account of his most intimate personal feelings, and this account is so impartial in its frankness that it comes to have the significance of universal truth."

At a time like the present, when England, isolated by the jealousy and assailed by the threats of powerful rivals, is rising to the situation, and showing that the heart of the nation is as sound after the long Victorian peace as it was in the days of the Armada, that the desperate if lawless enterprise of Jameson and Willoughby [leaders of a British force captured by the Boers in 1896, bringing about the Boer War, 1899–1902] is as near to the general heart of the people as were the not very dissimilar enterprises of the old Elizabethan captains, a want which has long existed, makes itself felt with increased intensity—the want of some book that shall satisfy the well-nigh universal desire to know the inmost truths of the experiences which actual battle alone bestows on the men engaged in it.

The want finds the book as the opportunity finds the man: Mr. Stephen Crane's *Red Badge of Courage* really supplies the want more completely, and therefore more satisfactorily, than any other book with which we are acquainted. Tolstoi, in his *War and Peace* and his sketches of Sebastopol, has given, with extraordinary depth of insight and extraordinary artistic skill, the effect of battle on the ordinary man, whether cultured officer or simple and rough soldier; but he takes no one man through the long series of experiences and impressions which Mr. Crane describes in its effects on young Henry Fleming, a raw recruit who first saw service in the last American Civil War. While the impressions of fighting, and especially of wounds and death, on an individual soldier have been painted with marvellously vivid touches by Tolstoi, the impressions of battle on a body of men, a regiment, have been also realized and represented with characteristic vigour by Mr. Rudyard Kipling in such admirable work as "The Drums of the Fore and Aft." With less imagination, but with an accumulated mass of studied knowledge altogether too laboured, M. Zola in *La Debacle* has done some excellent literary work, but work not so convincing as Kipling's, and work certainly far inferior to Mr. Stephen Crane's, whose picture of the effect of actual fighting on a raw regiment is simply unapproached in intimate knowledge and sustained imaginative strength. This we say without forgetting Merimee's celebrated account of the taking of the redoubt. The writing of the French stylist is, no doubt, much superior in its uniform excellence; but Mr. Crane, in the supreme moments of the fight, is possessed by the fiery breath of battle, as a Pythian priestess by the breath of God, and finds an inspired utterance that will reach the universal heart of man. Courage in facing wounds and death is the special characteristic of man among the animals, of man who sees into the future, and has therefore much to deter him that affects him alone. Indeed, man, looking at the past, might almost be described as the fighting animal; and Mr. Crane's extraordinary book will appeal strongly to the insatiable desire, latent or developed, to know the psychology of war, how the sights and sounds, the terrible details of the drama of battle, affect the senses and the soul of man. Whether Mr. Crane has had personal experience of the scenes he depicts we cannot say from external evidence; but the extremely vivid touches of detail convince us that he has. Certainly, if his book were altogether a work of the imagination, unbased on personal experience, his realism would be nothing short of a miracle. Unquestionably his knowledge, as we believe acquired in war, has been assimilated and has become a part of himself. At the heated crises of the battle he has the war fever the Berserk fury in his veins, he lives in the scenes he depicts, he drinks to the dregs the bitter cup of defeat and the bitter cup of fear and shame with his characters no less completely than he thrills with their frantic rage when repulsed by the enemy, and their frantic joy when they charge home.

The Red Badge of Courage a name which means, we may perhaps explain, a wound received in open fight with the enemy is the narrative of two processes: the process by which a raw youth develops into a tried and trustworthy soldier, and the process by which a regiment that has never been under fire develops into a finished and formidable fighting machine. Henry Fleming, the youth who is the protagonist of this thrillingly realistic drama of war, has for deuteragonist Wilson, the loud young boaster. Wilson, however, comes only occasionally into the series of pictures of fighting, and of the impressions that fighting produces on the hyper-sensitive nerves of the chief character. Fleming, a neurotic lad, constitutionally weak and intensely egotistic, fanciful and easily excited, enlists in the Northern Army, and finds himself a raw recruit in a new regiment, derisively greeted by veteran regiments as "fresh fish." Nights of morbid introspection afflict the youth with the intolerable question, Will he funk when the fighting comes? Thus he continues to question and torture himself till his feelings are raised to the nth power of sensitiveness. At last, after many false alarms and fruitless preparations, the real battle approaches, and whatever confidence in himself remained oozes away from the lonely lad. "He lay down in the grass. The blades pressed tenderly against his cheek. The liquid stillness of the night enveloping him made him feel vast pity for himself. . . . He wished without reserve that he was at home again." He talked with his comrades, but found no sign of similar weakness. He felt himself inferior to them: an outcast. Then, in the grey dawn, after such a night of fear, they start hastily for the front. . . .

He looked round him, but there was no escape from the regiment. "He was in a moving box." The experiences of the battle are led up to with masterly skill. First he is fascinated by the skirmishers, whom he sees running hither and thither, "firing at the landscape." Then comes one of Mr. Crane's vivid poetical conceptions: the advancing line encounters a dead soldier. . . .

An unreasoning dread swept over the young recruit; the forest everywhere seemed to hide the enemy, and might any moment bristle with rifle-barrels. He lagged at last, with tragic glances at the sky; only to bring down on himself the young lieutenant of his company with loud reproaches for skulking. The new regiment took its ground in a fringe of wood. Shells came screaming over. "Bullets began to whistle among the branches and hiss at the trees. Twigs and leaves came sailing down. It was as if a thousand axes, wee and invisible, were being wielded." Then the tide of battle moved toward them, and out of the grey smoke came the yells of the combatants, and then a mob of beaten men rushed past, careless of the grim jokes hurled at them. "The battle reflection that shone for an instant on their faces on the mad current made the youth feel" that he would have gladly escaped if he could. "The sight of this stampede exercised a flood-like force that seemed able to drag sticks and stones and men from the ground." At last, "Here they come! Here they come! Gunlocks clicked. Across the smoke-infested fields came a brown swarm of running men who were giving shrill yells. A flag tilted forward sped near the front."

The man at the youth's elbow was mumbling, as if to himself, "Oh! we're in for it now; oh! we're in for it now." The youth fired a wild first shot, and immediately began to work at his weapon automatically. He lost concern for himself, and felt that something of which he was a part was in a crisis. . . .

The description goes on, full of vivid realistic touches, of which we can only give a fragment or two. . . .

The book is crowded with vivid passages and striking descriptions, often expressed in original and picturesque diction. "A mass of wet grass marched upon rustled like silk"; "A dense wall of smoke settled slowly down. It was furiously slit and slashed by the knife-like fire from the rifles"; Bullets "spanged"; "Bullets buffed into men"; "His dead body lying torn and gluttering upon the field." One is not inclined to criticize the giver of such a book; but it will be observed that when the Berserk inspiration is not upon him, Mr. Crane writes as badly as, when his imagination is heated, he writes well e.g. "Too, the clothes seemed new."

—ATTRIBUTED TO SYDNEY BROOKS,
Saturday Review, January 11, 1896, pp. 44–45

HAROLD FREDERIC
"KAISER WORRIES BRITONS" (1896)

Harold Frederic, a novelist and an American correspondent for *The New York Times* in London and later a close friend of Stephen Crane, reports the popularity of *The Red Badge* in England. Frederic immediately recognized the work as a masterpiece.

Later Frederic and Kate Lyons, with whom he maintained a household and had children, became good friends of Stephen and Cora. They traveled to Ireland together and often visited one another. When Frederic died unexpectedly, the Cranes took in their children and raised money for them.

This is not a favorable week for literature, but the big "Life of Cardinal Manning" has been occupying a good deal of space in the [London] papers.

The general reader, however, is talking a hundred times more about "The Red Badge of Courage," written by Stephen Crane, who is presumably an American, but is said to be quite young and unknown, though he is understood to be living here. I have never known any other book to make its own way among the critics so absolutely swiftly. Everybody who read it talks of nothing else. *The Saturday Review* gives it nearly two pages at the head of its list today, and everywhere else it is getting exceptional attention.

—HAROLD FREDERIC,
"Kaiser Worries Britons,"
The New York Times, January 12, 1896, p.1

HAROLD FREDERIC
"STEPHEN CRANE'S TRIUMPH" (1896)

Harold Frederic followed up the previous announcement of the success of *The Red Badge* in England with this review. He expresses admiration for the boldness and originality of Crane's style, especially noting its visual aspects and its individual point of view. He asserts the book's originality and finds it "more vehemently alive and heaving with dramatic human action than any other book of our time." He states that the novel is more alive than actual accounts given in the four volumes of The Century's *Battles and Leaders of the Civil War,* and he credits Stephen Crane's "photographic revelation" for the book's success.

Who in London knows about Stephen Crane? The question is one of genuine interest here. It happens, annoyingly enough, that the one publishing person who might throw some light on the answer is for the moment absent from town. Other sources yield only the meagre information that the name is believed to be a real, and not an assumed, one, and that its owner is understood to be a very young man, indeed. That he is an American, or, at least, learned to read and write in America, is obvious enough. The mere presence in his vocabulary of the verb "loan" would settle that, if the proof were not otherwise blazoned on every page of his extraordinary book. For this mysteriously unknown youth has really written an extraordinary book.

The Red Badge of Courage appeared a couple of months ago, unheralded and unnoticed, in a series which, under the distinctive label of *Pioneer,* is popularly supposed to present fiction more or less after the order of *The Green Carnation,* which was also of that lot. The first one who mentioned in my hearing that this *Red Badge* was well worth reading happened to be a person whose literary admirations serve me generally as warnings what to avoid, and I remembered the title languidly from the standpoint of self-protection. A little later others began to speak of it. All at once, every bookish person had it at his tongue's end. It was clearly a book to read, and I read it.

Even as I did so, reviews burst forth in a dozen different quarters, hailing it as extraordinary. Some were naturally more excited and voluble than others, but all the critics showed, and continue to show, their sense of being in the presence of something not like other things. George Wyndham, M.P., has already written of it in *The New Review* as "a remarkable book." Other magazine editors have articles about it in preparation, and it is evident that for the next few months it is to be more talked about than anything else in current literature. It seems almost equally certain that it will be kept alive, as one of the deathless books which must be read by everybody who desires to be, or to seem, a connoisseur of modern fiction.

If there were in existence any books of a similar character, one could start confidently by saying that it was the best of its kind. But it has no fellows. It is a book outside of all classification. So unlike anything else it is, that the temptation rises to deny that it is a book at all. When one searches for comparisons, they can only be found by culling out selected portions from the trunks of masterpieces, and considering these detached fragments, one by one, with reference to the *Red Badge,* which is itself a fragment, and yet is complete. Thus one lifts the best battle pictures from Tolstoi's great *War and Peace* from Balzac's *Chouans,* from Hugo's *Les Miserables,* and the forest fight in 93, from Prosper Merimee's assault of the redoubt, from Zola's *La Debacle,* and *Attack on the Mill,* (it is strange enough that equivalents in the literature of our own language do not suggest themselves,) and studies them side by side with this tremendously effective battle painting by the unknown youngster. Positively they are cold and ineffectual beside it. The praise may sound exaggerated, but really it is inadequate. These renowned battle descriptions of the big men are made to seem all wrong. The *Red Badge* impels the feeling that the actual truth about a battle has never been guessed before.

In construction, the book is as original as in its unique grasp of a new grouping of old materials. All the historic and prescribed machinery of the romance is thrust aside. One barely knows the name of the hero; it is only dimly sketched in that he was a farm boy and had a mother when he enlisted. These facts recur to him once or twice; they play no larger part in the reader's mind. Only two other characters are mentioned by name—Jim Conklin and Wilson; more often even they are spoken of as the tall soldier and the loud soldier. Not a word is expended on telling where they come from, or who they are. They pass across the picture, or shift from one posture to another in its moving composition, with the impersonality of one's chance fellow-passengers in a railroad car. There is a lieutenant who swears new oaths all the while, another officer with a red beard, and two or three still vaguer figures, revealed here and there through the smoke. We do not know, or seek to know, their names, or anything about them except what, staring through the eyes of Henry Fleming, we are permitted to see. The regiment itself, the refugees from other regiments in the crowded flight, and the enemy on the other side of the fence, are differentiated only as they wear blue or gray. We never get their color out of our mind's eye. This exhausts the dramatis personae of the book, and yet it is more vehemently alive and heaving with dramatic human action than any other book of our time. The people are all strangers to us, but the sight of them stirs the profoundest emotions of interest in our breasts. What they do appeals as vividly to our consciousness as if we had known them all our life.

The central idea of the book is of less importance than the magnificent graft of externals upon it. We begin with the young raw recruit, hearing that at last his regiment is going to see some fighting, and brooding over the problem of his own behavior under fire. We follow his perturbed meditations through thirty pages, which cover a week or so of this menace of action. Then suddenly, with one gray morning, the ordeal breaks abruptly over the youngster's head. We go with him, so close that he is never out of sight, for two terrible crowded days, and then the book is at an end. This cross-section of his experience is made a part of our own. We see with his eyes, think with his mind, quail or thrill with his nerves. He strives to argue himself into the conventional soldier's bravery; he runs ingloriously away; he excuses, defends, and abhors himself in turn; he tremblingly yields to the sinister fascination of creeping near the battle; he basely allows his comrades to ascribe to heroism the wound he received in the frenzied "sauve qui peut" of the fight; he gets at last the fire of combat in his veins, and blindly rushing in, deports himself with such hardy and temerarious valor that even the Colonel notes him, and admits that he is a "jim-hickey." These sequent processes, observed with relentless minutiae, are so powerfully and speakingly portrayed that they seem the veritable actions of our own minds. To produce this effect is a notable triumph, but is commonplace by comparison with the other triumph of making us realize what Henry saw and heard as well as what he felt. The value of the former feat has the limitation of the individual. No two people are absolutely alike; any other young farm boy would have passed through the trial with something different somewhere. Where Henry fluttered, he might have been obtuse; neither the early panic nor the later irrational ferocity would necessarily have been just the same. But the picture of the trial itself seems to me never to have been painted as well before.

Oddly enough *The Saturday* Review and some other of the commentators take it for granted that the writer of the *Red Badge* must have seen real warfare. "The extremely vivid touches of detail convince us," says *The Review,* "that he has had personal experience of the scenes he depicts. Certainly, if his book were altogether a work of imagination, unbased on personal experience, his realism would be nothing short of a miracle." This may strike the reader who has not thought much about it as reasonable, but I believe it to be wholly fallacious. Some years ago I had before me the task of writing some battle chapters in a book I was at work upon. The novel naturally led up to the climax of a battle, and I was excusably anxious that when I finally got to this battle, I should be as fit to handle it as it was possible to make myself. A very considerable literature existed about the actual struggle, which was the Revolutionary battle of Oriskany, fought only a few miles from where I was born. This literature was in part the narratives of survivors of the fight, in part imaginative accounts based on these by later writers. I found to my surprise that the people who were really in the fight gave one much less of an idea of a desperate forest combat than did those who pictured it in fancy. Of course, here it might be that the veterans were inferior in powers of narration to the professional writer. Then I extended the text to writers themselves. I compared the best accounts of Franco-German battles, written for the London newspapers by trained correspondents of distinction who were on the spot, with the choicest imaginative work of novelists, some of them mentioned above, who had never seen a gun fired in anger. There was literally no comparison between the two. The line between journalism and literature obtruded itself steadily. Nor were cases lacking in which some of these war correspondents had in other departments of work showed themselves capable of true literature. I have the instance of David Christie Murray in mind. He saw some of the stiffest fighting that was done in his time, and that, too, at an early stage of his career, but he never tried to put a great battle chapter into one of his subsequent novels, and if he had I don't believe it would have been great.

Our own writers of the elder generation illustrate this same truth. Gen. Lew Wallace, Judge Tourgte, Dr. Weir Mitchell, and numbers of others saw tremendous struggles on the battlefield, but to put the reality into type baffles them. The four huge volumes of The Century's *Battles and Leaders of the Civil War* are written almost exclusively by men who took an active part in the war, and many of them were in addition men of high education and considerable literary talent, but there is not a really moving story of a fight in the whole work. When Warren Lee Goss began his *Personal Recollections of a Private,* his study of the enlistment, the early marching and drilling, and the new experiences of camp life was so piquant and fresh that I grew quite excited in anticipation. But when he came to the fighting, he fell flat. The same may be said, with more reservations, about the first parts of Judge Tourgee's more recent *Story of a Thousand*. It seems as if the actual sight of a battle has some dynamic quality in it which overwhelms and crushes the literary faculty in the observer. At best, he gives us a conventional account of what happened; but on analysis you find that this is not what he really saw, but what all his reading has taught him that he must have seen. In the same way battle painters depict horses in motion, not as they actually move, but as it has been agreed by numberless generations of draughtsmen to say that they move. At last, along comes a Muybridge, with his instantaneous camera, and shows that the real motion is entirely different.

It is this effect of a photographic revelation which startles and fascinates one in *The Red Badge of Courage*. The product is breathlessly interesting, but still more so is the suggestion behind it that a novel force has been disclosed, which may do all sorts of other remarkable things. Prophecy is known of old as a tricky and thankless hag, but all the same I cannot close my ears to her hint that a young man who can write such a first book as that will make us all sit up in good time.

—HAROLD FREDERIC, "Stephen Crane's Triumph,"
The New York Times, January 26, 1896, p. 22

GEORGE WYNDHAM
"A REMARKABLE BOOK" (1896)

George Wyndham was a veteran of war, a Member of Parliament, and chief secretary of Ireland, in addition to being a critic for prominent literary magazines. This is one of the best-written articles on *The Red Badge of Courage*. In it, Wyndham points out the images experienced in an actual war and shows how Crane effectively paints them in his novel. Wyndham focuses on Crane's technique of displaying those images: "In order to show the features of modern war, he takes a subject—a youth with a peculiar temperament, capable of exaltation and yet morbidly sensitive. Then he traces the successive impressions made on such a temperament."

Wyndham's praise is ebullient, but he backs it up with so much concrete and clearly analyzed data that there is no doubt in his mind or the reader's that Crane's work is worthy of such praise.

Mr. Stephen Crane, the author of *The Red Badge of Courage* (London: Heinemann), is a great artist, with something new to say, and consequently, with a new way of saying it. His theme, indeed, is an old one, but old themes re-handled anew in the light of novel experience, are the stuff out of which masterpieces are made, and in *The Red Badge of Courage* Mr. Crane has surely contrived a masterpiece. He writes of war—the ominous and alluring possibility for every man, since the heir of all the ages has won and must keep his inheritance by secular combat. The conditions of the age-long contention have changed and will change, but its certainty is coeval with progress: so long as there are things worth fighting for fighting will last, and the fashion of fighting will change under the reciprocal stresses of rival inventions. Hence its double interest of abiding necessity and ceaseless variation. Of all these variations the most marked has followed, within the memory of most of us, upon the adoption of long-range weapons of precision, and continues to develop, under our eyes, with the development of rapidity in firing. And yet, with the exception of Zola's *La Debacle,* no considerable attempt has been made to portray war under its new conditions. The old stories are less trustworthy than ever as guides to the experiences which a man may expect in battle and to the emotions which those experiences are likely to arouse. No doubt the prime factors in the personal problem—the chances of death and mutilation continue to be about the same. In these respects it matters little whether you are pierced by a bullet at two thousand yards or stabbed at hands' play with a dagger. We know that the most appalling death-rolls of recent campaigns have been more than equaled in ancient warfare; and, apart from history, it is clear that, unless one side runs away, neither can win save by the infliction of decisive losses. But although these personal risks continue to be essentially the same, the picturesque and emotional aspects of war are completely altered by every change in the shape and circumstance of imminent death. And these are the fit materials for literature—the things which even dull men remember with the undying imagination of poets, but which, for lack of the writer's art, they cannot communicate. The sights flashed indelibly on the retina of the eye; the sounds that after long silences suddenly cypher; the stenches that sicken in after-life at any chance allusion to decay; or, stirred by these, the storms of passions that force yells of defiance out of inarticulate clowns; the winds of fear that sweep by night along prostrate ranks, with the acceleration of trains and the noise as of a whole town waking from nightmare with stertorous, indrawn gasps—these colossal facts of the senses and the soul are the only colours in which the very image of war can be painted. Mr. Crane has composed his palette with these colours, and has painted a picture that challenges comparison with the most vivid scenes of Tolstoi's *La Guerre et la Paix* or of Zola's *La Debacle.* This is unstinted praise, but I feel bound to give it after reading the book twice and comparing it with Zola's Sedan and Tolstoi's account of Rostow's squadron for the first time under fire. Indeed, I think that Mr. Crane's picture of war is more complete than Tolstoi's, more true than Zola's. Rostow's sensations are conveyed by Tolstoi with touches more subtle than any to be found even in his *Sebastopol,* but they make but a brief passage in a long book, much else of which is devoted to the theory that Napoleon and his marshals were mere waifs on a tide of humanity or to the analysis of divers characters exposed to civilian experiences. Zola, on the other hand, compiles an accurate catalogue of almost all that is terrible and nauseating in war; but it is his own catalogue of facts made in cold blood, and not the procession of flashing images shot through the senses into one brain and fluctuating there with its rhythm of exaltation and fatigue. *La Debacle* gives the whole truth, the truth of science, as it is observed by a shrewd intellect, but not the truth of experience as it is felt in fragments magnified or diminished in accordance with the patient's mood. The terrible things in war are not always terrible; the nauseating things do not always sicken. On the contrary, it is even these which sometimes lift the soul to heights from which they become invisible. And, again, at other times, it is the little miseries of most ignoble insignificance which fret through the last fibres of endurance.

Mr. Crane, for his distinction, has hit on a new device, or at least on one which has never been used before with such consistency and effect. In order to show the features of modern war, he takes a subject—a youth with a peculiar temperament, capable of exaltation and yet morbidly sensitive. Then he traces the successive impressions made on such a temperament, from minute to minute, during two days of heavy fighting. He stages the drama of war, so to speak, within the mind of one man, and then admits you as to a theatre. You may, if you please, object that this youth is unlike most other young men who serve in the ranks, and that the same events would have impressed the average man differently; but you are convinced that this man's soul is truly drawn, and that the impressions made in it are faithfully rendered. The youth's temperament is merely the medium which the artist has chosen: that it is exceptionally plastic makes but for the deeper incision of his work. It follows from Mr. Crane's method that he creates by his art even such a first-hand report of war as we seek in vain among the journals and letters of soldiers. But the book is not written in the form of an autobiography: the author narrates. He is therefore at liberty to give scenery and action, down to the slightest gestures and outward signs of inward elation or suffering, and he does this with the vigour and terseness of a master. Had he put his descriptions of scenery and his atmospheric effects, or his reports of overheard conversations, into the mouth of his youth, their very excellence would have belied all likelihood. Yet in all his descriptions and all his reports he confines himself only to such things as that youth heard and saw, and, of these, only to such as influenced his emotions. By this compromise he combines the strength and truth of a monodrama with the directness and colour of the best narrative prose. The monodrama suffices for the lyrical emotion of Tennyson's *Maud;* but in Browning's *Martin Relfyou* feel the constraint of a form which in his *Ring and the Book* entails repetition often intolerable.

Mr. Crane discovers his youth, Henry Fleming, in a phase of disillusion. It is some monotonous months since boyish "visions of broken-bladed glory" impelled him to enlist in the Northern Army towards the middle of the American war. That impulse is admirably given:—"One night as he lay in bed, the winds had carried to him the clangouring of the church bells, as some enthusiast jerked the rope frantically to tell the twisted news of a great battle. This voice of the people rejoicing in the night had made him shiver in a prolonged ecstasy of excitement. Later he had gone down to his mother's room, and had spoken thus: 'Ma, I'm going to enlist.' 'Henry, don't you be a fool,' his mother had replied. She had then covered her face with the quilt. There was an end to the matter for that night." But the next morning he enlists. He is impatient of the homely injunctions given him in place of the heroic speech he expects in accordance with a tawdry convention, and so departs, with a "vague feeling of relief." But, looking back from the gate, he sees his mother "kneeling among the potato parings. Her brown face upraised and stained with tears, her spare form quivering." Since then the army has done "little but sit still and try to keep warm" till he has "grown to regard himself merely as a part of a vast blue demonstration." In the sick langour of this waiting, he begins to suspect his courage and lies awake by night through hours of morbid introspection. He tries "to prove to himself mathematically that he would not run from a battle"; he constantly leads the conversation round to the problem of courage in order to gauge the confidence of his messmates.

"How do you know you won't run when the time comes?" asked the youth. "Run?" said the loud one, "run?—of course not!" He laughed. "Well," continued the youth, "lots of good-a-'nough men have thought they was going to do great things before the fight, but when the time come they skedaddled." "Oh, that's all true, I s'pose," replied the other, "but I'm not going to skedaddle. The man that bets on my running will lose his money, that's all." He nodded confidently.

The youth is a "mental outcast" among his comrades, "wrestling with his personal problem," and sweating as he listens to the muttered scoring of a card game, his eyes fixed on the "red, shivering reflection of a fire." Every day they drill; every night they watch the red campfires of the enemy on the far shore of a river, eating their hearts out. At last they march:—"In the gloom before the break of the day their uniforms glowed a deep purple blue. From across the river the red eyes were still peering. In the eastern sky there was a yellow patch, like a rug laid for the feet of the coming sun; and against it, black and pattern-like, loomed the gigantic figure of the colonel on a gigantic horse." The book is full of such vivid impressions, half of sense and half of imagination:—The columns as they marched "were like two serpents crawling from the cavern of night." But the march, which, in his boyish imagination, should have led forthwith into melodramatic action is but the precursor of other marches. After days of weariness and nights of discomfort, at last, as in life, without preface, and in a lull of the mind's anxiety, the long-dreaded and long-expected is suddenly and smoothly in process of accomplishment:— "One grey morning he was kicked on the leg by the tall soldier, and then, before he was entirely awake, he found himself running down a wood road in the midst of men who were panting with the first effects of speed. His canteen banged rhythmically upon his thigh, and his haversack bobbed softly. His musket bounced a trifle from his shoulder at each stride and made his cap feel uncertain upon his head." From this moment, reached on the thirtieth page, the drama races through another hundred and sixty pages to the end of the book, and to read those pages is in itself an experience of breathless, lambent, detonating life. So brilliant and detached are the images evoked that, like illuminated bodies actually seen, they leave their fever-bright phantasms floating before the brain. You may shut the book, but you still see the battle-flags "jerked about madly in the smoke," or sinking with "dying gestures of despair," the men "dropping here and there like bundles"; the captain shot dead with "an astonished and sorrowful look as if he thought some friend had done him an ill-turn"; and the litter of corpses, "twisted in fantastic contortions," as if "they had fallen from some great height, dumped out upon the ground from the sky." The book is full of sensuous impressions that leap out from the picture: of gestures, attitudes, grimaces, that flash into portentous definition, like faces from the climbing clouds of nightmare. It leaves the imagination bounded with a "dense wall of smoke, furiously slit and slashed by the knife-like fire from the rifles." It leaves, in short, such indelible traces as are left by the actual experience of war. The picture shows grisly shadows and vermilion splashes, but, as in the vast drama it reflects so truly, these features, though insistent, are small in size, and are lost in the immensity of the theatre. The tranquil forest stands around; the "fairy-blue of the sky" is over it all. And, as in the actual experience of war, the impressions which these startling features inflict, though acute, are localised and not too deep: are as it were mere pinpricks, or, at worst, clean cuts from a lancet in a body thrilled with currents of physical excitement and sopped with anaesthetics of emotion. Here is the author's description of a forlorn hope:—

As the regiment swung from its position out into a cleared space, the woods and thickets before it awakened. Yellow flames leaped toward it from many directions. The line swung straight for a moment. Then the right wing swung forward; it in turn was surpassed by the left. Afterward the centre careered to the front until the regiment was a wedge-shaped mass . . . the men, pitching forward insanely, had burst into cheerings, mob-like and barbaric, but tuned in strange keys that can arouse the dullard and the stoic. . . . There was the delirium that encounters despair and death, and is heedless and blind to odds. . . . Presently the straining pace ate up the energies of the men. As if by agreement, the leaders began to slacken their speed. The volleys directed against them had a seeming wind-like effect. The regiment snorted and blew. Among some stolid trees it began to falter and hesitate. . . . The youth had a vague belief that he had run miles, and he thought, in a way, that he was now in some new and unknown land. The charge withers away, and the lieutenant, the youth, and his friend run forward to rally the regiment.

In front of the colours three men began to bawl, "Come on! Come On!" They danced and gyrated like tortured savages. The flag, obedient to these appeals, bended its glittering form and swept toward them. The men wavered in indecision for a moment, and then with a long wailful cry the dilapidated regiment surged forward and began its new journey. Over the field went the scurrying mass. It was a handful of men splattered into the faces of the enemy. Toward it instantly sprang the yellow tongues. A vast quantity of blue smoke hung before them. A mighty banging made ears valueless. The youth ran like a madman to reach the woods before a bullet could discover him. He ducked his head low, like a football player. In his haste his eyes almost closed, and the scene was a wild blur. Pulsating saliva stood at the corner of his mouth. Within him, as he hurled forward, was born a love, a despairing fondness for this flag that was near him. It was a creation of beauty and invulnerability. It was a goddess radiant, that bended its form with an imperious gesture to him. It was a woman, red and white, hating and loving, that called him with the voice of his hopes. Because no harm could come to it he endowed it with power. He kept near, as if it could be a saver of lives, and an imploring cry went from his mind.

This passage directly challenges comparison with Zola's scene, in which the lieutenant and the old tradition, of an invincible Frenchman over-running the world "between his bottle and his girl," expire together among the morsels of a bullet-eaten flag. Mr. Crane has probably read La *Debacle,* and wittingly threw down his glove. One can only say that he is justified of his courage.

Mr. Crane's method, when dealing with things seen and heard, is akin to Zola's: he omits nothing and extenuates nothing, save the actual blasphemy and obscenity of a soldier's oaths. These he indicates, sufficiently for any purpose of art, by brief allusions to their vigour and variety. Even Zola has rarely surpassed the appalling realism of Jim Conklin's death in Chapter X. Indeed, there is little to criticise in Mr. Crane's observation, except an undue subordination of the shrill cry of bullets to the sharp crashing of rifles. He omits the long chromatic whine defining its invisible arc in the air, and the fretful snatch a few feet from the listener's head. In addition to this gift of observation, Mr. Crane has at command the imaginative phrase. The firing follows a retreat as with "yellings of eager metallic hounds"; the men at their mechanic loading and firing are like "fiends jigging heavily in the smoke" in a lull before the attack "there passed slowly the intense moments that precede the tempest"; then, after single shots, "the battle roar settled to a rolling thunder, which was a single long explosion." And, as I have said, when Mr. Crane deals with things felt he gives a truer report than Zola. He postulates his hero's temperament—a day-dreamer given over to morbid self-analysis who enlists, not from any deep-seated belief in the holiness of fighting for his country, but in hasty pursuit of a vanishing ambition. This choice enables Mr. Crane to double his picturesque advantage with an ethical advantage equally great. Not only is his youth, like the sufferer in *"The Fall of the House of Usher,"* super-sensitive to every pin-prick of sensation: he is also a delicate meter of emotion and fancy. In such a nature the waves of feeling take exaggerated curves, and hallucination haunts the brain. Thus, when awaiting the first attack, his mind is thronged with vivid images of a circus he had seen as a boy: it is there in definite detail, even as the Apothecary's shop usurps Romeo's mind at the crisis of his fate. And thus also, like Herodotus' Aristodemus, he vacillates between cowardice and heroism. Nothing could well be more subtle than his self-deception and that sudden enlightenment which leads him to "throw aside his mental pamphlets on the philosophy of the retreated and rules for the guidance of the damned." His soul is of that kind which, "sick with self-love," can only be saved "so as by fire"; and it is saved when the battle-bond of brotherhood is born within it, and is found plainly of deeper import than the cause for which he and his comrades fight, even as that cause is loftier than his personal ambition. By his choice of a hero Mr. Crane displays in the same work a pageant of the senses and a tragedy of the soul.

But he does not obtrude his moral. The "tall soldier" and the lieutenant are brave and content throughout, the one by custom as a veteran, the other by constitution as a hero. But the two boys, the youth and his friend, "the loud soldier," are at first querulous braggarts, but at the last they are transmuted by danger until either might truly say:

> We have proved we have hearts in a cause, we are noble still,
> And myself have awaked, as it seems, to the better mind;
> It is better to fight for the good than to rail at the ill;
> I have felt with my native land, I am one with my kind,
> I embrace the purpose of God, and the doom assigned.

Let no man cast a stone of contempt at these two lads during their earlier weakness until he has fully gauged the jarring discordance of battle. To be jostled on a platform when you have lost your luggage and missed your train on an errand of vital importance gives a truer pre-taste of war than any field-day; yet many a well-disciplined man will denounce the universe upon slighter provocation. It is enough that these two were boys and that they became men.

Yet must it be said that this youth's emotional experience was singular. In a battle there are a few physical cowards, abjects born with defective circulations, who literally turn blue at the approach of danger, and a few on whom danger acts like the keen, rare atmosphere of snow-clad peaks. But between these extremes come many to whom danger is as strong wine, with the multitude which gladly accepts the "iron laws of tradition" and finds welcome support in "a moving box." To this youth, as the cool dawn of his first day's fighting changed by infinitesimal gradations to a feverish noon, the whole evolution pointed to "a trap"; but I have seen another youth under like circumstances toss a pumpkin into the air and spit it on his sword. To this youth the very landscape was filled with "the stealthy approach of death." You are convinced by the author's art that it was so to this man. But to others, as the clamour increases, it is as if the serenity of the morning had taken refuge in their brains. This man "stumbles over the stones as he runs breathlessly forward"; another realises for the first time how right it is to be adroit even in running. The movement of his body becomes an art, which is not self-conscious, since its whole intention is to impress others within the limits of a modest decorum. We know that both love and courage teach this mastery over the details of living. You can tell from the way one woman, out of all the myriads, walks down Piccadilly, that she is at last aware of love. And you can tell from the way a man enters a surgery or runs toward a firing-line that he, too, realises how wholly the justification of any one life lies in its perfect adjustment to others. The woman in love, the man in battle, may each say, for their moment, with the artist, "I was made perfect too." They also are of the few to whom "God whispers in the ear."

But had Mr. Crane taken an average man he would have written an ordinary story, whereas he has written one which is certain to last. It is glorious to see his youth discover courage in the bed-rock of primeval antagonism after the collapse of his tinsel bravado; it is something higher to see him raise upon that rock the temple of resignation. Mr. Crane, as an artist, achieves by his singleness of purpose a truer and completer picture of war than either Tolstoi, bent also upon proving the insignificance of heroes, or Zola, bent also upon prophesying the regeneration of France. That is much; but it is more that his work of art, when completed, chimes with the universal experience of mankind; that his heroes find in their extreme danger, if not confidence in their leaders and conviction in their cause, at least the conviction that most men do what they can or, at most, what they must. We have few good accounts of battles—many of shipwrecks; and we know that, just as the storm rises, so does the commonplace captain show as a god, and the hysterical passenger as a cheerful heroine.

It is but a further step to recognise all life for a battle and this earth for a vessel lost in space. We may then infer that virtues easy in moments of distress may be useful also in everyday experience.

—George Wyndham, "A Remarkable Book,"
New Review, January 1896, pp. 32–40

William Morton Payne
"Recent Fiction" (1896)

William Morton Payne was a critic, teacher, translator, and associate editor of the Chicago *Dial* from 1892 to 1915. His short review may be considered as the official position of the *Dial*, later expanded upon by the magazine's owner, A.C. McClurg, and spurring a rivalry and disagreement among English and American critics about who had first championed Stephen Crane's work.

━━━━━━ ━━━━━━ ━━━━━━

The Red Badge of Courage is a book that has been getting a good deal of belated praise within the past few weeks, but we cannot admit that much of it is deserved. There is almost no story to Mr. Crane's production, but merely an account, in roughshod descriptive style, of the thoughts and feelings of a young soldier during his first days of active fighting. The author constructs for his central character a psychological history that is plausible, but hardly convincing. We do not know, nor does the writer, that it is what actually does go on in the mind of a man who is passing through his baptism of fire. It may be retorted that we do not know any more that Count Tolstoi is giving us the real thing in his war-stories, or "Stendhal" in the *Chartreuse de Parme*, but the descriptions in these books at least seem inevitable while we are reading them, and Mr. Crane's descriptions do not.

—WILLIAM MORTON PAYNE, "Recent Fiction,"
Dial, February 1, 1896, p. 80

UNSIGNED "COMMENT ON NEW BOOKS" (1896)

This review points out the power of *The Red Badge*, but it undercuts any praise by decrying the novel's rough style and indicating its lack of "excellence of literary workmanship."

The Red Badge of Courage, by Stephen Crane (Appletons), is a narrative of the experience of a raw youth in battle, and of the steady screwing of his courage to the point of heroism. So vivid is the picture of actual conflict that the reader comes faces to face with war. He does not see its pomp, which requires a different perspective, but he feels the sickening horror of slaughter and becomes a part of the moving line of battle. The process of becoming a hero is so naturally unfolded that the reader no more than the hero himself is aware of the transformation from indecision and cowardice to bravery. This picture, so vivid as to produce almost the effect of a personal experience, is not made by any finished excellence of literary workmanship, but by the sheer power of an imaginative description. The style is as rough as it is direct. The sentences never flow; they are shot forth in sharp volleys. But the original power of the book is great enough to set a new fashion in literature.

—UNSIGNED, "Comment on New Books," *The
Atlantic Monthly*, March 1896, p. 422

UNSIGNED "THE RAMBLER" (1896)

Although this review in an American literary magazine is quite positive, it does little to analyze the novel. The author points out the "high pitch at which it is sustained" and the "multiplicity of detail" found in *The Red Badge* but does not explain how these two elements function in the text.

Mr. Stephen Crane's story, *The Red Badge of Courage*, has received higher praise than it is usual to bestow, with sincerity, upon the work of a living writer. It certainly sounds extravagant to say (as has been said) that his work is "inspired," and that, if he has not himself experienced the sensations of a soldier in the heat of battle, his achievement in writing the story is "a miracle." Yet the story is so remarkable that one may be pardoned for saying almost anything about it while the flush of its reading is still upon one. Two things in this tale strike most persons very forcibly: the high pitch at which it is sustained throughout a good-sized volume, and the multiplicity of detail with which it is heaped and rounded up.

In a conversation, recently, Mr. Crane said that he began the tale as a pot-boiler, intending to make a short story for a newspaper; that he selected a battle as his subject as affording plenty of "color" and range for the imagination, although he had, of course, never been in a battle in his life. But as he went on, the story grew under his hand, and he determined to put the best work into it of which he was capable. "I don't believe in inspiration," said he. "I am one of those who believe that an enthusiasm of concentration in hard work is what a writer must depend on to bring him to the end he has in view." And he went on to say that he had kept this story in hand for nearly a year, polishing and bettering it. Perhaps this is the most amazing thing about a thoroughly amazing book. If he had said he wrote it in three days (as he wrote the *Black Riders)* one might understand such a *tour de force.* But to be able to keep the *Red Badge* in his desk and do days' work upon it—to assume at will the frame of mind which would seem necessary to set down such a memorandum of a whirlwind—this is astonishing, indeed. The story is like a picture by Verestchagin in its seemingly commonplace sward of homely words through which one suddenly sees the pale faces of dead men tumbled headlong into twisted and horrifying shapes. The reader of the story is caught up into the chariot, and forgets any mechanical flaws in the English in the excitement of being present at such a dance of death. . . .

Somebody said, quite gravely, the other day, that he believed the soul of some great soldier—not a general, but a fighter in the ranks—had gone into Stephen Crane at his birth, and that the *Red Badge* came from his mind as spontaneously as the galley-slave's tale was told by the pale-faced London lad in Kipling's "'Greatest Story in the World.'" Should this ingenious theory be true, Mr. Crane will never write any good stories except of battles; but it is pretty safe to assume that the writer of the *Red Badge* is not a man of one story; he is bound to write many more which shall brighten the shining reputation he has already gained. And yet, this theory of reincarnation is a fascinating one, for it would explain how Mr. Crane, who "has never been in battle in his life," has been able to write down descriptions in such a guise of seer's authority as to compel the reader to accept his statements without thought of question.

—Unsigned, "The Rambler,"
Book Buyer, April 1896, pp. 140–141

A.C. McClurg "The Red Badge of Hysteria" (1896)

A.C. McClurg was a soldier, publisher, book collector, and more importantly, at the time of this review headed the publishing firm that owned the *Dial*. His letter responds to critics who had taken *The Red Badge* seriously, including the reviewer for the *Dial*. McClurg, a veteran of the Civil War who served in the Chickamauga and Chattanooga campaigns, attacks the novel, English reviewers and magazines, cowards and deserters, and the lack of proper censorship of modern literature.

This assault on the novel and Stephen Crane engendered a battle among critics and brought much attention to the novel itself.

———

Must we come to judge of books only by what the newspapers have said of them, and must we abandon all the old standards of criticism? Can a book and an author, utterly without merit, be puffed into success by entirely undeserved praise, even if that praise come from English periodicals?

One must ask these questions after he has been seduced into reading a book recently reprinted in this country entitled *The Red Badge of Courage, an Episode of the American Civil War*. The chorus of praise in the English papers has been very extravagant, but it is noticeable that so far, at least, the American papers have said very little about the merits or demerits of the book itself. They simply allude to the noise made over it abroad, and therefore treat its author as a coming factor in our literature. Even *The Dial's* very acute and usually very discerning critic of contemporary fiction (Mr. Payne) treats the book and the author (in your issue of Feb. 1) in very much this way—that is, as a book and an author to be reckoned with, not because of any good which he himself finds in them, but because they have been so much talked about.

The book has very recently been reprinted in America, and would seem to be an American book, on an American theme, and by an American author, yet originally issued in England. If it is really an American production one must suppose it to have been promptly and properly rejected by any American publishers to whom it may have been submitted, and afterward more naturally taken up by an English publisher.

It is only too well known that English writers have had a very low opinion of American soldiers, and have always, as a rule, assumed to ridicule them. . . .

Under such circumstances we cannot doubt that *The Red Badge of Courage* would be just such a book as the English would grow enthusiastic over, and we cannot wonder that the redoubtable *Saturday Review* greeted it with the highest encomiums, and declared it the actual experiences of a veteran of our War, when it was really the vain imaginings of a young man born long since that war, a piece of intended realism based entirely on unreality. The book is a vicious satire upon American soldiers and American armies. The hero of the book (if such he can be called—"the youth" the author styles him) is an ignorant and stupid country lad, who, without a spark of patriotic feeling, or even of soldierly ambition, has enlisted in the army from no definite motive that the reader can discover, unless it be because other boys are doing so; and the whole book, in which there is absolutely no story, is occupied with giving what are supposed to be his emotions and his actions in the first two days of battle. His poor weak intellect, if indeed he has any, seems to be at once and entirely overthrown by the din and movement of the field, and he acts throughout like a madman. Under the influence of mere excitement, for he does not even appear to be frightened, he first rushes madly to the rear in a crazy panic, and afterward plunges forward to the rescue of the colors under exactly the same influences. In neither case has reason or any intelligent motive any influence on his action. He is throughout an idiot or a maniac, and betrays no trace of the reasoning being. No thrill of patriotic devotion to cause or country ever moves his breast, and not even an emotion of manly courage. Even a wound which he finally gets comes from a comrade who strikes him on the head with his musket to get rid of him; and this is the only *Red Badge of Courage* (!) which we discover in the book. A number of other characters come in to fill out the two hundred and thirty-three pages of the book,—such as "the loud soldier," "the tall soldier," "the tattered soldier," etc., but not one of them betrays any more sense, self-possession, or courage than does "the youth." On the field all is chaos and confusion. "The young lieutenant," "the mounted officer," even "the general," are all utterly demented beings, raving and talking alike in an unintelligible and hitherto unheard-of jargon, rushing about in a very delirium of madness. No intelligent orders are given; no intelligent movements are made. There is no evidence of drill, none of discipline. There is a constant, senseless, and profane babbling going on, such as one could hear nowhere but in a madhouse. Nowhere are seen the quiet, manly, self-respecting, and patriotic men, influenced by the highest sense of duty, who in reality fought our battles. It can be said most confidently that no soldier who fought in our recent War ever saw any approach to the battle scenes in this book—but what wonder? We are told that it is the work of a young man of twenty-three or twenty-four years of age, and so of course must be a mere work of diseased imagination. And yet it constantly strains after so-called realism. The result is a mere riot of words. . . .

It is extraordinary that even a prejudiced animus could have led English writers to lavish extravagant praise on such a book; it is still more extraordinary that an attempt should be made to foist it upon the long-suffering American public, and to push it into popularity here. Respect for our own people should have prevented its issue in this country.

There may have been a moderate number of men in our service who felt and acted in battle like those in this book; but of such deserters were made. They did not stay when they could get away: why should they? The army was no healthy place for them, and they had no reason to stay; there was no moral motive. After they had deserted, however, they remained "loud soldiers," energetic, and blatant,—and they are possibly now enjoying good pensions. It must have been some of these fellows who got the ear of Mr. Crane and told him how they felt and acted in battle.

—A.C. McClurg, "The Red Badge of Hysteria,"
Dial, April 16, 1896, pp. 227–228

D. Appleton & Company "The Red Badge of Courage: A Correction" (1896)

This letter, probably written by Ripley Hitchcock in response to A.C. McClurg's "The Red Badge of Hysteria," seeks to show the American support that *The Red Badge of Courage* had received. Hitchcock was a journalist, critic, historian, and the one who contracted to publish *The Red Badge of Courage*. His letter mentions the reviews in *The New York Times* and the *Philadelphia Press*, as well as many other favorable reviews the book had received in this country.

It is with a certain hesitation that we write you to correct the author of a somewhat bitter letter published in your journal for April 16, for we recognize the signature as that of a gallant soldier, as well as a student of literature. But as the author of that letter labors under several misapprehensions, we think that he will be glad to learn the facts.

The Red Badge of Courage was read and accepted by us in December, 1894, and, in book form, it was first published in this country in October, 1895. Although the book was copyrighted in England at the same time, it was not formally published there for two months. Meantime the American journals had reviewed it and had begun an almost universal chorus of eulogy. October 19, 1895, the *New York Times* devoted a column and a half to a strong review of "this remarkable book." On October 13, the *Philadelphia Press* compared Mr. Crane and Bret Harte, not to the disadvantage of the former. On October 26, the *New York Mail and Express*, in one of several notices, said, "The author has more than talent there is genius in the book." On October 26, the *Boston Transcript*, in speaking of "this tremendous grasping of the glory and carnage of war," added at the close of a long and enthusiastic review, "The book forces upon the reader the conviction of what fighting ready means." Other favorable reviews appeared in October issues of the following American newspapers: *New York Herald, Brooklyn Eagle, Cleveland World, St. Paul Pioneer Press, Boston Daily Advertiser, New York World, St. Paul Globe, New York Commercial Advertiser, Kansas City Journal, Chicago Evening Post, Boston Courier, Cleveland Plain Dealer, Boston Beacon, Hartford Times, Sioux City Times, New Haven Leader,* and *Minneapolis Journal,* and to these names, taken almost at random, we might add many others. These journals reviewed *The Red Badge* favorably in October, and others, including weeklies like *The Critic* and *The Outlook,* followed in November with emphatic recognition of the strength and high talent shown in the book.

It was not until the end of November, two months after publication here, that the first reviews appeared in England. By that time American reviewers from Maine to California had "greeted" the book with the highest "encomiums." The English "encomiums" became specially marked in late December, January and February.

We state these facts in view of your correspondent's remarks that "So far, at least, the American papers have said very little about the merits or demerits of the book," and, "The book has very recently been reprinted in America," and, "Respect for our own people should have prevented its issue in this country." "Our country" was the first to recognize Mr. Crane's genius, and our people have read his book so eagerly that it continues to be the most popular work of fiction in the market, and it has been the one most talked of and written about since October last.

A glance at the back of the *Red Badge* title-page would have shown that the book could not have been "first published" in England and "reprinted" here, while the literary departments of journals throughout our country, and the opinions of American men of letters like Mr. Howells and Mr. Hamlin Garland, have proved, happily, that Americans are ready to recognize American talent, and that, *pace* your correspondent, a prophet is not without honor even in his own country.

As to other points, against the opinion of the gallant veteran who criticizes the book might be put the opinions of other veterans who have found only words of praise.

—D. Appleton & Company, "*The Red Badge of Courage*: A Correction," *Dial*, May 1, 1896, p. 263

J.L. Onderdonk "A Red Badge of Bad English" (1896)

J.L. Onderdonk was a lawyer, newspaper editor, and Idaho state legislator. After publishing this review supporting McClurg's attack on *The Red Badge*, Onderdonk released his *History of American Verse: 1610–1897*, which contains no mention of Stephen Crane's volume of poetry, *Black Riders* (1895). McClurg was instrumental in arranging the publication of that book.

In this review, Onderdonk carefully quotes sentences from *The Red Badge* that have errors in standard English, and he connects the book with "*fin de siecle* poetasters," evoking the image of Oscar Wilde and others accused of moral lapse and decadent behavior near the end of the nineteenth century.

The animus of the articles in British magazines during our Civil War, as quoted by "A. C. McC." in your issue of April 16, sufficiently explains the English enthusiasm for that literary absurdity called *The Red Badge of Courage*. The trend of the whole work to prove the absence of such a thing as a gentleman in the union army may be justly expected to arouse the resentment of the class of whom "A. C. McC." is such a striking and honorable example. If this work is realism, it is realism run mad, rioting in all that is revolting to man's best instincts, and utterly false to nature and to life. The Federal army doubtless possessed its share of ruffianly officers and stupid brainless men, but to select such and to hold them up as types is not true realism. Yet this is the work which one London periodical compares favorably with the writings of Tolstoi and Zola, and concerning which another London periodical says: "There is no possibility of resistance when once you are in its grasp."

The examples of hysterical composition given by "A. C. McC." might be supplemented by others fully as absurd taken from nearly every page of the book. Amid so much that is strained and affected there is not one agreeable character, hardly one praiseworthy sentiment, and certainly not a new or original thought. But as the book is heralded as one of the literary successes of the year, it is but fair to call attention to a few examples of its latter-day English. We can bear with equanimity the author's vulgarisms and mannerisms, his use of the split infinitive, and of such words as reliable, standpoint, and others which the slipshod fashion of the day has authorized by general usage. We may even attribute to "typographical errors" such careless constructions as the following:

> A shrill lamentation rang out filled with profane illusions to a general.
>
> His anger was directed not so much against the men whom he knew were rushing.
>
> Tottering among them was the rival color bearer, whom the youth saw had been bitten.
>
> But what is to be said of the following bright gems, culled almost at random while turning over these 'irresistible' pages?
>
> Set upon it was the hard and dark lines.
>
> There was no obvious questions, nor figurings, nor diagrams. There was apparently no considered loopholes.
>
> He departed ladened. The youth went with his friend, feeling a desire to throw his heated body onto the stream. Once he found himself almost into a swamp.
>
> The majesty of he who dares give his life.
>
> He could not flee no more than a little finger can commit a revolution from the hand.

Eugene Field [newspaper columnist, translator of Horace, author of "Little Boy Blue"], not long before his death, remarked: "The one crime that cannot be righteously charged against our *fin de siecle* poetasters is slovenliness." Unhappily our *fin de siecle* prose writers are peculiarly susceptible to the charge. Can this general butchery of the language be the nemesis of "dialect literature," which has done so much to bring sensible and intelligible English into ill repute?

—J.L. ONDERDONK, "A Red Badge of
Bad English," *Dial*, May 1, 1896, p. 263

CHARLES DUDLEY WARNER
"EDITOR'S STUDY" (1896)

Charles Dudley Warner was an American essayist and novelist, born of Puritan ancestry, in Plainfield, Massachusetts. He joined the editorial staff of *Harper's Magazine* in 1884.

Although he believes the intensity of color to be overdone in The Red Badge of Courage, he recognizes the work as one of imagination, and a good one at that, but he questions whether it can be called realism.

———————— ———————— ————————

We read of an ethical motive as "a yellow light thrown upon the color of his ambitions"; in the army a soldier is part of "a vast blue demonstration"; we read of "liquid stillness" and "red rage," a "black procession" of oaths, the "red sickness of battle," and so on, and so on. The attempt in the book from which these expressions are taken is to make every page blaze with color, in order to affect the mind through the eye. It is all very interesting. Every page is painted, perhaps I should say saturated, with this intensity of color. Undeniably the reader is strongly affected by it—though the effect is weakened in time. The natural eye cannot stand a constant glare of brilliant light, and the mind soon wearies of the quality that has come to be called "intensity" in literature. Great literature is always calm, and produces its effects by less apparent effort. This is of course a truism, but at the same time the reader does love warmth and color and the occasional show of vivid pictures on the printed page.

The story to which I have referred is in many respects a remarkable one. It is the description of the feeling and experience of a raw soldier lad in a couple of days of battle, and it has gained foreign approval as one of the most real pictures of war ever made, one that could only have been drawn from personal experience. I believe, in fact, that it is purely the work of imagination, and it might not have been written but for Tolstoi's *Sevastopol*. And yet it is quite original in its manner. I have been curious to hear what the "Realists" would say about it. The conversations are plainly vernacular, and there is no attempt to idealize the persons of the vivid drama. There is a studied commonplaceness about the talk and the characters, which seems nature itself. But I have talked with many soldiers of what they actually saw and felt in great battles, and I never got from any of them such a literary appreciation of a battle as this, nothing, in fact, half so interesting. I would not dare to say, from internal evidence, that this young soldier was "not in it," but any man who could see these pictures, have these sensations, and go through this mental and moral struggle in such circumstances ought not to be food for powder. He is needed in the New York drama. I do not wish to be misunderstood. I liked the book very much. I was carried along by its intensity, and felt at the end as if I had experienced a most exciting and melodramic dream, which I could not shake off when waking. I do not know how much of this effect was due to the scheme of color. It is almost a poem—quite, except in form. It is real, in a way. But what worried me was the thought of the verdict of the Realists. Would they not call it lurid realism?

—CHARLES DUDLEY WARNER,
"Editor's Study," *Harper's New
Monthly Magazine,* May 1896, p. 962

UNSIGNED "THE RED BADGE OF COURAGE" (1896)

This unsigned review from the English literary magazine the *Spectator* finds *The Red Badge* "remarkable." It points out that the novel is "an interesting and painful essay in pathology" and compares its effect to the works of Tolstoy and Ambrose Bierce.

The Red Badge of Courage: an Episode of the American War is a remarkable book, and has been received by English reviewers with an unanimity of praise which we are in no wise desirous that its author—a young man, as it is understood—should have been deprived of. But we believe that Mr. Stephen Crane, the author in question, has received his good marks not exactly on right grounds. His episode has been praised as a novel; we are inclined to praise it chiefly as an interesting and painful essay in pathology. The substance and "thesis" of the book, as the serious theatrical reviewers might say, consists in a presentation of the effects of physical danger, in the thousand forms which danger wears in modern warfare, upon the human nervous system. Nor is this all; the nervous system on which Mr. Crane chooses to illustrate his prelection is not a normal organism but an abnormal one,—morbid, hypersensitive, and over-conscious. Mr. Crane notes the effect upon his patient of each day and hour and minute of pained experience with a precision which would do credit to Mr. Lauder Brunton or a brother specialist. We are inclined to believe that his notes are the exact production by an extraordinary memory of moments that have been lived; yet it is believed that Mr. Crane has seen nothing of actual fighting. As an achievement in imagination, in the art of placing one's self in the situation of another—of an exceptional other in exceptional surroundings—Mr. Crane's document can hardly be praised too much. It convinces; one feels that not otherwise than as he describes did such a man fall wounded and another lie in the grasp of corruption. But when we are asked to say that a specialised record of morbid introspection and an exact description of physical horrors is good art we demur; there *is* art in *The Red Badge of Courage*— an infelicitous title by the way—but the general effect which it leaves behind it is not artistic.

But it is time to cease generalising. The scene, to come to detail, is laid in the American Civil War, and the hero is one Harry Fleming, who is spoken of invariably as "The Youth." We may note here an adroitness of Mr. Crane's. A narrative told in the first person must have been a limited affair. The author desires primarily to show us the nervous system under fire. But "The Youth," left to tell his story, could have given us only his own blurred impression of the terrible background of war which Mr. Crane, in the interest of the truth, as he conceives it, desires to present to us. Accordingly, "The Youth's" impressions are given in the third person, and he is presented to us *totus, teres, atque rotundus,* and against the lurid background of his adventures. It is a tactful arrangement. "The Youth" then enlisted in a Northern regiment, and has been some months a soldier when we are introduced to him. He has never met the enemy, and is weary of the tedium which has succeeded the first excitement of leaving home with his regiment. He has had time to fall back on his nerves, and the problem has begun to front him: will he or will he not run away?—

A sufficient time before he would have allowed the problem to kick its heels at the outer portals of his mind, but now he felt compelled to give serious attention to it. A little panic-fear grew in his mind. As his imagination went forward to a fight, he saw hideous possibilities. He contemplated the lurking menaces of the future and failed in an effort to see himself standing stoutly in the midst of them. He recalled his visions of broken-bladed glory, but in the shadow of the impending tumult he suspected them to be impossible pictures.

At last he finds himself face to face with danger, and Mr. Crane's descriptions of approaching conflict are wonderfully right and picturesque:—

The sun spread disclosing rays, and one by one, regiments burst into view like armed men first born of the earth. The youth perceived that the time had come. He was about to be measured. For a moment he felt in the face of his great trial like a babe, and the flesh over his heart seemed very thin. He seized time to look after him calculatingly. But he instantly saw that it would be impossible for him to escape from the regiment. It enclosed him. And there were iron laws of tradition and law on four sides. He was in a moving box.

The recorded sensations which follow in the youth's mind are far too many and too minute to pursue. But there are conspicuous moments which may be given as examples of many. The youth, it should be said, did run away at first, his regiment, it must be understood, retiring in disorder:—

He wondered what they would remark when later he appeared in camp. His mind heard howls of derision. Their density would not enable them to understand his sharper point of view. He began to pity himself acutely. He was ill-used. He was trodden beneath the feet of an iron injustice. He had proceeded with wisdom and from the most righteous motives under Heaven's blue, only to be frustrated by hateful circumstances.

In this key of self-pity and self-defence he stumbled on a dead man:—

> He was being looked at by a dead man, who was seated with his back against a column-like tree. The eyes, staring at the youth, had changed to the dull hue to be seen on the side of a dead fish. The mouth was open. Its red had changed to an appalling yellow. Over the grey skin ran little ants. One was *trundling some sort of a bundle along the upper lip.*

Presently he came on a line of wounded men, the description of whom is the best thing in the book. This encounter was his salvation. He got back with them to the body of the regiment, and the sight of his comrades, notably the heroic death of one of them, made a beginning of the end in his egoism. After a series of endeavours to play the man he succeeded, was the first in a rush by the men of his regiment, and won his way not to glory but to self-respect:—

> He found that he could look back upon the brass and bombast of his earlier gospels and see them truly.
> He was gleeful when he discovered that he now despised them. With this distinction came a store of assurance. He felt a quiet manhood, non-assertive, but of sturdy and strong blood. He knew that he would no more quail before his guides wherever they should point. He had to touch the great death to find that, after all, it was but the great death. He was a man.

A story like this is a mosaic. It is impossible to illustrate its effect by fragments. Tolstoi and another author, whose war stories are too little known, though it seems probable that Mr. Crane knows them—Mr. Ambrose Bierce to wit—have given us the aspect of war as war is seen by ordinary men; and Tolstoi, of course, with the epic touch of a great literary artist. But as a bundle of impressions received by a temperament especially sensitive, *The Red Badge of Courage* is a remarkable performance, and we believe without example.

—Unsigned, "The Red Badge of Courage,"
Spectator, June 27, 1896, p. 924

Unsigned [G.H. Putnam] "Stephen Crane: The English as So-Called Discoverers of His Talent" (1897)

In this interview, the unknown reporter and G.H. Putnam try to explain the timeline of *The Red Badge*'s publication in order to determine ultimately whether English or American critics first embraced the book. Putnam was

the head of the publishing firm that his father, G.P. Putnam, had established.
Here he blames the "slipshod and haphazard" system of book reviewing for
the mix-up over reviews of *The Red Badge*, with some assessments written
immediately and others appearing months after publication of the novel.

"There is a great deal of slipshod and haphazard book reviewing on both
sides of the Atlantic," said Mr. G. Haven Putnam to a reporter for *The New
York Times*. He was speaking of the controversy which from time to time
breaks out in regard to the first recognition of Stephen Crane. Some of the
London reviewers still labor under the hallucination that they "discovered"
Mr. Crane.

"There is no adequate, thorough system of reviewing," said Mr. Putnam, "on
the press of either continent. To prove that assertion I have only to cite the fact
that I have seen an elaborate review of a book eighteen months after the whole
edition was exhausted, and when a review was of no use either to the reading
public or the publishers. An announcement of the appearance of a book a year
and a half after the public have become familiar with it is an absurdity.

"In the case of Mr. Crane, if every leading journal had a system of reviewing
books carefully and thoroughly on their merits, without prejudice as to
nationality or subject, this controversy could have arisen, and 'Trilby' would
not have been neglected in England until after the Americans had taken it up
and given Du Maurier the recognition which his genius deserved.

"It is not stupidity on the part of book critics—it is neglect, lack of system,
with streaks of prejudice and dyspepsia.

"What is wanted is a careful, honest review of a book, or none at all. To
be of value to reading people a review should be timely. It should be made as
promptly on the appearance of a work as possible, but not so promptly that the
critic does not really know whether the work is to be praised or condemned.
Better to have fewer book reviews and have them reliable, authoritative. It ought
to be the ambition of the literary men on the papers to have their criticisms
recognized, to have them serve as a guide to intelligent readers."

D. Appleton & Co., who brought out *The Red Badge of Courage*, have
watched with amusement, if not amazement, the claims of the English
"discoverers" of Mr. Crane. The true and exact history of the publication of
"The Red Badge of Courage" is that it was read and accepted by D. Appleton &
Co. in December, 1894, almost a year before the book was printed. It was the
intention then to publish the volume immediately, but Mr. Crane was absent
from the city and could not be reached conveniently when the proofs were
ready, and the work was, as a consequence, delayed. The electrotype plates

were all made in the Spring of 1895, but as it was deemed inadvisable to put the book on the market at that time of year, the publication was deferred until Autumn. The book was brought out on the 1st of October in this country. Although the work was copyrighted abroad at the same time, it did not appear and was not reviewed in Europe until nearly two months afterward. The first edition was entirely exhausted in the United States and a second one was on the market before the book was published in London. The American journals began reviewing it and praising it in October, fully sixty days before there was anything seen of it in England. On Oct. 19, 1895, *The New York Times* devoted a column and a half to a review of the work, pronouncing it "a remarkable book." The book was commanding attention from one end of the United States to the other when the Englishmen first heard of it.

By the end of November the American reviewers from Maine to California had greeted the new book and the new author, bestowing high encomiums on them. Then the book made its appearance in England and began slowly to make its way there. There were some favorable notices at the first, but generally given in a grudging spirit. The London Academy is surely accepted as an authority on literary matters in that part of the world, and here is what that publication said on the 15th of February, 1896. Mark the date, for it goes far to settle in a single paragraph the absurd claim that the English reviewers first took up the young American author. Feb. 15 would be three months after the principal review of the book appeared in *The New York Times*, and three and a half months after the volume was generally on the market. Here is the language of the *Academy*.

> "Another American book is *The Red Badge of Courage*, being an episode of the civil war. The author, in quaint, bantering style, describes some military operations and presents us with a running analysis of a young soldier's varying emotions during the course of the campaign. It must be confessed that the narrative soon becomes tiresome. A serio-comic effect seems to be intended throughout, and Mr. Crane is no doubt highly gifted with that grotesqueness of fancy which is peculiarly a transatlantic production; but the humor is scarcely of a sort to be appreciated by readers on this side, and not a few of them will lay the book down before getting half way through."

Nor is this the worst of it. The book actually secured quite a run in the English market in December, particularly around the holidays, without much stimulus from the reviewers. The reading people found that it suited their taste and did not wait to be told by the critics whether to read the book or not. In view of this fact and such friendly notices as were given, more or less perfunctorily, what backwardness the London *Academy* shows in the recognition of American genius when it publishes such an unjustified slap at Mr. Crane as late as Feb. 15, 1896! The same publication has since eulogized *The Red Badge of Courage*, and no doubt today is among those journals on the other side of the ocean which flatter themselves that they "discovered" Mr. Crane.

—Unsigned [G.H. Putnam], "Stephen Crane:
The English as So-Called Discoverers of His
Talent," *The New York Times*, April 3, 1897, p. BR4

John W. DeForest "Authors at Home: J. W. DeForest in New Haven" (1898)

John W. DeForest was a novelist and a Civil War veteran. He is perhaps best known for his novel of the war, *Miss Ravenel's Conversion from Secession to Loyalty* (1867), which was considered by some to be too realistic in its portrayal of the conflict's blood and violence and denounced by others as having too much romanticism. Stephen Crane had almost certainly read the book.

John W. DeForest says in this interview: "You have read Stephen Crane's 'Red Badge of Courage'? It seems to me to be a really clever book, with a good deal of really first class work in it. His battle scenes are excellent, though I never saw a battery that could charge at full speed across a meadow. His style is short, sharp, jerky; a style that never would have been tolerated in my day. How different it is from the pure, swinging style of Irving, from Holland, from Mrs. Stowe!"

—John W. DeForest, "Authors at Home:
J. W. DeForest in New Haven," *The New York
Times*, December 17, 1898, p. BR856

Unsigned "Stephen Crane's Master Work" (1900)

The writer of the following article, which appeared a few weeks after Stephen Crane's death, credits *The New York Times* with bringing *The Red*

Badge to the attention of the public and alludes to the English claim of "discovering" the work. It also announces a new edition of the novel.

———·ᔕᔕ·— —·ᔕᔕ·— —·ᔕᔕ·—

The new edition of the late Stephen Crane's remarkable imaginative work, *The Red Badge of Courage*, contains a good portrait of the author and a preface by Ripley Hitchcock, who stood sponsor to this "episode of the American civil war" when it was first given to the world in book form. Mr. Hitchcock now tells about the origin of the book:

It was in December, 1894, that Mr. Crane was asked if he had a story long enough for publication in book form. He replied hesitatingly that he had written one rather long story, which was appearing in a Philadelphia newspaper, and "some of the boys in the office seemed to like." He was asked to send the story at once and presently there appeared a package of newspaper cuttings containing "The Red Badge of Courage," which was promptly accepted for publication. Owing to Mr. Crane's absence in the South and West, where he acted as correspondent for a newspaper syndicate, there was delay in the proof reading, and the book was not issued until the Autumn of 1895. It differed from the newspaper publication in containing much matter which had been cut out to meet journalistic requirements.

Crane had studied some books on the civil war and had in mind the Battle of Chancellorsville. He found he could not gain much insight from talks with veterans. Mr. Hitchcock dwells admiringly upon the power of the young author's imagination, shown "in the analysis of a young recruit's soul, which is as vivid and clear as the finest anatomical dissection and yet distinct with life and palpitating with emotion." He finds points of coincidence between the attitude of Tolstoi in "War and Peace" and the attitude of Crane in this story. He tells well the brief tale of Crane's life and death and the work he did.

In this newspaper *The Red Badge of Courage* was first reviewed Oct. 19, 1895, from an "advance copy" of the story. We believe this was the first long notice of the work printed. All the merits of the narrative were extolled and stress was laid on the fact that, although the author was a youth who had never seen war, the story struck the reader as "a statement of facts by a veteran." The vigor, directness, emotional force, and great imaginative power of the book were cordially praised. A long while afterward somebody in England "discovered" the story. It reads as well as ever, now. It has not grown old. It is a book that will not soon be forgotten.

—UNSIGNED, "Stephen Crane's Master Work,"
The New York Times, July 14, 1900, p. BR4

GEORGE'S MOTHER

FRANK RINDER (1896)

In this review in the English periodical *Academy*, Frank Rinder, an artist, illustrator, and critic, points out the sensitive portrait of the title character, George's mother, but he finds the portrayal of George somewhat unbelievable.

———— ———— ————

George's Mother, despite certain marked defects, is a strong study of life among the poor of an American city. Every line in the drawing of Mrs. Kelcey's character is carefully thought out, each serves to intensify the vivid impression which we gain of her. The picture of this lone woman, who worships her son as only a mother can—who, in the evening, watches for his return from work with all the keen expectancy of a sweetheart; who is quietly content even when George is surly or silent; who anticipates the time when her son shall become "a white and looming king among men"; whose whole life is sacrificed to his well-being, and who dies believing in him against the evidence of her own senses—is invested with all the pathos of real life. George is less satisfactorily portrayed. It is hard to think of him as one who dreamed "of the indefinite woman and the fragrance of roses that came from her hair," "of the chariot of pink clouds coming for him." In several places the author permits his ready pen to run away with him, notably in the scene where the temporarily penitent George accompanies his mother to a prayer-meeting. In the circumstances, surely it is too much to say that, because the old lady insisted on marching slowly up the aisle to a foremost place, "he felt he could have assassinated her," and "his hands were to him like monstrous swollen hides."

—FRANK RINDER, *Academy,* July 25, 1896, p. 64

HARRY T. PECK (1896)

Contrary to his positive assessment of Crane in 1895, here Harry Thurston Peck finds little to commend in *George's Mother*.

———— ———— ————

This is sorry stuff. Even if it were well done, it is not worth the doing; and it is not well done. There is absolutely no reason why it should have been done at all. The whole thing is simply an incoherent fragment, told with no purpose and fraught with no interest. Who cares about what George said to the bartender or what the bartender said to George? There is no meaning to any of it. Someone will say that it is a bit of intense realism; but that is just what it isn't. Anyone can hang around a bar-room and jot down the conversation and also print it, but his is not realism. Literary realism would perhaps take such wretched material as this for its own purposes, but it would use it with some insight, some psychology, some grasp upon the essential meaning of it all. We are not going to object to the narrative of a squalid debauch, but we do assert that if a writer forces it upon our notice, he shall justify himself by limning it with some power and artistic sense, as Zola drew, in *L'Assommoir*, that Rabelaisian revel at which Coupeau and Lantier met and opened up the way for the final *debacle*. Rhyparography is the lowest form of art, but at least it should be good of its kind. Mr. Crane's rhyparograplhy is in this book incongruous, formless, and deadly dull.

The book is a small one, yet its publication seems to us to involve a principle. When an English author by any chance attains a sudden and definite success, he is always extremely solicitous that his earlier and imperfect books should not be dragged out and thrust upon the public in a violent effort to take advantage of his "boom." He rather suppresses them altogether, as Anthony Hope has tried to do with some of his early stories, or at least he rewrites them, as Thomas Hardy rewrote *Desperate Remedies*. And he does this partly out of regard to his own literary reputation, and partly from an honourable feeling of what is due to the public that admires him. We commend this precedent to Mr. Crane, and beg to suggest that an author who within a single year has forced critics to compare his work with that of the greatest living realists, ought not, as a mere matter of self-respect, to rake over his literary ash barrel and ask us to accept his old bones and junk as virgin gold.

—HARRY T. PECK, *Bookman*,
July 1896, pp. 446–447

JOHN D. BARRY "A REASSESSMENT" (1896)

John D. Barry, a painter and literary critic in San Francisco, finds much to praise in *George's Mother*, so much that he finds the book "teeming with life."

When I told a friend that I was going to write an article on *George's Mother*, he said, contemptuously, "Why, that was *dead* long ago." Well, perhaps it was, if anything may be said to be dead that had hardly any life, for as soon as the book appeared a battalion of enraged reviewers fell upon it, hacked it and then turned exultingly away from the remains with the self-congratulatory manner of people who have done a good work. But isn't there some animal that has a way of pretending to be dead and then springing up full of energy? I have a feeling that *George's Mother* is like that animal.

I couldn't read *The Red Badge of Courage*. I suspect that there are others— but I'll let that pass. So when *George's Mother* first appeared I didn't take the trouble to find what it was like. Then, when I saw the first of the reviews to deal the book a sharp cut, I felt pleased with myself. That review gave a quotation from the story that seemed to me vulgar and commonplace. When, the other day, by the merest chance, the book came in my way and I read it, because there happened to be nothing else at hand to read, I saw why the reviewer had chosen that quotation. It was the only detachable bit that could misrepresent the story as he wanted to misrepresent it. Out of the context it had no meaning; in its place it was the keystone of the whole structure. But the reviewer didn't speak of that; he had a point to make.

The first chapter of *George's Mother* seemed to me just gratuitously low. When I had finished the last I know what the first chapter meant, and I changed my mind. In other words, the construction of the story is absolutely logical. Taken as a whole, there is nothing insignificant, nothing that does not make for the completeness of the picture, for the consummation of the ghastly tragedy. Then the truth of it, the nice observation and the exquisite humors revealing itself in a thousand little touches, so that you read slowly, not skipping a words, and, greatest of all, the awful pathos of it that makes you every now and then hurriedly lay the book down and sit perfectly still for a while!

Yet this is the book, teeming with life, that is said to be dead. This is the book that raised a howl of rage and disgust from earnest reviewers who are supposed to encourage literature. For many reasons I feel profoundly grateful for it—not to the author, however, for a more *impersonal* story has never existed; if you think of him at all, it is only as the agent through which tremendous forces in nature have been marshaled and expressed. One of these reasons is that it has formulated to myself the justification of the use in literature of utterly squalid material. I can imagine Mr. Crane's theme treated in a way that would make it the really debasing thing the reviewers have called *George's Mother*. But Mr. Crane's book is its own justification; it teaches us what the lesson of the life it depicts would teach us if we were to know it at first hand, the dreadful pity of it. I don't see how any one could resent or blame the characters in *George's Mother*; given the conditions surrounding them, and they had to be what they were. In this lies the whole pathos of all human life!

The mystery of the treatment which *George's Mother* has received bewilders me when I think of the intense humanity of the story. It is the most heart-rending picture of mother-love that I have ever seen in literature, and mother-love is a theme that ought to touch even critics. Yet the book is not for one instant either mawkish or morbid! How exquisitely humorous is the sketch of that fierce little mother doing battle with her household gods before her boy's return from work, pausing for rest, and then going wildly into the fray again. And how fine is the picture of the great Youngman at the little table at home leaning back in his chair "in the manner of the man who is paying for things," while the eager little mother "perched on the edge of her chair, ready to spring to her feet and run to the closet or the stove for anything he might need." The description of their going to meeting together is a unique example of impressionism in literature, as wonderful as a picture by Claude Monet. For the matter of that the whole book is the work of a master of literary impressionism.

Whatever Mr. Crane may be in *The Red Badge of Courage*, he is not a realist in *George's Mother*. The little mother is real, but the son stands for a class, not an individual. Mr. Crane's conversation I don't believe in for a moment, nor do I believe that life is exactly as he depicts it, any more than I think the pictures of the impressionists are like the life they see. But the impressionists think they see what they describe, and that is enough. In *George's Mother* Mr. Crane has written a great book, and I shall be amazed if it does not have a revival.

—JOHN D. BARRY, "A Reassessment,"
Daily Tatler, November 1896, pp. 6–7

THE LITTLE REGIMENT

GEORGE PARSONS LATHROP (1896)

George Parsons Lathrop was an associate editor of the *Atlantic Monthly* from 1875 to 1877. The husband of Nathaniel Hawthorne's daughter, he published a study of Hawthorne in 1876 and edited an edition of his works in 1883–84. He finds *The Little Regiment* inferior to *The Red Badge*.

In speaking of *The Little Regiment*, by Stephen Crane, as a companion volume to *The Red Badge of Courage*, and as a completion of the story of the *Red Badge's* hero, Messrs. D. Appleton & Co. lead us to think that the new book is a single tale, whereas it is a collection of sketches, some or all of which have previously been printed. After the first flush of disappointment, however, we enjoy reading, or perhaps it is rereading, these sketches, for do we not know that they will send gorgeous blue thrills of red patriotism down our spine?

A certain nine-year-old devotee of Cooper's tales always reads them with a band of turkey quills tied around his curly head—"to get the spirit of it," he explains. And so the reader of Stephen Crane's war stories should wear a tattered, gory, mud-bespattered, blue uniform for the same laudable purpose.

There are three Stephen Cranes—the one who is advertised by his loving friends; the one who is reviled by his adverse critics, and the man he really is. The last we may only know from the things he really says. Aside from and beneath his bizarre color-schemes, his profanity and bad English, and his magnificent collection of adjectives, there is a marvelous fount of originality, a great and daring imagination, and a power of forcible, graphic description.

Added to these is a decided talent for exaggeration, which is perhaps the keynote of his popularity. But "nothing is reprehensible if you're clever at it," and clever at his exaggerations Mr. Crane certainly is. It goes without saying that these war stories cannot compare with *The Red Badge* in merit. Mr. Crane's bright sayings are decidedly of the note-book order, and no note-book, however fat, could stand such repeated drafts upon it. And though in the new volume the diction is improved, and the profanity modified, yet we find the same springy turfs and rolling mists and long wavering lines of soldier; and the human emotions are painted with the same splashes of pure color till we long for the yellow and green plaid laugh, or a black and red striped oath, and are relieved when a few mountains turn up that are even to Mr. Crane *inexpressibly* blue. Especially in these stories is the phrase "eyes like two points of metal" horribly overworked.

The stories in *The Little Regiment*, read at a sitting and viewed as a whole, leave on the mind the same impression as an exhibition of Pain's fireworks—noise, color, and fire. But, read separately and taken seriously, we find real types and typical realities, and there are well worked up bits of human nature that show appreciative insight and sympathetic intuition.

—George Parsons Lathrop,
Daily Tatler, November 9, 1896, p. 5

Unsigned (1897)

This English reviewer of *The Little Regiment* finds it equal to *The Red Badge*; he points out that Stephen Crane proves his mastery of the short story with this collection.

Mr. Crane has attempted the bold and dangerous task of writing two books on exactly the same subject, from exactly the same standpoint, and making use of exactly the same background. This has proved a stumbling-block to many more experienced authors, and it is high praise to say that *The Little Regiment*, in every way a companion volume to *The Red Badge of Courage*, is not one whit behind it in power or picturesqueness. It is true that war is a far-reaching, inexhaustible subject, but Mr. Crane does not content himself with bird's-eye views of the battlefield. He takes his stand with the rank and file of the army, with the men who fight wherever their feet are planted until more orders come, knowing absolutely nothing of the general significance of their actions. The awful monotony of his pictures is almost depressing: there is no room for variety of any kind.

The present volume is made up of six episodes. The story entitled "The Little Regiment" stands out from the others as the most finished, the most complete piece of work Mr. Crane has given us. It is a short sketch, but brimful of the grim reality of war. Although individuals seem almost insignificant in such a picture, each man is perfectly realized. Dan and Billie live before our eyes, and we feel sure we should recognize "the man who sat on the horse-hair trunk" among a thousand. As a word painting "The Little Regiment" is truly wonderful. In every sentence we can hear, even more clearly than in *The Red Badge of Courage*, the panther-like screaming, the witches' crooning of the shells, the cracking of the skirmishers, the spattering and zipping of the bullets, while through all these pulsates the fierce elation of the men amid the horrors. Great dashes of crimson and blobs of blue break occasionally through the dim and mystic clouds of grey mist, and the whole demoniacal howling of the battle quivers in our brain for hours.

Mr. Crane relies for his effects on daring and original colour similes. He is a word artist of infinite resource, and for everything he invents a special hue. The sense of smell which plays such a prominent part in Zola's *Débacle* is conspicuous by its absences. We certainly miss the *odeur de la guerre*.

Mr. Crane's peculiar genius is admirable adapted to the exigencies of the short story. He writes at such fever heat, and puts so much of the rush and turmoil of battle into his short, quivering sentences, that a long-continued story like *The Red Badge of Courage* comes as a strain to the mind of the average reader, who closes the book with a genuine sigh of relief. In these episodes the pace is faster, the intensity more striking than ever; but the pauses between the stories give time for breathing. Compared with "The Little Regiment," the other episodes are sketchy and less compact. "An Indiana Campaign" is a pleasant piece of comedy, which comes as a relief amid the all-pervading gloom; but Mr. Crane lacks the necessary lightness of touch. "The

Veteran," the story of an old man who meets his death in the flames while trying to rescue some colts, is a trifle theatrical and commonplace. A woman figures in "Three Miraculous Soldiers" and "A Grey Sleeve," but she seems out of her element and only half realized. "A Mystery of Heroism," a new version of an episode in the Cave of Adullam, and a splendid psychological revelation of the feelings of a desperado, is, in its way, as perfect a piece of work as "The Little Regiment," though the tone is quieter and more subdued.

—UNSIGNED, *Academy*,
February 20, 1897, pp. 231–232

UNSIGNED "STORIES OF AMERICA, BY YOUNG AMERICANS" (1897)

Despite quibbling about the effects Stephen Crane may have sometimes carried too far, this reviewer finds much power in the stories in *The Little Regiment*, especially the story "The Veteran."

The six short stories which Mr. Crane has printed under the title of *The Little Regiment* seem to have been produced in response to the public demand, familiar enough nowadays, that a writer who has done a striking thing once should promptly proceed to do it over again. These war stories are without exception variations upon the underlying motive of *The Red Badge of Courage*, namely, a study of the human animal under the stress of unreasoning terror. The people who were troubled by the grammar of *The Red Badge* and by some of its structural defects, will find less fault with these short sketches. They exhibit the same wayward experiments in color, sometimes extraordinarily successful, but often spoiled by effectivism and overloading of the brush. They have the same Maeterlinckian vagueness of outline and trick of imparting to every inanimate object a grotesque and sinister significance. The close of each story in *The Little Regiment*, however, is a clever attempt to redeem the fundamental cynicism of the author's point of view, and the impression made by the volume as a whole, when compared with his earlier book about war and warriors, is distinctly less depressing.

The power of Mr. Crane's art is undeniable. His method is frankly individualistic. He ignores literary conventions and escapes the commonplace. His impressions are rendered with a vividness and nervous energy that compel attention, as is evidenced by the recognition which his work has already received. Whether his war stories have the characteristics that will enable the normally minded lover of literature to turn to them again and again, for their permanent pleasure-giving quality, is quite another matter. They are seriously handicapped by morbid psychology and by mannerisms. Interesting as is the color-notation, for instance, it is frequently obtruded upon the reader at the very moment when his attention should be engrossed with the personages or the action of the story. A sympathetic spectator of the struggle would not notice—nor wish to notice—many of the nuances of atmospheric effect to which Mr. Crane invites his scrutiny, and it is sometimes difficult to resist the conclusion that the author himself did not at bottom care so much for the essentials as for the picturesque accidents of the tale. He takes great risks, likewise, as every impressionist must, in his phraseology. When we are told that a wounded horse is "turning its nose with a mystic and profound eloquence towards the sky," or that another horse "with his great mystically solemn eyes looked around the corner of his shoulder at the girl," or that "the feedbox was a mystic and terrible machine," the entire effect depends upon one's mood at the moment. If he is under sufficient emotional excitation, he is ready to believe that anything or everything is "mystic" when he is told so, but there is always a chance that some one may laugh or that the showman himself may wink. In either case the exhibition suffers. Again, Mr. Crane's favorite motive, the mania of terror, precludes him from characterizing his personages. "The tall soldier" or "the other soldier" is indeed characterization enough, if abject fear or emotional insanity is a moment later to obliterate the human traits of these men. In "The Veteran," the finest story in the volume, we are informed that at the alarm of fire the old man's face "ceased instantly to be a face; it became a mask, *a gray thing*, with horror written about the mouth and eyes." We get a striking phrase, but it dehumanizes the hero. In "A Gray Sleeve" "the troopers threw themselves upon the grove like wolves upon a great animal." In a night skirmish between two bodies of troops, in another story, "it seemed as if two gigantic animals were engaged in a mad floundering encounter, snarling, howling, in a whirling chaos of noise and motion." All this is singularly graphic, but the truth is that most readers approach the depiction of war with prepossessions in favor of the distinctively human traits of loyalty, faith, deliberate self-sacrifice, cool-headed heroism. Literature has doubtless done something to encourage them in this prejudice. "A soldier's a man," sings poor drunken Cassio; and certainly this view of the case, whether right or wrong, affords more attractive literary material than does the theory that a soldier is an animal, with predisposition to phobomania.

—Unsigned, "Stories of America,
by Young Americans," *Book Buyer*,
January 1897, pp. 983–984

THE THIRD VIOLET

Unsigned "New American Fiction: Characteristic Books by W.D. Howells, Stephen Crane, Frank R. Stockton, and Others" (1897)

This reviewer likes little about *The Third Violet* except for the dog and "one or two touches of nature."

There is a good dog, too, in Stephen Crane's new story, a large orange and white setter, whose geniality and constancy almost reconcile one to Mr. Crane's manner of telling a story. For Mr. Crane is no longer fighting over again old battles. He has made a study of the common life of people in his own sphere.

A young man who has acquired some sort of reputation as an artist in New York goes home to the farm in Sullivan County for a Summer visit. Upon his refined nature the voices and manners of the folds at home jar as much as they do upon the refined nature of the reader. There is a Summer hotel in the neighborhood, and the artist falls in love with a nice girl who is staying there. He cannot understand her nature or translate her moods. He is dull and uncomfortable in her company. His ignorance of her feelings continues almost to the end, when she promises to marry him. There are married women and girls at the hotel who are deeply interested in the progress of the courtship. There is a writer of fiction who helps his friend, the artist, all he can. There is a small, bad boy who intends to be a full-back at Yale in 1907.

The mother and sisters of the artist are jealous of the nice girl. The dilapidated father is silently sympathetic. In the grimy Bohemia near his New York studio there is a model named Florinda (so she says) who is very sorry when she learns that Hawker is smitten; but she will not kill herself, or even lose her appetite.

In other words, Mr. Crane deliberately tells a story that is no story at all. His object is, seemingly, to paint humanity just as it is. But he stops at the surface. The ungrammatical, elliptical speck; the dialect of everybody; the littleness and dryness of it all are unquestionably true. People do use bad English and express their thoughts badly. Life is, on the whole, prosy and humdrum and ugly. But why dwell on it? If it were not for the dog and one or two touches of nature in which the sympathy of the poet is betrayed, we should not like *The Third Violet* at all.

—UNSIGNED, "New American Fiction:
Characteristic Books by W.D. Howells,
Stephen Crane, Frank R. Stockton, and Others,"
The New York Times, May 22, 1897, p. BR4

UNSIGNED (1897)

This review in an English magazine found positive aspects in *The Third Violet,* which was largely neglected by critics. It points out a "vividness of portraiture" that other reviewers did not see and detects in the work something of the style of Henry James.

As we began to read Mr. S. Crane's novel *The Third Violet* we thought it was outside the list of his works of genius, and an attempt at a new departure into which less brain-power had been put. It makes little demand upon the reader, and flows almost as smoothly as the "Dolly Dialogues." But before the middle of this American love story was reached we found reason to change our view, and to recognize a vividness of portraiture which puts *The Third Violet* on a high level—higher, we think, than Mr. Crane's very different *Maggie*, though perhaps lower than *The Little Regiment*, which is also very different. In his present book Mr. Crane is more the rival of Mr. Henry James than of Mr. Rudyard Kipling. But he is intensely American, which can hardly be said of Mr. Henry James, and it is possible that if he continues in his present line of writing he may be the author who will introduce the United States to the ordinary English world. We have never come across a book that brought certain sections of American society so perfectly before the reader as does *The Third Violet*, which introduces us to a farming family, the boarders at a summer hotel, and to the young artists of New York. The picture is an extremely pleasant one, and its truth appeals to the English reader, so that the effect of the book is to draw him nearer to his American cousins. *The Third Violet* incidentally contains the best dog that we have come across in modern fiction. Mr. Crane's dialogue is excellent, and it is dialogue of a type for which neither *The Red Badge of Courage* nor his later books had prepared us. For example, a reference to China, before an artist hero, produces the reflection: "There are innumerable tobacco jars in China. . . . Moreover, there is no perspective. You don't have to walk two miles to see a friend." Some understanding will really have to be come to between us and the Americans, and our colonists in Australia and elsewhere, as to the English language. If they are going to produce writers who are so certain to be read throughout the English world as Mr. Stephen Crane, our people will have to learn the meaning of many American phrases. There are passages in the present book which will be spoilt for many English readers by the fact that they may be unaware that, across the Atlantic, "bug" means a flying insect. "Snickered" we suppose means *sniggered*. "So long" of course we know to be a salutation on departure; but in England that fact is not generally understood, though it is known in parts and among certain classes. There is one phrase which, with all our admiration for Mr. Crane, we find simply horrible: "mucilaged to their seats," for *glued*.

—UNSIGNED, *Athenaeum*, May 22, 1897, p. 678

UNSIGNED (1897)

The ongoing rivalry between English and American critics is obvious in the following American review of *The Third Violet*.

The only writers whom English critics seem to consider typically American, are Mrs. Gertrude Atherton and Mr. Stephen Crane. No American who has any respect for his country's literature can read with patience the praise bestowed by certain English papers—*The Athenaeum* and *The Academy* among others—on Mr. Crane's latest story, *The Third Violet*. I think that these papers take delight in picking out our most commonplace, vulgar books to praise for their "Americanism." They call them "racy," and say they are the sort of books American authors should write, instead of those that show cultivation and a decent regard for grammar. What have such barbarians as we to do with "literature." Let us describe American life as the English believe it to be—then they will applaud. They would praise cowboy poets, they abuse Mr. Lowell (as *The Athenaeum* did recently), and they would no doubt pat us on the back for Blind Tom, while they would let Mr. MacDowell's musical genius go unnoticed. In other words, they only care for things American when they are "freakish." No one can accuse me of Anglophobia, but I must admit that I lose patience when I see such a book as Mr. Crane's *Third Violet* singled out for unqualified praise in England. That book is called there a genuine American product, but *The Scarlet Letter*, *The Sketch Book*, *The Conduct of Life*, *Hiawatha*, *The Biglow Papers*, *The Luck of Roaring Camp*, etc.—these are English!

—UNSIGNED, "On the British Reception,"
Critic, June 1897, p. 444

HARRISON S. MORRIS
"WITH THE NEW BOOKS" (1897)

Harrison Smith Morris, a poet, novelist, and essayist, was managing director of the Philadelphia Academy of the Fine Arts, editor of *Lippincott's Magazine*, and art editor of *Ladies' Home Journal*.

Conceived in the style of Maeterlinck and brought forth in the way of Ibsen, the tales of Stephen Crane are teeming with modernity. They are undigested, ungrammatical, slangy, boyish, and yet they rise often into the loftier simplicity of literature. *The Third Violet* is a story as abrupt in form as the *Sentimental Journey*, but there the analogy disappears. Were it told in straightforward chapters, each blending with the next, it is doubtful if it would arrest a reader. Even the dash of Bohemia in the metropolis is tame beside the reality, and here we should have fancied Mr. Crane to be strong and picturesque. His vein is naturally an heroic one. He needs the tragic background of war or peril. In "The Open Boat," which has just appeared in *Scribner's Magazine*, he surpasses himself in his achievements as well as in defects. In *The Third Violet* his theme is the flirtation of a hotel porch, terminating in the capture of an heiress. Imagine the panting sentences of *The Red Badge of Courage*, thus degraded, and you have the result.

—HARRISON S. MORRIS, "With the
New Books," *Book News*, July 15, 1897, p. 562

THE OPEN BOAT AND OTHER TALES OF ADVENTURE

JOSEPH CONRAD (1897)

In this letter to Stephen Crane, Conrad praises the art of Crane's short story "A Man and Some Others," which appears in *The Open Boat and Other Tales of Adventure*.

But *my* great excitement was reading your stories. Garnett's right. "A Man and Some Others" is immense. I can't spin a long yarn about it but I admire it without reserve. It is an amazing bit of biography. I am envious of you—horribly. Confound you—you fill the blamed landscape—you—by all the devils—fill the seascape. The boat thing is immensely interesting. I don't use the word in its common sense. It is fundamentally interesting to me. Your temperament makes old things new and new things amazing. I want to swear at you, to bless you—perhaps to shoot you—but I prefer to be your friend.

You are an everlasting surprise to one. You shock—and the next moment you give the perfect artistic satisfaction. Your method is fascinating. You are a complete impressionist. The illusions of life come out of your hand without a flaw. It is not life—which nobody wants—it is art—art for which everyone—the abject and the great—hanker—mostly without knowing it.

—Joseph Conrad, letter to
Stephen Crane, December 1, 1897

Joseph Conrad (1897)

In this correspondence, Conrad writes directly to Edward Garnett about "A Man and Some Others" and "The Open Boat."

I had Crane here last Sunday. We talked and smoked half the night. He is strangely hopeless about himself. I like him. The two stories are excellent. Of course, "A Man and Some Others" is the best of the two but the boat thing interested me more. His eye is very individual and his expression satisfies me artistically. He certainly is *the* impressionist and his temperament is curiously unique. His thought is concise, connected, never very deep—yet often startling. He is *the only* impressionist and *only* an impressionist. Why is he not immensely popular? With his strength, with his rapidity of action, with that amazing faculty of vision—why is he not? He has outline, he has colour, he has movement, with that he ought to go very far. But—will he? I sometimes think he won't. It is not an opinion—it is a feeling. I could not explain why he disappoints me—why my enthusiasm withers as soon as I close the book. While one reads, of course he is not to be questioned. He is the master of his reader to the very last line—then—apparently for no reason at all—he seems to let go his hold. It is as if he had gripped you with greased fingers. His grip is strong but while you feel the pressure on your flesh you slip out from his hand— much to your own surprise. This is my stupid impression and I give it to you in confidence. It just occurs to me that it is perhaps my own self that is slippery. I don't know. You would know. No matter.

—Joseph Conrad, letter to
Edward Garnett, December 5, 1897

Harold Frederic "London on the War" (1898)

Harold Frederic praises "The Open Boat" in his column in *The New York Times.*

The most important literary event of these last few days has been the issue of Stephen Crane's new book, of which the title story, "The Story of the Open Boat," would, even if he had written nothing else, have placed him where he now undoubtedly stands. The heart of a nation of sailors goes out to him who spelled at the oar with the oiler, while even the most microscopic critic can find no wasted stroke of the pen in his pages. The genius of this young son of America is being keenly felt here, and there is a quickening touch in this volume of stories which will put a new face on British appreciation, though the average indolent reviewer has been too staggered by their form to be able to see the true inwardness of his poems, for the British critic, with all his good qualities, is at heart a literary Tory and somewhat cramped by the iron rules of precedent. Just as it has been candidly said of the present Poet Laureate that he is too facile a maker of rhymes ever to be a poet, so it is true of Stephen Crane that he is too real a poet to be a rhymester. No living English prose writer of his years approaches his wonderful gift of original and penetrating observation, while no writer of English is today prouder of being an American. Possibly this steady, unswerving loyalty to his native land has helped to make him so many friends among Englishmen, ho, even when men of letters, are sportsmen enough to like that man who stands up for his own regiment. Maybe Crane little knows himself what a powerful factor he has been of late in drawing England Westward.

—HAROLD FREDERIC, "London on the War,"
The New York Times, May 1, 1898, p. 19

Unsigned "Review of Books" (1898)

This review praises "The Open Boat" and finds vigor in the collection overall.

Four men in a boat. That is all. But the conditions? What are they? Concentrated in that frail dinghy are all human agonies. At the mercy of the waves are four men, the Captain, the cook, the oiler and the correspondent. The boat, no longer than a bathtub, is at the mercy of the raging sea, and that craft "pranced and reared and plunged like an animal, " and at each moment during the raging storm every man, Captain, cook, oiler, correspondent, thought his last moment had come. The cook bailed, the Captain gave his orders, and they all fought it out manfully during that terrible night. And now they neared the shore, and there was again the certainty of death, because of the surges. Then, finally, when at their last gasp, they were saved. That is all, but told in such a dramatic way that the reader takes his place in the dinghy and battles with death, and has his heart in his mouth, and when, finally, the rescue comes he feels so sorry for his poor comrade, the oiler, who floats, dead, in the shallow water. It is a story to be simply styled "immense," one that bites right into your soul, for you will not forget it, and Mr. Stephen Crane never wrote a stronger or more impressive story. It is a bit of plain English, for be it said to his praise, the author of *The Red Badge of Courage* uses no dialect, and for that, too, we are grateful. The little touches of nature are even pathetic. The men are starving, for so suddenly had they abandoned their sinking ship that they have no morsel of food. "Billie," said the cook, murmuring dreamfully, "what kind of pie do you like best?" "Pie!" said the oiler and the correspondent, "Don't talk about those things, blast you!" "Well," said the cook, "I was just thinking about ham sandwiches, but—"

The story called "Flanagan," descriptive of a filibustering expedition, is opportune, if it be nothing else, but it has, too, its distinguishing merit. Flanagan took the position of Captain of that leaky old craft the Foundling simply for the "fun of it," but nobly, heroically, did he carry out his duty, and when his poor, limp body floated ashore it was that of a man whose "calm face" was of "an Irish type." "The Bride Comes to Yellow Sky" has its peculiarities. The groomsman, Sheriff Potter, would have been wiped out had it not been for the bride, who hung so awkwardly on her husband's arm. That uncommon ruffian "Scratchy" Wilson, would have killed the Sheriff on sight if not for the fact that he was loath to disturb a honeymoon. In the eight stories in this little volume there is shown an amazing amount of vigor, with that peculiarity of touch which is singular to Mr. Stephen Crane.

—UNSIGNED, "Review of Books,"
The New York Times, May 7, 1898, p. RBA308

WILLIAM L. ALDEN
"LONDON LITERARY LETTER" (1898)

William L. Alden had praised *The Red Badge of Courage* and panned *Active Service*; in this review, he finds *The Open Boat and Other Tales of Adventure* to be more akin to the former work.

It is true, however, that there are some authors to whom war is a benefit. Mr. Stephen Crane is one of these. When men's thoughts are of battle by sea and land Mr. Crane, with his marvelous kinemetascope, brings the terrible scenes visibly before them. I have not the slightest doubt that hundreds of people have read his *Red Badge of Courage* since the war broke out who would not have thought of reading it in time of peace. His reputation as a painter of battle pieces will unquestionably secure a good sale for his new book, *The Open Boat*. It has been received by the London press with unanimous approval. Those of his books which have appeared since the *Red Badge of Courage* have been disappointing to his admirers, at any rate to those on this side of the Atlantic, but the "Open Boat" shows him at his best, and, in spite of certain trifling defects which will disappear when Mr. Crane is older, there is no one who can touch him at his best. I remember how the *Red Badge of Courage* came to me like a revelation. I have never lost my enthusiasm for it, nor my belief that Mr. Crane is destined to do great things.

—WILLIAM L. ALDEN, "London
Literary Letter," *The New York Times*,
June 4, 1898, p. BR368

UNSIGNED "RECENT SHORT STORIES" (1898)

This glowing review from the English magazine finds the stories in *The Open Boat* even better than Crane's previous work.

Mr. Stephen Crane grows, and this is no small thing to say of a writer who sprang full-armed on the public with his first book. When it transpired that *The Red Badge of Courage* was the work of a mere boy, that it was the result of intuition, not experience, one felt misgivings whether the experience when it came would not blur the visions which came unsought into the crystal mirror of Mr. Crane's imagination. His new volume, *The Open Boat,* based in regard to the story which gives its name to the collection on Mr. Crane's escape from the steamer *Commodore,* conclusively dispels this anxiety. Mr. Crane has never done anything finer than this truly wonderful picture of four men battling for their lives in a cockleshell off the coast of Florida. How finely it begins: "None of them knew the colour of the sky. Their eyes glanced level, and were fastened upon the waves that swept toward them. These waves were of the hue of slate, save for the tops, which were of foaming white, and all of the men knew the colours of the sea." Here at once we are confronted with a device—borrowed, perhaps, from Maeterlinck—which Mr. Crane employs with great effect in this and other sketches,—the device of iteration. In the dialogue it emphasises the dreary monotony of the long agony; in the descriptive passages it is like the *ritornello* of a song; but in both the effect is entirely artistic. Very touching, again, is the way Mr. Crane illustrates the "subtle brotherhood" established between the four comrades by the stress of a common peril, and the drowning of the poor "oiler" when within an acre of rescue brings the recital to a harrowing conclusion. Here, again, we are tempted to quote the last words, so characteristic of Mr. Crane's method, of this enthralling narrative: "The welcome of the land for the men from the sea was warm and generous, but a still and dripping shape was carried slowly up the beach, and the land's welcome for it could only be the different and sinister hospitality of the grave. When it came night, the white waves paced to and fro in the moonlight, and the wind brought the sound of the great sea's voice to the men on shore, and they felt that they could then be interpreters." That drives home the point we endeavoured to make at the outset. Mr. Crane is no longer a clairvoyant, he is an interpreter as well. In "A Man, and Some Others" we have a wonderfully vivid account of a night attack by Mexican "greasers" on the camp of a "sheep-herder" and a chance comrade,—both Americans. Here is a "nocturne" in Mr. Crane's most striking manner:—

> Long, smouldering clouds spread in the western sky, and to the east silver mists lay on the purple gloom of the wilderness. Finally, when the great moon climbed the heavens and cast its ghastly radiance on the bushes, it made a new and more brilliant crimson of the camp fire, where the flames capered merrily through its mesquit branches, filling the silence with the fire chorus, an ancient melody which surely bears a message of the inconsequence of individual tragedy,—a message that is in the boom of the sea, the sliver of the wind through the grass-blades, the silken clash of hemlock boughs. No figures moved in the rosy space of the camp, and the search of the moonbeams failed to disclose a living thing in the bushes. There was no owl-faced clock to chant the weariness of the long silence which brooded upon the plain. The dew gave the darkness under the mesquit a velvet quality that made air seem nearer to water, and no eye could have seen through it the black things that moved like monster lizards toward the camp.

We have no space left to dwell in detail on the humour of the strange home-coming of the town-marshal of Yellow Sky and his newly wedded wife, on the thrilling night-escape on horseback of an American traveller from a den of Mexican cutthroats, or on the splendid portrait of the filibustering Captain Flanagan, whose expedition, for reasons which Mr. Crane so vividly sets forth, never became historic. We hope, however, that we have said enough to induce the curious reader to make acquaintance with the most striking and irresistible of all the younger American writers.

—UNSIGNED, "Recent Short Stories," *Spectator,*
July 23, 1898, pp. 120–121

WAR IS KIND

UNSIGNED [ASHLEY A. SMITH] "SPRING VERSE: THREE HANDFULLS [SIC] OF VOLUMES—EIGHTEEN IN ALL—FROM POETS MOSTLY YOUNG" (1899)

This review finds the poems in *War Is Kind* to "have little claim to commendation."

The initial poem of Mr. Crane's collection gives the title to the entire volume. The book is a collection of impressions, with little of rhyme or rhythm. One would say that here evidently is a disciple of Walt Whitman. Dealing as he does with much of the matter, and certainly after the manner, of that poet, Mr. Stephen Crane will certainly be called most unconventional in his thought and the expression of it.

Judged by almost any poetic standard, from that of Mr. Poe, who called poetry "the rhythmical creation of beauty," to that of Mr. Matthew Arnold, who called it "a criticism of life," the verses of Mr. Crane have little claim to commendation.

There is little, also, of those elements which Milton asserted to be the dominating ones of true poetry: "Simplicity, sensuousness, and passion." In the entire volume of ninety pages, a single line occasionally occupying an entire page, there is nothing which reaches the dignity of the best work of the modern masters.

Still, it is only fair to say that in one respect Mr. Crane's work is remarkable, that is, in its "verbal magic," he paints with words; a faint echo of that power which was seen to such a degree in his war story, "The Red Badge of Courage," is also shown in his verse. This power of epithet is one of his most distinctive characteristics; he condenses sentences, pages, even, into a single word. Especially noticeable and remarkable in this regard is the poem on Page 36 (for these poems are titleless) commencing "On the desert a silence." It is also seen in the first poem.

He does not describe so much as, by the use of a single word or phrase, he suggests the description. The imagination of the reader is always active, and under his verbal direction each reader pictures, as for instance, in the first poem, the battlefield, for himself.

The open couplet to the poem on Page 27 is one of the finest, perhaps the most poetic, in the volume:

"I have heard the sunset song of the birches,
A white melody in the silence."

But this is quite in contrast with the austere realism that dominates the greater part of his work.

He always chooses words with "color" in them. Such a method in verse writing could be well termed—to borrow a much abused word of the painter—impressionistic. To this book of verse bys Mr. Crane might be applied the couplet which Mr. A. B. Frost once applied to the work of Mr. F. Hopkinson Smith:

"A little paint, a little work,
And lots of empty paper."

The book is handsomely bound, and is printed on blue-gray paper. There are several drawings—some of the full-page—by Mr. Will Bradley, and these add, in no small degree, to the beauty and worth of the volume.

It must be admitted frankly by those who have waited so long for the delayed publication of this volume that, while it shows some of the stronger characteristics of Mr. Crane's earlier prose work, as a poetic production it is closely akin to a genuine disappointment.

—Unsigned [Ashley A. Smith],
"Spring Verse: Three Handfulls [sic] of Volumes—
Eighteen in All—From Poets Mostly Young,"
The New York Times, May 27, 1899, p. BR337

John Curtis Underwood (1899)

John Curtis Underwood, a poet and critic, dislikes much of *War Is Kind* but finds that Crane is indeed a poet. He does not, however, appreciate the illustrations done by Will Bradley.

No one who reads this book can say justly that Mr. Crane is not a poet. He has enriched our literature with prose that rises almost to the level of epic song at times, but he will never be able to make prose of poetry, and his wisdom in following Walt Whitman's footsteps is not overwhelmingly apparent. He has neither the supreme sense of melody that harmonises Whitman's rugged lines nor the force and breadth of grasp that makes the "Song of the Open Road" the biggest thing in American literature.

Among the best things in the book are the epigrams. They are obviously prose, nothing more. Stripped of the gray paper, the black drawings, the printing of four solitary lines at the top of one page, they stand for the thought in them, but the illusive glamour of verse has fled. . . .

Technically, the book is in some respects an advance on *The Black Riders*, Mr. Crane's former metrical effort. There is manifested at times, not always, a nice sense of cadence, and the colour effects where we escape from the prevailing fog are fascinating. It is this fogginess, this groping in vagueness of feeling, the natural foe of clear thought, that has doubtless permitted the insertion of such inanities as the lines about the dead knight, such crudities as the description of the successful man. And again this same mystic shadowing has wrought true art in the witchery of the desert serpent-charmer.

There is no doubt that Mr. Crane has begun to arrive, but there is grave doubt of his ultimate success along these lines. Evidently he takes himself seriously, in spite of what seems occasional freakishness. There is room for his individuality in fiction—so striking a personality will always find hearers—but in the strait domain of true poesy he can only win to greatness by a closer regard for the conventionalities of rhyme and reason that the centuries have taught us are the best. The less said of Mr. Bradley's drawings the better.

—JOHN CURTIS UNDERWOOD,
Bookman, July 1899, pp. 466–467

UNSIGNED [T.W. HIGGINSON] (1899)

Higginson is dismissive of Crane's final volume of poems, finding them to be too experimental.

Men are liable to become, it is said, the slaves of their own actions, and the volume on dark-gray paper composed by Mr. Stephen Crane and illustrated by Mr. Will Bradley, entitled *War Is Kind*, may afford a useful illustration of this maxim. We were among those who frankly acknowledged the strong point of Mr. Crane's *Black Riders*, yet called attention to the disastrous outcome of such modes of work. It would be hardly worth while to repeat any such warnings now, since Mr. Crane has chosen his part, and the world now finds other experimenters more interesting. Mr. Bradley's share in the book is perhaps worse than Mr. Crane's, being purely imitative, but even Mr. Crane has written his own epitaph neatly on one page as follows (p. 56):

> A man said to the universe:
> "Sir, I exist!"
> "However," replied the universe,
> "The fact has not created in me
> "A sense of obligation."

—UNSIGNED [T.W. HIGGINSON],
The Nation, November 16, 1899, p. 378

ACTIVE SERVICE

UNSIGNED "NEW FICTION: WORKS BY EGERTON CASTLE, STEPHEN CRANE, SIENKIEWICZ, ANDREW LANG, AND OTHERS" (1899)

This review mostly details the plot of *Active Service,* but it shrewdly suggests that Stephen Crane may have been satirizing the contemporary "yellow journalism." Although no other critics come to this conclusion, Crane's dislike of such journalistic practices is especially clear in one of his poems.

Whatever glamour Mr. Stephen Crane can manufacture, he furnishes to Rufus Coleman, the "Sunday Editor of the Eclipse." It is questionable whether the author of "Active Service" himself really sees anything remarkable in his newspapery hero. One is half inclined to think that all the time Mr. Stephen Crane is laughing at his principal personage, and that the book itself is a satire on current "yellow journalism."

Despite his cleverness and dash, Rufus is not a lovable person, and parents would side with Prof. Wainwright when he questions whether the "Sunday Editor of the Eclipse" would be a fitting husband for his daughter Marjorie. Rufus has plenty of pluck, but is not a well-bred man. He has a decided liking for poker and champagne, bad company, and talks slang.

The Professor, wanting to save Marjorie from such a marriage, makes up his mind "to cart her off." He takes her to Greece, and he carries off with him, in his train, his rather hard-headed wife, and some half-dozen students who have archaeological proclivities. Marjorie, who is rather an obstinate young person, loves Rufus. Now comes the chance for the "Sunday Editor of the Eclipse." May he not join together his love and a newspaper job? It is just at the time when Greece has joined issue with the Turks. News has come to the United States that the Wainwright party has been lost. What a splendid sensation it would make if the Eclipse could organize a rescue party! How superb would be the Scare heads! Rufus goes to Greece and undertakes the business. The editor of the Eclipse supplies the means.

But why did Mr. Stephen Crane mar what might have been a really nice, proper story by interjecting into it Nora Black, the vulgar variety actress? The author carries her to Greece, where she does her "turn." What may have been the former intimacy between Rufus and Nora is not stated, but may be imagined. Finally, by a bit of good luck, the "Sunday editor of the Eclipse" stumbles over the Wainwright party, and by his courage and push does get them out of a very uncomfortable situation. The professor changes his mind about Rufus, and finally Marjorie, the prim Professor's daughter, at some trysting place, bathed by the waters of the blue Aegean, combs the hair of the "Sunday Editor of the Eclipse" with her taper fingers, and then the man cries "with a kind of diffident ferocity, 'I haven't kissed you yet—'"

Mr. Stephen Crane's text abounds with baseball argot, and we regret to state that some of the slang does not belong to the period of the Greek and Turkish war, but is Bowery of the moment, the freshest coinage of today. The smartness of Mr. Stephen Crane, his epigrammatic way, need never be questioned. Perhaps, after all, "Active Service" is banter, or the arraignment of the "heros maigre lui."

—Unsigned, "New Fiction: Works by Egerton Castle, Stephen Crane, Sienkiewicz, Andrew Lang, and Others," *The New York Times*, November 18, 1899, p. BR772

William L. Alden
"London Literary Letter" (1899)

Although William L. Alden had praised *The Red Badge of Courage,* in this review he criticizes *Active Service.*

It is a pity that there cannot be a law requiring every man who wishes to write a book to pass an examination in Herbert Spencer's "Essay on Style" before receiving permission to publish. The number of young authors who have been wrecked on the rock of style must be enormous. They fancy that words have another office besides that of conveying ideas, and that style consists in finding some new way of arranging words. Spencer taught that there is a right way in which every sentence should be written, and that every other way of writing it is wrong. The youth searcher after style thinks that to make words perform difficult acrobatic feats is the main object of writing, and that the more boldly an author's sentences stand on their heads, the more attractive is the style.

Mr. Bernard Capea affords a conspicuous illustration of this curious belief in the merits of word juggling, but Mr. Stephen Crane, in his last book, "Active Service," is, of the two, by far the worse offender. I greatly admire Mr. Crane's genius, and was among the first to perceive the power which he displayed in his "Red Badge of Courage." His "Active Service" is in several respects a decidedly clever book, but it is marred by his persistent effort to use words in a way that is novel. In so doing Mr. Crane not only defies reason, but he mocks at grammar. There are readers who will probably mistake Mr. Crane's eccentricities for genius, but the average reader will forget the author's story to wonder at his efforts at word juggling.

This sort of thing usually grows on a man. Mr. Capea's style was much more sane and intelligible in his first book that it is in his last; and Mr. Crane goes on steadily from bad to worse. He needs to be dealt with sharply. I am not so absurd as to fancy that I can have any influence with him, but if the majority of the critics would show him plainly that his present style is vicious, and to a certain extent vulgar, it might have some effects upon him. It would not be of the slightest consequence were Mr. Crane an ordinary man, but he is not an ordinary man. He is a writer who is capable of great things, and who, in at least one of his books, has come very near to achieving them. But if he persists in the delusion that words have some other and more important office than that of conveying ideas easily and plainly he is lost. The public will weary of him, and he himself will lose sight of substance in striving after form. I hope he may het be saved, but after reading "Active Service" I have little expectation that he will repent and strive to enter the right path. It is easier for a drunkard to give up his habit than it is for the author who has once delivered himself over to the bondage of an artificial style to emancipate himself, and to write as a sane man should write.

—William L. Alden, "London Literary Letter,"
The New York Times, December 23, 1899, p. BR898

UNSIGNED (1899)

This unfavorable review compares two characters in the novel to biblical counterparts in Genesis 39: 7–20, which discusses the temptation of Joseph by Potiphar's wife.

———

In *Active Service* Mr. Stephen Crane has applied his literary method, which aptly suits the unusual, to the commonplace. A battlefield stands Mr. Crane's descriptive staccato. A newspaper office does not. So far as the reader goes, the result is a story which opens with interest and closes with confused dull talk and incident. Mr. Crane has taken the new Sunday supplement newspaper man, had him fall in love with the daughter of a professor of Greek, put the professor, his family, and a chorus of students in the vortex of the Greek war and let the hero rescue them, with a comic opera singer thrown in to play Potiphar's wife to the Sunday supplement man's Joseph. This ought to be interesting to the end, but it is interesting only about to the middle, the illusion of reality being lost midway. Now Mr. Crane is a realist.

—UNSIGNED, *Book News*, December 1899, p. 202

RUPERT HUGHES (1900)

Rupert Hughes, who had previously written positively of *Maggie: A Girl of the Streets*, in this review praises much of Stephen Crane's work, especially *Active Service*, which is the focus of much of the article, but he incorrectly remembers the subtitle of *Maggie*. Although most criticism, contemporary and later, has found this novel to be little more than a potboiler, Hughes finds it among Crane's best work. In a later part of this review not included here, the critic also acclaims *The Monster and Other Stories*, concluding that Crane is a "big genius."

———

That Stephen Crane is a genius I have been convinced ever since I read that little fatherless yellow-covered book *Maggie, a Tale of the Streets*, by Johnston Smith. To this belief I have clung in spite of many jolts and jars, for the retainer of this author must hang on like the watcher in the crow's nest of a ship, which ploughs splendidly forward, but with much yawing and buffeting and many a career.

Mr. Crane's faults are not surreptitiously stowed away; they are carried aboveboard like a defiant figurehead or a pirate's black flag. For instance, there's his grammatical carelessness; he takes the natural liberty of a writer handling so elastic a language as ours and carries it to license, to criminal excess, for which there is no excuse. First, you blame the proof-reader; then you realize that no proof-reader could live and let slip the things that get into Mr. Crane's books unless his hands were tied behind him by definite orders. Of all the writers I have ever read with respect, Mr. Crane makes the greatest number of solecisms. Many of them bear the look of absolute illiteracy; they are as inconsistent with his capabilities for discriminating and recherché compositions Wordsworth's off-hours are with his inspiration. That superb work, *The Red Badge* of *Courage*, and the later, *Active Service*, fairly bristle with these things.

Then he is wont to take it into his head to send his glorious argosy on some fool's errand of wanton affectation and triviality. These outlandish junketings marked many, though not all, of his *Black Rider* lines, much of *George's Mother*, the general idea (though, strangely, not the detail) of *The Third Violet*, and almost all of that crazy nightmare, *War is Kind*.

Yet, withal, Mr. Crane seems to me to be the most definite and individual of all our book-writers; and I credit him with having written some of the best pages America has contributed to literature, in *Maggie*, *The Red Badge*, certain of the *Black Rider* lines, *The Open Boat* and in the two books just published from his hand.

Active Service enambers some of Mr. Crane's impressions of Greece, which he saw as a war correspondent. The hero is far from ideal; he stumbles into heroism more or less unintentionally; he takes good and ill fortune with a bad grace generally; he is in short a hero by accident, an average flawful character, peevish and irritable at worst and not very good at best. But because he is like the great average of humanity, he is the more worthy of consideration. Though the book drags a bit at first, it later enchains and hales along the interest unflaggingly, and this without sacrificing probabilities.

The heroine is a fine study, an American girl, whose deep emotions are held in strict leash by a sturdy self-respect. Her frumpish and shallow mother and her petty and professorial father are well characterized, and an actress is brought in to mix things up. As a psychological study of motives the book is keen; as a piece of narrative construction, the latter half of it shows an ability Mr. Crane has given little evidence of before.

But, chiefly, the book is worthy for its details. There is an abundance of that minute observation that distinguishes Mr. Crane's manner. There is, furthermore, a warmth of amorous life that is unusual in his prose; the love of the heroine for the man is beautifully painted, and when, after many misunderstandings, they reach the great understanding in a crisis of danger, there is a nobility of situation. All is petty again when a silly contretemps cuts the Gordian knot of love. There is a deep and faithful pathos in the scene where the heroine, so strong in public, is found, by her foolish old father, alone in the dark and crying over her broken heart. Then, when the man of text-books becomes for the nonce a man of action and reunites the lovers, there is a new height of power, all is ecstatic, rose-colored, and blissful. Now Mr. Crane writes like a lover, with just the right luxury and extravagance. . . .

—Rupert Hughes, *Criterion*,
January 6, 1900, p. 24

THE MONSTER AND OTHER STORIES

Robert Bridges (1898)

Robert Bridges, an editor at Scribner's and Sons from 1880 until 1930, was instrumental in launching the new *Life* magazine. He, along with Cyrus McCormick and Woodrow Wilson, graduated from Princeton University in 1879. The novella *The Monster* first appeared in *Harper's Magazine* in August 1898, and this review is concerned with only that part of the later volume. The collection of short stories that took its title from the novella was not published until November 1899.

Bridges points out the complex nature of Stephen Crane's story, but he still finds elements of which he is skeptical, describing them as the result of perhaps too much "dexterity" on Crane's part.

There are more kinds of things well done in Stephen Crane's story, *The Monster*, than in any previous work of his. It is really a small novel of thirty thousand words, though published in a single number of *Harper's*. The motive of it is intensely psychological, and yet there is scarcely a single reflective paragraph in it. It is incident, action, character, in quick succession—and often apparently disjointed and irrelevant. But when the last block is put in place the whole design flashes into an orderly picture—like the landscape painted on six separate boards by a variety artist, and suddenly clapped into a gilt frame.

The adjective which seems best to describe this talent is "dexterity." He always makes you feel a certain dashing confidence behind his work; he is a juggler who is perfectly sure that he will catch the knife by the handle every time. The reader can't escape the suspicion that perhaps Mr. Crane is not juggling with real knives—and if he did catch the wrong end it would not hurt him. All kinds of dexterity are apt to breed a similar skepticism.

To name the things well done in the story is almost to name each incident. The comedy of the Dutch barber shop and of the negro dandy's call upon his sweetheart is irresistible. There is no attempt at being smart or funny; he simply tells you what they said. Then the aspect of the square at night in a rural town which calls itself a city; the strange thrill of the fire alarm, the humors of the volunteer companies, the tragedies of the burning house—all these things follow with increasing gloom to the subtle horrors of the close.

And in depicting horrors he shows more restraint than he has previously thought wise. To paint a horror and pile it on thick have seemed to be a part of his stock in trade. But in this tale he follows the admirable Hawthornesque plan of suggesting the horror by showing its effects upon various observers. The black veil over *Johnson's* disfigured face is far more terrible than any gruesome anatomical details.

There is also unexpected elevation in the motive of the story. The quiet heroism of the Doctor is admirably indicated. He is the central figure of the drama, and yet he says least and seldom appears.

—Robert Bridges, *Life*,
September 1, 1898, p. 166

Julian Hawthorne "The Monster and Other Stories" (1900)

Julian Hawthorne, an American writer and journalist, was the son of novelist Nathaniel Hawthorne. He worked in numerous genres: poetry, novels, short stories, mystery/detective fiction, essays, travel books, biographies, and histories. As a journalist, he reported on the Indian famine for *Cosmopolitan* magazine and the Spanish-American War for the *New York Journal*. He later served time in an Atlanta penitentiary for mail fraud, the result of his sale of stock in a nonexistent silver mine. Although he and Stephen Crane reported on the Spanish-American War for the same newspaper, the two men seem to have had little in common.

Hawthorne's review is one of many negative assessments of *The Monster*. He finds Stephen Crane anything but an artist: "His outfit for literary purposes consists of a microscopic eye, and a keen sense of the queer, the bizarre, the morbid. His minute analysis produces nothing."

What is a man to do with a monster which exists owing to his efforts? The problem has been attacked by Mrs. Shelley in her "Frankenstein," which everybody has heard of, but not so many of this generation have read, insomuch that many suppose that "Frankenstein" was the monster. Now comes Stephen Crane, with his modern, realistic style, and tries his hand at the same proposition.

He takes us to a town up-country, in New York, and proceeds to paint a picture of its various aspects. They are painted with the utmost truthfulness of detail, and verisimilitude. This minuteness is applied not merely to the scenery and personages as pictorially viewed, but also to the idiosyncrasies of the thought and action of the latter.

In the midst of the orthodox country town stupidity, the factory whistle blows, and the idle population rushes to the fire which is burning down the doctor's house. Faster than all runs the negro hostler, who is the little boy's friend; he dashes into the flames, rescues the boy from all but a slight scorching, but is himself caught in a painful manner under a table in the doctor's office, and his face is burned off, all but one eye, which is left without a lid; his mind is also gone. The doctor, by his skill, animated by gratitude for the man's having, at such expense to himself, saved his son, brings him out alive, but—a monster. People who see him are thrown into fits of terror or horror; they lose their appetite, and pine away. The doctor sends the unhappy creature to a neighboring darky's hut, to be kept out of the way there; but though the darky is paid $5 a week for the accommodation, he cannot stand it; his wife and children and himself are utterly thrown off their base by the hideous affliction. While he is remonstrating, the monster escapes, and spreads devastation through the town; there is nothing for it but that the doctor should keep him on his own premises. But hereupon a new complication arises; for what patient would call in a doctor who keeps a monster in his house?

The mere association of the doctor and the monster makes the doctor look like the monster to the diseased eye of the patient, and forbids the success of his most skillful treatment. Not only that, but the citizens of the town will not any longer exchange the civilities of social intercourse with the doctor; and his wife, on her reception day, is left with fifteen untouched cups and saucers and slices of cake; and is found thus, in hopeless tears, by her husband. What is he to do about it? That is the question that same self appointed committee of the solid citizens asks him; they suggest that he send the monster out of town somewhere; that he house him in a public institution; anything, only don't keep him here. The doctor can only reply that the creature saved his son's life, and to that owes his monstrous condition; abandoning him is therefore out of the question. And if you will believe it, Crane leaves the matter in that condition, without the faintest pretense of doing anything whatever to relieve it!

I call this an outrage on art and humanity; and the splendid descriptive ability of the author, his vividness and veracity, only render it more flagrant. Something is fundamentally out of gear in a mind that can reconcile itself to such a performance. There is abundance of humor in many of the details; but it is an easy thing to be humorous about microscopic things, the essence of humor being in a kindly or amused smile at the weaknesses and absurdities of human nature; but it is one thing to be humorous when writing a history of the French Revolution, like Carlyle; and quite another to be humorous about the tiny trivialities of a New York country town. Anybody can look down on that, and see the fun of it. Crane never gets more than a few feet above the ground, and often falls below even that moderate elevation. Of constructive ability he shows not a vestige. His outfit for literary purposes consists of a microscopic eye, and a keen sense of the queer, the bizarre, the morbid. His minute analysis produces nothing. He is anything but an artist. He has everything belonging to art to learn; and he evinces no disposition or ability to learn it. We all know, nevertheless, how successful he has been; but in these days we are thankful for what we can get, if it be genuine so far as it goes; and Crane's work is no doubt that.

—JULIAN HAWTHORNE, "The Monster
and Other Stories," *Book News*,
February 18, 1900, pp. 337–338

UNSIGNED (1901)

This review is highly complimentary of the collection of stories, recognizing the value of not only the title story but of "The Blue Hotel," "Twelve O'Clock," and other individual stories. The critic paints Stephen Crane as a gifted writer and the book as "intensely alive and intelligent."

If Mr. Crane had written nothing else, this book would have wrested from the world an acknowledgment of his curious, searching gifts, and would have made him a reputation. Not that he is wholly represented here. The Crane of *The Open Boat*, of *Maggie*, of *Death and the Child*, of *The Red Badge of Courage*, is absent, or only fugitively present; but the quick, nervous, prehensile mind that in an instant could select the vital characteristics of any scene or group, is notably here; and here also in superabundance is the man's grim fatalism, his saturnine pleasure in exhibiting (with bitter, laughing mercilessness) the frustrations of human efforts, the absurd trifles which decide human destiny. There is one story, for example, "Twelve

O'Clock," which tells how a young cowboy's excitement on hearing a cuckoo-clock for the first time led indirectly to murder—all done with perfect credibility. Nothing but a kind of savage impatience with the accidentalism of the scheme of things could have caused a man to set down this particular story; but it is finely done—a triumph of narrative art. "The Blue Hotel" is another excellent piece of work—the history of a quarrelsome night and its fatal issue—a nocturne in blood and whisky, with a curious thread of grotesque running through it, and a very peculiar knowledge of human nature in every line. The question, "Is it worth while?" had better, perhaps, not be asked. To our mind the art justifies it. "The Monster" itself, the title-story, has been praised in America with that warmth of praise for which the country is famous; but it is not better than "The Blue Hotel." It is, however, an amazing story, with deeper interest, and the questions, "is it worth while?" is far less likely to be put. "Manacled" is an exercise in the horrible that does not quite succeed. "His New Mitten" belongs rightly to *Whilomville Stories*. The last story of all, "An Illusion in Red and White," is a very delicate piece of gruesomeness. Altogether, the book is intensely alive and intelligent, and not by any means the kind of thing for nervous fold or for the "art-for-anything-else's-sake-but-art" school.

—UNSIGNED, *Academy*,
March 16, 1901, p. 230

WHILOMVILLE STORIES

UNSIGNED (1900)

This review of *Whilomville Stories* finds little to commend. Maintaining that Stephen Crane's writing had deteriorated during his time in England, the critic refers to "uncertainties of style" and "artificial expressions" without ever giving specific examples of these supposed faults. Any merit the book has is attributed to William Dean Howells and William Allen White.

Stephen Crane's *Whilomville Stories* are put forth by the Harpers in a handsome edition, which seems almost to be a memorial one, with a frontispiece portrait (too photographic and "nicified") of Crane, and in excellent type and paper—and, of course, with Newell's pictures, which are in his best vein, and which are outwardly the most attractive feature of the volume. Crane is just now much in fashion, the *Red Badge* being out in a new edition, and the as yet unpublished romance—as yet unfinished, too—much talked about.

There is good reason why he should be a part of the vogue of the time—especially as he is dead. It would be interesting to know how Crane's reputation will stand fifteen years from now, when the world will be vibrating with the successes of the great new Filipino-American poet and romanticist, Emilio Coaklobogan Jones, or agonizing over the latest translation from the Bulgarian of Varchef Bogomsky.

Even the admirers of Stephen Crane, however, may fear that a certain conscious uncertainty and literary fickleness that there was in the man has really so impaired the quality of his work that the coming generation will fail to find in it the steady high note that compels lasting admiration. Crane does not seem to have known how he wanted to write. He polished and sophisticated his style, after the critics told him—what was certainly true—that the *Red Badge* was in bad English—and he never wrote so vividly again as he did in that book. Perhaps his nearest approach to it was in that sharp and clear running account of his experiences in the Spanish war which he contributed to Lady Randolph Churchill's *Anglo-Saxon Review.*

Crane was a sensitive plant, and changed as the wind blew on him. He went to England—and was lost. If he had been kicked about, unappreciated, on this rude continent, for ten years longer, he might have been great. In the *Whilomville Stories*, true to the main points of child life as they are, you can hardly glance at a page without finding some of these conscious uncertainties of style—these artificial expressions which Crane seems to have picked up in England along with the English accent which he had in his last two years, and which with him was no affectation; he simply could not help adopting it.

And as we go on, we find many and many a paragraph that makes us sigh for the rude Saxon tumult of words in the *Red Badge* or the pat compression of the *Black Riders.*

As to the matter of the book, it has all been put in better shape by Mr. Howells and Mr. William Allen White, if not by several others. Yet, there are gleams of the great Crane that the author really is, as in the description of the boy who could answer the questions in the Sunday-school class:

"He had the virtue of being able to walk on very high stilts, but when the season of stilts had passed, he possess no rank save this Sunday-school rank, this clever-little-Clarence business of knowing the Bible and the lesson better than the other boys; the other boys, looking at him meditatively, did not actually decide to thrash him as soon as he cleared the portals of the church, but they certainly decided to molest him in such ways as would establish their self-respect. Back of the superintendent's chair hung a lithography of the martyrdom of St. Stephen."

—Unsigned, *Literary News,*
September 1900, p. 273

Unsigned "Books and Authors: Stories by Stephen Crane" (1900)

This review decries the fact that *Whilomville Stories* "do not, upon the whole, commend themselves." The critic sees Stephen Crane presenting children who are "boasting, bullying, cowardly, cruel little wretches, apparently soulless—simply a gang of selfish little roughs" and prefers the more "realistic" children in the Tom Brown series or in *Little Women.*

It seems an ungracious deed to write a work breathing any save kindly criticism of the latest work of the brilliant boy who has done so much that is worthy and who all too soon has "laid the weary pen aside." The word becomes well-nigh impossible as one looks at the pathetic portrait prefixed to these sketches, so youthful, so full of promise, and remembers how he crowded his brief years with work and missed the maturity of his powers by too eagerly anticipating it.

Eliminating as much as may be the influence of the writer's personality, we must confess that the "Whilomville Stories" do not, upon the whole, commend themselves to our approbation. Mr. Crane's literary touch makes itself felt, though he will occasionally indulge in the split infinitive. The stories contain many laughable situations, many bits of nature, and not a little food for reflection to the parents of "angel children"; but many of the scenes are so long drawn out as to be decidedly boring; more than once the reader is very much too vividly reminded of parallel occurrences in "Tom Sawyer"; the gibes at Sunday schools are cheap and unworthy; and as a delineation of the child nature the book is singularly inadequate.

It is not a little odd that while teachers and physicians are making a cult of child study, and are frightening plain-minded parents out of their wits by fine-drawn and microscopic analyses of the complex little psychical organisms to be trained and influenced, the children of fiction are becoming more and more simple, possessing more and more the elemental characteristics we have been wont to ascribe to the Bushman or the South Sea Islander. This is, of course, a reaction against the sentimental view of childhood almost universal in literature until the present generation. Let a child appear in a novel thirty years ago, and the reader knew his heart was to be torn. In the tears that have been shed over the soul-harrowing experiences of saintly children persecuted by worldly elders a whole army of Little Alices and her "creatures" might swim. Biography, too, delighted in anaemic, abnormally spiritual children who sank into an early tomb, such as "The Young Cottager," or poor little seven-year-old Nathan Dickerman, appropriately bound in slim black volumes and supposed to be edifying "Sunday reading" for the average child. Dickens laid the hand of genius upon the accepted ideal, but did not venture to change it; and so we have Little Nell, Paul Dombey, and Tiny Tim still radiant survivors of the children of sentiment.

Dear Marjorie Fleming in biography, Tom Brown and *Little Women* in fiction, substituted real children for the shadowy, haloed throng of impossible little saints, and the eager welcome these books received stimulated the vast host of followers who have at last pushed realism into the unreal.

For, we submit, while children are not all soul and sentiment, they certainly have soul and sentiment. Manly piety is found even among schoolboys. The veriest urchin of the streets knows something of unselfish love for somebody, but we should never discover these things from the most prominent literature of the day. We should be sorry to have "Stalky & Co." stand for the normal type of English schoolboy, or "Whilomville Stories" for the village children of our own country. Mr. Crane's children are boasting, bullying, cowardly, cruel little wretches, apparently soulless—simply a gang of selfish little roughs, devoid even of cohesive loyalty among themselves. No doubt he paints correctly one phase, and that the least attractive phase, of childlife, but he has left a whole world untouched, and so his picture must be pronounced a most unfair one. If "of such" as Mr. Crane's declared "hoodlums" were "the kingdom of heaven," there would be little to choose between that and the kingdom of Beelzebub!

And so, although "Whilomville Stories" provoke a smile, they and all their kin arouse serious protest. "Shades of the prison-house" have closed with a vengeance "upon the growing boy" of fiction. Such a brutal young savage is he portrayed that, because of his altogether evil influence, long—suffering elders begin to lament that books about boys should be at the same time books for boys. Surely the literary pendulum must be ready to swing back again, if not to the solemn little prigs of good Mr. Da and Mrs. Barbauld, at least to the boys of Thomas Hughes. For the real boy, full of animal spirits, full of mischief, full of faults though he be, does pause sometimes to feel in his shy, dumb way the stirrings of a soul within him, and is not without worthy aspirations.

—Unsigned, "Books and Authors: Stories by
Stephen Crane," *The New York Times*,
September 8, 1900, p. BR12

Unsigned (1900)

This even-handed review points to both the strengths and weaknesses of Stephen Crane's stories of childhood. The critic points out the "delightful sympathy" and "humour" of the book, following through with an example with which the reader can immediately identify, and noting that this volume even includes female characters who are not the syrupy little girls that populated fiction of the period.

Whilomville Stories, the last book Stephen Crane wrote before his death, comes to us from the press of Harper and Brothers. It is a study of child-life, done in the form so popular nowadays and so effective—a series of sketches, each complete in itself, but with the same background and characters throughout. With delightful sympathy and humour Mr. Crane chronicles for us the ways of the average boy—that boasting, bragging, teasing young animal, with his funny little code of ethics, in which so much depends on the question of who "kin lick." There are girls in the sketches, too, notably one angel child, who comes down from New York occasionally, attended by her admiring parents, to queen it over the Whilomville children and lead them into such pieces of mischief as have not occurred to them before. We have all met this angel child, we have all longed to say, as the goaded Dr. Trescott said to her worshipping papa, " . . . Spank her! Spank her, confound you, man! She needs it! Here's your chance. Spank her, and spank her good! Spank her!" Of course, she didn't get spanked; they never do. But, oh, if the parents of the ubiquitous angel child could but recognize their portraits in this book! . . . There are some clever hits in *Whilomville Stories* at sham and convention and the various inconsistencies of society. But it is with children—not older folk—that Mr. Crane is here concerned chiefly, and these glimpses into the heart of the child-nature, never glossing over its meannesses, its unattractive phases, but entering so into its cherished make-believes and the small affairs that seem to it so big, show on his part an insight keen and rare. The book has faults, but they are the faults of immaturity mainly, faults he would have conquered in days to come had not his hand been so untimely stilled.

Therefore, we may well forget blemishes in pure delight of his genius, of his vigour, his earnestness and his fun.

—UNSIGNED, *Bookman*,
October 1900, p. 165

ARTHUR STANLEY "STEPHEN CRANE'S CHILDHOOD STORIES" (1904)

While the literary world was not especially kind to Stephen Crane's *Whilomville Stories*, the public was more receptive to the realism of childhood interactions. This letter and the following one show that, four years after the volume's publication, readers still retained admiration of it, even though by this time Crane was largely ignored and unread.

With all due respect to the judgment of *The Book Review* concerning the stories of E. L. Sabin, I would suggest a harking back to the work of the late Stephen Crane for the "real thing" in literature anent childhood. Crane himself was wont to refer to his work in this line somewhat rudely, but the stories found a place in Harper's Magazine some years ago, and were later published in book form under the title, I think, of "Whilomville Stories. ." They have all the realism of Mr. Sabin's sketches, with more poignancy, and all the humor of Miss Daskam's "Memoirs," with less smartness, though it must be confessed that they lack the sugary quality which seems to appeal to many of your correspondents in the "Bruvver Jim" book. Crane's story, "The Monster,"—which, by the way, was held by the author to be his best effort—while not strictly a study of childhood, gives, too en passant, an uncannily accurate view of boy nature. It is probable that Crane had no very exalted estimate of the innate sweet reasonableness of the human being, even when caught young, for he lived close to the madding crowd, and therefore his baby stories may not appeal to those who prefer to believe every young hopeful an Angel of Light, capable of reforming entire communities by mere effulgent existence. On the other hand, there is in these stories none of that metallic cleverness which mars the "Memoirs of a Baby," and which has aroused the gentle to wrath through the medium of your columns. In this connection it occurs to me to venture the opinion that no one of your correspondents has done Miss Daskam the justice of giving her credit for inaugurating a reaction against the tide of sloppy mush that sweeps through the present school of childhood fiction. To treat the "Memoirs" as a mere study of a child, and to ignore the very wholesome irony of the treatment of the subject, seems to me to argue in the reader a lack of the sense of humor. But then, the American reader of fiction is not noted for his, or, more properly, her, appreciation of realistic humor, and if any notice whatever is taken of this small suggestion of mine in favor of Crane's stories, I shall expect it to take the form of a howl against ungentle treatment of the innocents.

Arthur Stanley Wheeler,
Grove Beach, Conn., July 31, 1904

—ARTHUR STANLEY, "Stephen Crane's
Childhood Stories," *The New York Times*,
August 6, 1904, p. BR535

A.A. McG. (1904)

It was good to find some one who remembered and who spoke a good word for the "Whilomville Stories" of Stephen Crane among all the overwrought discussions of children's books which have been appearing in print of late. The marvel is that Crane's wonderfully searching delineations of the child nature, with all its subtle reserves and resources for deception, or rather secrecy with its elders, should have been felt out of such a discussion up to the present moment. If I am not mistaken his stories were recommended in an approved list of books for teachers on the study of child life.

A.A. McG.
New York, Aug 6, 1904

—A.A. McG., "Crane's Whilomville Stories,"
The New York Times, August 13, 1904,
p. BR550f

WOUNDS IN THE RAIN

This collection of Spanish-American War stories, *Wounds in the Rain*, was published posthumously in September 1900 by Frederick A. Stokes in the United States and Methuen in England. Planned before his death, the book is dedicated to Moreton Frewen, who owned the old manor, Brede Place, where Crane spent his last months before being taken to the Black Forest. Based on Crane's journalistic pieces on the war, this volume features soldiers who differ from the youth of the *Red Badge*, both in their experience and in their realistic outlook on battle.

UNSIGNED (1900)

Although this review of *Wounds in the Rain* ends by calling the volume "a brilliant last word," it is somewhat derisive in its attention to Stephen Crane's "inward" look at war and its repetition of the sound used to depict Spanish gunfire.

No one can escape, in reading this last of Mr. Crane's extraordinary work, from the reflection that it ridiculously resembles his first. Almost every impression was preconceived in *The Red Badge of Courage*, and for verisimilitude the author might have stayed for the one as for the other in his own armchair, and never have gone at all to the wars. This might lead to either of two conclusions: that the reporter was obsessed by the author's battles in the brain, or that the author had successfully divined truth which the reporter's observation could but verify. Which, it were not easy to decide; especially because a large part of the observation, and that the most characteristic, is concerned altogether with the inner man. The objectives operations are of secondary importance, and, as Mr. Crane tells them, are not always easy to follow; that which mainly interests him is the variation, under certain abnormal conditions, in the fundamental conceptions of time and space, the sharpening of the senses or their temporary anesthesia, the effects of fear, the strange sources from which in emergency courage may derive; and what he is interested in, that he desires to express. "The battle broke with a snap far ahead. Presently Lige heard from the air far above a faint, low note as if somebody were blowing in the mouth of a bottle. It was a stray bullet that had wandered a mile to tell him that war was before him." Then what? It may be observation, but the author of *The Red Badge* would easily have divined it: "he early broke his neck in looking upward." Forthwith the Spanish guns become as it were articulate. "Ss-sa-swow-ow-ow-ow-pum"—that is how they talk; also "flut-flut, flut, fluttery-flut-fllluttery-flut," they say. Bullets sing, sping, spang, snap, snatch, shiver, sneer. The war correspondent in the derelict steel boiler meanwhile "dreams frantically of some anthracite hiding-place, some profound dungeon of peace, where blind mules chew placidly the far-gathered hay." With nerves (to use his own phrase) standing on end like so many bristles, he writes like a man hag-rid by a terror of common things. . . . To our mind the finest work in the volume is the last story, "The Second Generation." It is of wider scope than the rest, treating with serious purpose and in less unmeasured language of the consequences of inherited wealth and position. On the whole, however, this posthumous volume is a brilliant last word from one who had discovered himself completely from the beginning.

—Unsigned, *Academy,* October 6, 1900, p. 281

CAROLYN SHIPMAN (1900)

Carolyn Shipman sees this last book as an "advance" when compared to Stephen Crane's earlier writing; it omits "some of the early crudeness" that she apparently detected in those works.

———— ———— ————

These stories of the Spanish War, *Wounds in the Rain*, show the author's encouraging grasp of the grammatical demands of the English language as a means of literary expression—a great gain to the mind of any reader that is at all sensitive to solecisms. The beauty of the scenery is vastly marred if one's wagon has no springs and the road is full of rocks. Some of the early crudeness has disappeared in these vivid pictures of soldier life, and with it some of the Manet splashes of color in word-painting. The vigor and fearlessness are here, without the apparent aim at effect. The book is a distinct advance, but we shall never know whether or not it would have been its author's swansong before literary death. Those who knew the man say No.

—CAROLYN SHIPMAN, *Book Buyer*,
November 1900, p. 300

UNSIGNED (1901)

Despite the fact that there was not much contemporary recognition of *Wounds in the Rain*, the book sold well. Stephen Crane's untimely death cannot account for the fact that the volume, published posthumously in September 1900, was already into its fourth edition in slightly less than a year.

———— ———— ————

Stephen Crane's "Wounds in the Rain" has gone into its fourth edition at the Frederick A. Stokes Company's. It is a collection of tales, tragic and humorous, whose scenes for the most part are laid in Cuba during the time of the Spanish-American war. It may be recalled that Mr. Crane was for many months in Cuba during and after the war, and his sketches have a basis of facts, and are not simply the work of the imagination.

—UNSIGNED, *The New York Times*,
August 17, 1901, p. BR15

Chronology

1871 On November 1, Stephen Crane, the fourteenth and last child of Jonathan Townley Crane and Mary Helen Peck Crane, is born in Newark, New Jersey. From 1874–1880, Crane's father serves as minister of various Methodist churches in New Jersey.

1880 Crane's father dies unexpectedly on February 16.

1883 Mrs. Crane moves with the family to Asbury Park, New Jersey.

1884 Crane's favorite sister, Agnes, dies at the age of twenty-eight.

1885–87 Stephen is a student at Pennington Seminary boarding school.

1888 Crane enrolls in Claverack College and Hudson River Institute, where he is in the military cadet corps. During the summers of 1888–1892, Crane assists his brother Townley as a reporter for local newspapers and the *New York Tribune*.

1891 In January, Crane transfers to Syracuse University, living in the Delta Upsilon fraternity house and playing on the varsity baseball team. He begins writing *Maggie: A Girl of the Streets*. His mother dies on December 7.

1892 In October, Crane moves to New York, living in a boarding house in Manhattan with a group of medical students.

1893 Using money from coal stock left by his mother's estate, Crane has *Maggie* privately printed. He becomes acquainted with Hamlin Garland, who introduces him to William Dean Howells.

1894 Crane shows some of his poems and the manuscript of *The Red Badge of Courage* to Garland. In an abridged version, *The Red Badge* is serialized in newspapers by the Bacheller syndicate in early December.

1895 Crane is sent by the Bacheller syndicate on a trip through the West and into Mexico. In May, *The Black Riders* is published by Copeland & Day, and in September, *The Red Badge of Courage* is published by Appleton.

1896 *Maggie* and *The Little Regiment* are published by Appleton. *George's Mother* is published by Edward Arnold. After defending Dora Clark, a prostitute, against the New York City Police Department in a suit for false arrest, Crane is unable to continue as a reporter in New York. In late November, the Bacheller Syndicate sends him to Jacksonville, Florida on his way to report the Cuban insurrection. He meets Cora Taylor, the proprietor of the Hotel de Dream.

1897 On the last day of 1896, Crane boards the *Commodore* to sail for Cuba. The ship sinks off the coast of Florida, and Crane and three others spend thirty hours in a dinghy before getting to land. In May, *The Third Violet* is published. Crane and Cora go separately to England and then to Greece to report the Greek-Turkish War. They return to England, living at Ravensbrook, Surrey, as Mr. and Mrs. Stephen Crane. They journey to Ireland in September with Harold Frederic and Kate Lyon.

1898 Crane publishes *The Open Boat and Other Tales of Adventure*. On April 13, he sails for New York on his way to Cuba to report the Spanish-American War. He returns to New York on December 24 and sails for England on December 31.

1899 Stephen and Cora move to Brede Place, Sussex. *War Is Kind*, *Active Service*, and *The Monster and Other Stories* are published. In late December, Crane collapses from a tubercular hemorrhage.

1900 In April, Crane suffers new hemorrhages. Cora arranges for him to go to a sanitarium in Badenweiler, Germany, where he dies on June 5 at the age of twenty-eight. *Whilomville Stories* and *Wounds in the Rain* are published posthumously.

Index